The Incarnation

The Incarnation of Freedom and Love

Ruth Page

SCM PRESS
London

British Library Cataloguing in Publication Data

Page, Ruth
The incarnation of freedom and love.
1. Jesus Christ
I. Title
232

ISBN 0–334–02490–0

First published 1991
by SCM Press Ltd
26–30 Tottenham Road, London N1 4BZ

Typeset at The Spartan Press Ltd, Lymington, Hants
and printed in England by
Clays Ltd, St Ives plc

Contents

Prologue

Everything bends
to reenact
the poem lived,
lived, not written,
the poem spoken
by Christ, who never
wrote a word,
saboteur
of received ideas
who rebuilt Rome
with the words he
never wrote:
whether sacred,
whether human,
himself a sunrise
of love, enlarged,
of love, enlarged.[1]

This book begins and ends in narrative description. Its content, the action of freedom and love in salvation, is imaged first in the initial representations of God and Jesus, then in the interwoven conclusion. These chapters may be read together without any of the intervening argument. The choice of this form was deliberate and appropriate, for the whole enterprise depends on free access to the love of God and therefore requires a medium which is itself accessible and mediates immediacy. That could be a description of Jesus Christ, but it is also in its own way true of the flesh made word again in christologies.[2] In that case a christology should do more than survey tradition, construct arguments and defend conclusions which may be neither accessible nor indicative of divine presence. It should also endeavour, as far as possible for the writer, to arouse the imagination (a far more potent influence on belief and action) to see the concurrence of divine and human in Jesus Christ.

> The arrangement contains the desire of
> The artist. But one confides in what has no
> Concealed creator.[3]

Imaginative representation *tout court* does not always have the effect one hopes for. In the poem quoted here Wallace Stevens, in reaction against an artfully posed portrait, declares that for preference he 'walks easily the unpainted shore'. This does not suggest that he sees the shore with an innocent eye, untouched by language, culture or experience, but there at least he is not being presented with the polished finality intended by another's composition. (The irony is that Stevens expresses this preference in a composition which is definitely not 'unpainted'. If expression and communication are to take place, such irony, like the irony of the flesh made word again, or the volumes on the man who never wrote anything, cannot be avoided.) Similarly, 'the story of Jesus' or 'the drama of salvation' presented in such a way that the creator is concealed may equally fail to arouse confidence. Why these particular representations?

Creators, of course, may still conceal something unconsciously in the most academic of discussions, but between the opening and final descriptions I have assembled reasons from the Bible, tradition, present knowledge and experience for the form and content of this christology. More exactly, the difference between representation and discussion is one of emphasis, for imagery reflects and may even advance an argument (as in the traditional 'begotten, not made'), while reason does not operate independently of the imagination. No order is perfect, and this one has difficulties in the separation of description and discussion. But for practical reasons also it seemed better to proceed in this way. The descriptive chapters embody the conclusions of the discussion, so that one may begin and end with positive portrayals and not with embroilment in christological problems. Moreover to mix argument and portrayal is to weaken both by interruption. Undoubtedly 'the arrangement' of the whole still 'contains the desire of the artist', but at least something of that desire, with its values, priorities, models and reasons is laid out for inspection.

With two thousand years of Christian tradition shaping mind and eye there is no 'unpainted' Galilean shore for a christologian to walk today. Yet in relation to the diverse heritage from the past there is here 'continuity and discontinuity, criticism and respect, acceptance and rejection, agreement and disagreement – for dialogue, interplay between past and present is inevitably involved'.[4] And if Christ continues to be the 'saboteur of received ideas' (in Plomer's phrase), he may still somewhere bring about an inverse miracle, whipping any flat doctrinal calm on the Sea of Galilee into disturbing life.

PART ONE

The Content of the Given

1 · God

The being of God

God is mystery. Whatever it is which we call God exceeds the finitude of human language, thought and being and is therefore mystery. Yet, because people have believed this mystery, have attended to it and found that it has touched and changed their lives, they have used language and reason, image and story to express it humanly, without denying the mystery.

God is one, not limited by the co-existence of other gods or powers. The one God must be infinite and therefore free, in that there is nothing outside which could curtail or condition the divine being. The boundlessness of infinity includes within itself the freedom of God throughout what humans experience as space and time. There is no time or space where God is not, but the divine exceeds time and space infinitely. So God is presence without absence.[1]

Since God is infinite and omnipresent, all creation must be 'in' God. There is nowhere else for it to be. It is the bounded presence of time and space within infinite presence. So God is never absent from creation. The sense of creation within God is caught in a warm image from Julian of Norwich, who saw the world as 'a little thing, the quantity of a hazel nut' which 'might fall suddenly to naught for littleness', except that God 'enwraps us and envelops us, embraces us and encloses us'.[2]

A God who is continually present in and with creation can no longer be thought of as 'up there' while the world is 'down here', separated by empty distance. All the images from the past of up and down, descending and ascending, no longer apply. A God who was thought of as at home 'up there' could be absent from 'down here', having to send emissaries such as angels, Wisdom,

Son or Spirit to be present in the world. The specialness of such means remains, but takes on a different character when God's continuous presence with creation is a presupposition for everything else. This book is concerned with what that means in the case of the Son.

Creation encounters God in relationship, so the being of God with which we ourselves are acquainted is being-in-relation. That has been expressed in all the wealth of human social relationships which have filled the tradition, like king, shepherd, father, friend. God, being God, relates perfectly, so the best imaginable models of relationship are used. But these are always human images from human society, and therefore as society changes, so do the roles in which the continuing relationship is understood. In a small hierarchical society in which the king's power and glory are evident, God is described as the wise, just and righteous ruler. When Israel fought for its land, God was Lord of the army. Now, in an age when personal autocracy is more suspect, when international power is known to be often covert and dubious, and when the power individuals actually encounter is more likely to be the facelessness of bureaucracy then the clemency, say, of a king, the earlier images of hierarchical relating are supplemented by those which are experienced as the best and warmest in our own society, like friend or companion. Images of parenthood remain potent, for they may change their content as perceptions of parenthood change, like the development of 'father' in this century from a primarily chastising authority to one who draws out a child's potential. Thus the images are varied from various societies, but what they have in common is the belief, expressed in human, temporal terms, that God provides the perfect relationship. That is also to say that the perfection of God's being is something which is expressed in open, continuous relating rather than in closed quantitive and qualitative completion.

Yet this very belief means that there is more to God than can be known in relationship and in the roles in which that relationship takes place. All relationship expresses the person relating, although a person is more than social relationships. Something of the being of the God known in relationship, may be pictured, but not much. Relationship requires openness to, respect for and understanding of the other; perfect relating implies perfect openness and perfect understanding, including respect in the sensitive application of knowledge and power. If God relates perfectly, therefore, to everything at all times, there must be within infinity something indescribable which might be pictured as an eternal 'well' of absolute potency beyond human conception or relation on which God can draw in order to have whatever knowledge and power are needed when they are needed.

Now these are needed in action, in relationship. Thus the perfection of God's knowledge and power are not these which foreordain or even foreknow the response of the other, nor are they those which will overwhelm the other, for both such characteristics would defeat the mutuality of relationship. Instead, God's perfect knowledge and power are those which draw on absolute potency to enable perfect relating. God is neither weak nor ignorant, having always the knowledge and power needed in the circumstances to relate with perfect understanding and sensitivity to all creation, including a hydrogen atom, methane gas, viruses, peonies, piranhas, pandas, humans or whatever. Unlike men and women, who have to relate to all else from a particular, limited human point of view and content of knowledge, an infinite God has complete understanding of all points of view and may relate to non-human creation in humanly unimaginable ways, but with perfect sensitivity of knowledge and power.

God's being, therefore, to the extent that we can begin to name it, is an everlasting potency which is actualized in every instance of divine relationship in space and time, while all creation exists within that nurturing environment. This christology is concerned with that understanding of divinity.

The freedom of God expressed in creation

God created the world: not as an artisan fabricates a technology he can then control, nor as an artist paints her own self-expression on to a canvas, nor as a mother gives birth to one of her own kind. God created the world by letting it be, by giving it the possibility of being and the freedom to develop.

Freedom is the character of the Creator, of the creating process and of the resulting creation as such. First, the Creator's infinity guarantees freedom from all external imposition, so God must have freely chosen to let be what is not-God. Infinity, however, need not mean having no boundaries at all. It may also imply having boundaries which are chosen, not imposed. Thus God may choose to respect the otherness of the other, for no relationship can be established or endure without such respect. Therefore, although the world is in God, it is not overwhelmed by the divine presence and remains distinct from the divine being. It is different, and although dependent upon divine possibility it is free to develop into what it may become. Creation responded to God's gift of possibility and respect for the other by coming into being in all its various ways through processes which are still continuing and still have freedom to develop.

The freedom of God is single and infinite. In one sense the freedom of creation is single as well – the freedom to develop without interference from God. But creaturely freedom is also finite; that is, it is bounded by time, space and other creatures who are also finitely free. The various ways in which past freedom has already shaped the world of possibility for better or worse give the context in which present freedom has to be exercised alongside others who are also using their possibilities of freedom. As a result there have been co-operative relationships in evolution and history, but there have also been competition, conflict and disaster. And there is always change, for anything new will succeed only if it rearranges or overturns the *status quo*. The continuing freedom of individuals or societies to rearrange their part of the world means that any existing order, however long it has lasted, is always vulnerable to upset through change, directly or in consequence of other changes.

Although it is the exercise of freedom in the world which has brought about its ambiguous character, if there were no freedom in creation there would be no 'world' as we know it at all. It is only because continuing possibilities have been acted upon that the diversity of species, societies and cultures has come into being. Freedom and possibility go together, and while the two endure, nothing in creation is finally fixed beyond all hope or fear of change. This does not make the world chaotic, though it does make it manifold. Instead of being chaotic, disordered or divinely preordered, the world is fluid with possibilities and hence orderable – for ever orderable and re-orderable, always determinable by whatever can make a difference, whether humans in their milieu or insects in theirs, whether locally or internationally.

Such freedom to respond and develop would be removed if God intervened to change things here and there, producing intermittently another originally disconnected set of conditions and their developments, overriding creaturely freedom of response in particular situations. A God who intervened would have to intervene sometimes or always, and both these options have serious difficulties. A God who intervened occasionally but left most suffering and disaster to take its course would hardly demonstrate relationship and love, and would not evoke worship and commitment. But if God were to intervene every time there was any kind of disaster to any creature, there would be no regularities left in the world and no dependable order would be possible in it. God does make all the difference to the world, but it is not the difference of intervention. This is true in the case of Jesus of Nazareth as well, for he was a man who responded freely to God, without that freedom being overridden by divine intervention. Even when multiple finite freedom produces disaster or misery, God does not intervene.

Suffering, hardship, inequality or extinction within creation would be impossible to connect with God's perfect relating unless creation is held to be free and thus accidentally or deliberately responsible. Some of the evils in the world are 'metaphysical', that is, they are inherent in the variety of finite freedom which came into being. Tectonic plates, volcanoes and quicksands all developed as the world evolved in response to God, but they were finite responses whose existence could at any point cause disaster to other beings. Their effects may be tragic, but one cannot blame volcanoes for being volcanoes. Nor is God to be blamed for letting them be, unless the evil consequent upon multiple finitude appears to outweigh all other considerations of creation. In that case creation as it is could be judged to be not worth the cost. The alternatives, however, if there were to be creation at all, would be one with no freedom, no multiplicity or no finitude. If there were no freedom, creation would be the puppet of God, who would have no respect for its otherness. It is difficult to see what kind of satisfaction or purpose would be achieved by such a toy. Moreover, without the variability which leads to multiplicity the possibilities of creation would be stringently reduced and relations would be stereotyped.

Finally, an infinite creation is a contradiction in terms. This is not the best of all possible worlds, and it is one which has developed and redeveloped contingently and often painfully, but if there is to be creation at all it is not obvious what other basic conditions could apply.

The evil which happens deliberately, carelessly or through wilful ignorance among humans, or between humans and the rest of creation, is a different matter. All order, including human order, is made, not found, in the orderable world of possibility. Order is needed, for just as stable conditions are necessary to any species, including humanity, for food, shelter and reproduction, so they are necessary to any society for such institutions as politics, religion or education, for instance. In the making and maintaining of order certain values will be expressed and particular kinds of relationships preferred. This is as true of family order as it is of international relations. In the process there is often a shifting mix of better and worse for the participants, and even for the devisers of order, for the world is rarely so manageable that everything goes according to plan. Yet it is through the values embodied in relationship or the denial of relationship that human social evil may occur.

No order is likely to be ideal for everyone, and values change like everything else in time. Nevertheless, distinctions may still be made. Some orders are imposed rather than agreed, ignoring mutuality of relationship and respect for the other in the implementation of values which serve only the interest of the dominant individual or group. A whole household may be organized, for example, on the principle of giving father peace and quiet, or a country under military dictatorship may be run for the benefit of the dictator and his supporters, no matter what may happen to others. If the quality of relationship within a world of multiple finite freedom is important, then these examples become instances on a scale of moral evil.

The quality of relationship does matter, because God is known in relationship, and the divine relationship becomes the model, the stimulus and criterion for all the relationships within the world and the values such relationships enact. In that case human response to God includes the use of freedom to bring about the best relationships possible within the finitude and diversity of the world and its inhabitants. Perfection throughout any relationship and goodness in all relationships are not humanly possible, and no one can be judged against an impossible ideal. But denial of relationship in spite of the interrelatedness of creation, and failures of relationship when something better was genuinely possible, make the world a place of greater inequality and grimmer hardship than it might have been.

So God in creation let be a finitely free complex diversity in a changeable world where humans implement values in shaping their societies in which relationships may be those which enlarge and fulfil or those which cripple or negate.

The love of God exercised in salvation

If freedom were the only decisive characteristic of God and creation, both would be diminished. God, like the God of the Deists, would in that case let the world be and show no further concern over its actual state. The situation would be indistinguishable from the one Hume imagined where the world, created by a superannuated deity too feeble to control it, simply 'ran on at adventures'.[3] Moreover, a creation whose only important feature was freedom might be adequately described in the cold terms of competition and conflict, with efficiency, the demolition of enemies and the weak, and the achievement of dominance being the signs of success. Freedom would then exist (however finitely) for the advancement of a self, a clan, a group, a society. Such a view has not been unknown in history, and is not absent from the present.

But, by complete contrast, it has been affirmed in the religious tradition that God is love. Enjoyment of creation on the one hand, and on the other care, support and indeed yearning for those in the toils of compromise, guilt and wrongdoing are the character of God's relationship which promises forgiveness for all failure. There is no way of demonstating that God is love, as one may show, given the premise of God's existence, that God is free. For God, who cannot have competitors for ultimacy, must be one, hence infinite, hence free. The love of God admits of no such logical inference, just as no human may infer from logic alone that one person loves another. In both cases the conclusion arises from the personal conviction of the loved one or the recognition of loving behaviour by those who see it.

It is often denied that the divine behaviour may be called loving, since God has not intervened to save in the great and small horrors of history. In that case salvation is being thought of only as rescue from the way the world is or from instances of wickedness. But that is only one way of understanding love and its consequences. Another way has to be found, for God will not remove the freedom of creation nor the regularities upon which the world depends for its very existence. Intervention is a model at home with the old understanding of God normally remote in transcendence, for such a God has to intervene or to act through agents and secondary causes to have an effect upon a world from which the divine is otherwise absent. But if creation is in God, the divine presence permeates the world without absence, even though it may sometimes be felt to be distant. In that case God does not have to intervene from without, being already part of every situation. But further, God allows the other to be *other* and so neither takes over nor manipulates creation in the process of giving it possibility to become what it might be. Intervention would in the end be unloving and a demonstration of partiality – quite apart from the question whether it is, strictly speaking, conceivable within the interrelationship of history. Instead of being a descent from heaven to rescue, the loving behaviour of God is more like a being-there, a disturbing and supporting companionship of all creation throughout ambiguous life with an accessibility which simply needs to be turned to, but will not be forced on anyone.

Such a God is vulnerable, both to the inattention and carelessness of creation and to the sharing of its pain as well as its joy. God does not let creation continue to be from a point of security above all the suffering, the compromises and the contradiction. Rather, God shares them all in all their multifariousness. Divine involvement is not like that of a scientist observing an experiment (not even an experiment in 'soul-making'), nor like that of a king/politician calculating that a greater good for many will come out of the suffering of some. Instead of that, God is more like a companion, relating in love to each individual and knowing perfectly the components and possibilities of every situation – consoling, confronting, forgiving and encouraging as the world is shaped and reshaped.

With this understanding of God's action, rescue is only one form of salvation, and in any case it refers to the rescue of a person who responds to a relationship which values and encourages. There may also be the rescue of a situation where relationships are changed in line with God's relation. But in neither case is there rescue by means of circumstances being changed from outside. All that love can do in an enhancing and fruitful relationship which bestows worth and purpose, even within the ambiguities of the world, is offered to creation by God who not only lets it be in freedom, but accompanies it in love. So salvation is not a new departure for God at some specific point, but the other aspect of divine relationship with creation from the start. Whatever the final state of things may be, the state Paul described as God being 'everything to everyone' (I Cor. 15.28), salvation as it is known here and now is the discovery that one is already loved, companioned, energized and forgiven by God.

In every good relationship there is giving as well as taking, so the discovery of God's love leads to creation's love of God and the sharing of God's concern for the world in its joy and sorrow. Just as all that was said about God's freedom has to be understood and rounded out by discovery of divine love, so human freedom to express value and shape the world is given its point by love. Our very being is one response to God, but beyond that there is the response of using what freedom we have to express love's values where we are. Thus the relationship in which each is free and each freely loves becomes the criterion for all relationships and the motivation for using the orderability of the world to bring about these values.

Two passages from the Old Testament illustrate vividly first, the relationship of freedom and love; secondly, the ordering of the world in accordance with these values. One of the most poignant expressions of freedom and love between God and humanity is given by Hosea's rendering of the relationship in terms of married love.[4] The prophet observes that God's people in their freedom have turned away to give their devotion to other gods, like a wife deserting her husband in promiscuity. God laments: 'What shall I do with you, O Ephraim? What shall I do with you, O Judah? Your love is like a morning cloud, like the dew that goes early away' (Hosea 6.4). But God's love endures this rejection, and the love he seeks in response cannot be commanded, nor can it be made a matter of duty or obedience; it can only be elicited from the other. 'Therefore, behold, I will allure her, and bring her into the wilderness, and speak tenderly to her . . . And in that day, says the Lord, you will call me "My husband" and no longer will you call me "My Baal"' (2.14, 16).

Israel and Judah are guilty of deserting God and of emptying religious rituals of substance: 'I desire steadfast love and not sacrifice, the knowledge of God rather than burnt offerings' (6.8). In Hosea, as in so many prophets, there are forceful passages on guilt and blame. God is free, and free to judge Israel. But surrounding the denunciations Hosea paints the picture of family love, of a God who prefers to forgive rather than to condemn, to be husband rather than judge. 'It was I who taught Ephraim to walk, I took them up in my arms . . . How can I give you up, O Ephraim, how can I hand you over, O Israel . . . My heart recoils within me, my compassion grows warm and tender' (11.3, 8f.). What Israel must do in that case is to seek out God as God has sought his wife: 'Take with you words and return to the Lord; say to him "Take away our iniquity; accept that which is good"' (14.2), God's response then is: 'I will heal their faithlessness; I will love them freely' (14.4).

The pattern of relationship here is based on the steadfast love of God which yearns for and seeks the other before that other is even aware of it. But it cannot be known in its full quality until the other in turn seeks God. Each is free so that the relationship, when it is recognized, is mutual. This is no dominating husband, no Baal. Yet God, the husband, is not so tied to his people that he cannot see their faults, nor is Israel so tied to God that she cannot go her own way. Nevertheless, there is a relationship to be sought and found between them which is not the ecstasy and agony of romance, but the steady comfort, encouragement, intimacy and co-operation of the best imaginable married love.

'Whoever is wise, let him understand these things', says Hosea in conclusion (14.9), and the relationship the prophet portrays has affinities with another Old Testament account of humankind's search for and rejoicing in Wisdom, a personified figure of the divine source of human wisdom. Instead of the bold direct imagery of God as husband to Israel this version takes Wisdom as a female mediator between God and all humanity. But the same motif of loving through seeking and finding recurs (as indeed it does in the love poem, the Song of Songs). Wisdom was created before all things, the delight of God and 'delighting in the sons of men' (Prov. 8.30f). Like God, she goes seeking in the streets and markets (1.20) and she herself is to be sought. Having set up her pillars and spread her table, she calls on others to come and gain insight from her (9.1–6).

It is not so much the forgiveness of guilt which is at issue here as the acquiring of wisdom for practical and just living. After the Jewish kingdom was destroyed, images of kingship for God became less compelling. God himself seemed distant. Yet religion continued to be practised within families where the wife (like the 'woman of worth' of Proverbs 31, who also had to be sought) with her practical ways, her teaching, counselling and loving could provide an image of how to live which could be linked with God, the creator of all wisdom. Thus personified Wisdom mediated between God and humanity. By the process of personification God through the figure of Wisdom could be seen to act, instructing the simple, guiding rulers. And because of the vividness of the picture, 'one responds not to the abstract concept of wisdom, but to the woman who takes a stand, cries out, offers love and builds a house'.[5]

Here, then, are two pictures of God's love which seeks the other but will not be imposed. One of them concerns forgiveness for failure and the tenderness of love, the other the insight for ordering affairs. One is mediated through the image of married love, the other through a lively figure which gathers together and gives a divine focus to the variety of human experience. Each is a way of expressing salvation, that metaphor, like redemption or reconciliation, for entering on the experience of the steadfast love of God in warm companionship, forgiveness and wisdom for living. To move from these moments of the Old Testament to Jesus Christ is to move from illustration and personification to that enactment of salvation in a human person which is incarnation.

2 · *Jesus*

Parables of response

Late one evening a Scot was walking alone through an American city when he found himself beside a large, dimly-lit parking-lot. At that very moment a tall muscular black appeared at the other end of the deserted street coming towards him. Just as they approached each other a public telephone began to ring from a pole in the lot. The black looked at the phone, then at the Scot, and said, 'Too bad. We ain't home, brother, are we?' To which the Scot replied, 'We sure ain't,' and they went their ways.

This scene actually happened, but in its quality as story it has much in common with the kind of parables Jesus told. I have kept the account almost as bare as the biblical tales, honed to the action without any latter-day psychological commentary on what either character felt or thought. But I shall depart from Jesus' practice by explaining why I have used it and what I believe the story has to tell. Jesus' parables are carried by what *happens*, while the 'inner' dimension remains implicit for his hearers to discern and apply. Such discernment is made possible in the first place because many of his stories have ordinary settings like farming, or easily understood ones like feasting. The setting has to be mundane, so that it does not pre-empt attention while possible but surprising things happen in it. The pavement/sidewalk in front of a car park is a contemporary urban equivalent which is easily assimilated. It requires no difficult act of the imagination.

Like many of Jesus' stories this one leads rapidly to a note of *tension*, for in our culture (British or American) it is easy to think of the meeting of black and white in a deserted place as a chancy affair the peaceful outcome of which could not be assumed. And mayhem in a parking-lot is a repeated motif of films. The desirable state of affairs would be to have a society in which this story would raise no apprehension, but as things most commonly are, we, white or black, can feel for this account all the unsettling background knowledge and imaginative understanding which Jesus' contemporaries could put into a story like the Good Samaritan. We are attuned to the depth of feeling and potential for violence which often exists between white and black, so that it does not have to be brought explicitly into the story. But now that the freshness of response has gone from hearing Jesus' parable after two thousand years of retelling and explanation we have to work at understanding the pristine shock it gave by portraying a despised foreigner as a neighbour in action. *The acceptance of disrupted relationships within his society, or fixed expectations of how relations were to be conducted often formed the initial position from which Jesus wished to dislodge his hearers.*

Because of the tension, the process of telling the American story, like the parables, raises the question 'What happens next?', and later the self-involving reflection 'What would I do in such a situation, supposing I allowed myself to get into it?' For these days there is an element of *risk* in walking alone at night through a city, as in Jesus' day there was risk in going down from Jerusalem to Jericho, in allowing a son to go his own way, or in giving money out to stewards. Unlike the setting, the opening action of Jesus' stories often involves a departure from *normal. So it may be that people who never risk putting themselves into the position of meeting what is strange to them, or whose instinct on encountering strangeness is to scuttle for safety, have not understood these parables.*

The tension of the story may be followed by a sudden twist of *surprise*, which is no more justified, but is just as likely to happen, as surprise at the charitableness of a Samaritan of all people, or the finding of royal guests in alleyways or back streets. In this case the surprise is not only the fortuitous ringing of the eerie telephone, but the response of the black in its everyday wit and inclusion of the white as 'brother'. Had the man been vicious or vengeful, the accident of the telephone would not have altered his purpose. Instead, the black resolves the situation in fraternity, enabling the white to respond in kind. 'We sure ain't' is not normal British speech, but to have said 'We certainly are not' would have put almost as much difference and distance between the two as not to have gone along with the black's interpretation. Even the fact that they spoke to each other in this way created a small spark of relationship which silence would never have ignited. Although the history of black and white has contained so much violence of domination or reaction of revolt, there is no sign of either in this encounter.

That leads to another parabolic aspect of the story – it produces *insight*. In our polarizing and frightened societies people are increasingly given to seeing others in predetermined categories, a matter particularly easy when based on something as obvious as the colour of skin. Such categories may then be used to define what relationship, if any, is possible. Some groups are marked off as dangerous or harmful to our own, and therefore to be avoided or met only with a show of strength. But here we have wit and humanity occurring between two who might have been in opposition, while the peaceful initiative comes from the one whose race has suffered more, and who has a white man at a disadvantage. It is possible to dismiss the story (and the thousands like it which occur daily) with a cynical comment like 'He was lucky to get off so lightly' or 'Whites always expect the worst of blacks'. But in the terms Jesus used, such a response is a refusal to see and hear, a refusal to be affected and changed by the story. When it becomes parable this small incident raises large questions: 'Could I have behaved like that? How do I behave to people of another colour, or to someone whose kind has done mine harm? Can I respond to openness with openness of my own?' Whether Jesus' stories disclose the extraordinary possibilities of relationship in ordinary settings or less unusual relations, like a father asking his two sons to do some work for him, *the story hinges on the quality of response which changes the whole situation.*

In this case both whites and blacks may have their different horizons enlarged and new perspectives on relationship opened up. The story does not excuse or deny the history of white exploitation or the present marginality of so many blacks. Rather, it shows that in the midst of our complex, troubled and violent times it remains possible to encounter one of another group in peace and equality, as if there were no 'groups'. One could begin the story with 'the kingdom of God is like a Scot who was walking alone in an American city . . .'. The kingdom, of course, is not like a Scot any more than it is like a man finding treasure in a field. The kingdom of God becomes visible in the perceptions and actions of the key characters in the stories.

The proximate kingdom

The kingdom of God was the substance of Jesus' good news. What he did put into action its attitudes, character, values and behaviour, while what he said encouraged other people to catch the vision and share in its happening. When Jesus observed the sacrifice and devotion of a widow putting her copper coins into the Temple treasury, he was seeing as he called on others to see. When he noticed Zacchaeus up a tree and invited himself to dine with the tax-collector, he put into action the overturning of categories and the establishing of relationship which characterize the kingdom. Of course this behaviour was not thought proper by many, for to be proper is to do the expected thing, so in a phrase the fine scorn of which can still be heard it was said that he was 'a friend of tax-collectors and sinners', (Matt. 11.19). By making himself freely available to the poor, the sick, the prostitutes, the lepers, the undesirable elements of society, to heal them, encourage them and forgive them Jesus enacted the accessibility of the love of God who is no respecter of persons. By having women in the group which travelled with him, he simply by-passed current conceptions of their appropriate place and role. His was an openness and sensitivity which ignored accepted social categories *if they put distance and difficulty between people and the kingdom.*

He exercised the same freedom, for the same reason, in regard even to the Jewish law. He did not abrogate the law, but would have nothing to do with its interpretation as a set of rules to be obeyed, however pious and self-denying the intention. The law, the way of life for the covenant community, was meant for the good of the men and women in it, to give them a framework of identity and morality in relation to God. But when pleasing God was interpreted primarily in terms of moral purity, the law came to be seen as a set of regulations for living more strict than seeking out Wisdom. Thus they became precise in definition and proliferated, as rules must, to cover every eventuality. Punctiliousness concerning rules is not simply a feature of first-century Jewish society. It has appeared regularly in Christian history and is alive and well in secular society.

I was warden of a student hall when its domestic staff became unionized. To the outrage of our cook, a cook was defined by the union as one who put two or more ingredients together or applied heat. According to the rules no one but the cook might perform these tasks, so, strictly speaking, no kitchen helper might even boil the water for tea. In the same way the sabbath rest, interpreted as a rule, required precise definitions of work so that work could be avoided. When Jesus' disciples plucked and husked ears of corn on the sabbath they were quite correctly accused of working 'within the meaning of the act', as it were. Jesus' response to this was not to supersede the law. He did not say, 'Forget the sabbath, it's people who count'. He considered neither the sabbath on its own nor people on their own but concentrated on the fruitful relation between the two: 'The sabbath was made for man, not man for the sabbath' (Mark 2.27). The sabbath had a purpose of rest and worship for all Jews which had become obscured by the paraphernalia of regulations, and it was to that purpose, the spirit rather than the letter, that Jesus appealed. He put into their right relationship an institution and the people for whom it was made, for otherwise any social institution may impede the kingdom.

What did Jesus mean by the kingdom of God? He never defined it, so although it may to some extent be described, its real understanding is intuitive and self-involving, like the parables. It is easier to say what it is not than what it is, for no concentrated power in the present and no Jewish tradition of God's rule captures the use to which Jesus put the metaphor. Today, for instance, one of the models of power is the cohesive organization of an international conglomerate, with carefully encouraged loyalty from its staff. None of that shows in Jesus. One of the delights of reading the Gospels in an age when managerial and entrepreneurial models of relationship proliferate is to find that he was not organized in that sense. He conducted no strategic evangelization crusade. Instead, he put himself where people of all kinds were and let the encounters come *ad hoc*. These encounters occurred because Jesus drew people to himself, and with his spontaneity and sensitivity he could address their situation. He saw the kingdom as leaven working invisibly through a loaf, or as salt sprinkled all over to change the taste of the world. Again, fidelity to the kingdom is not achieved by an organization's judicious mixture of reward and pressure (a kind of secular version of the roles heaven and hell used to play in 'preaching for conversion').The spontaneity of Jesus' approach is met (sometimes) by spontaneity of response, for the kingdom is more a matter of organic inter-relationship than of hierarchical organization. Organization, moreover, distances those at the centre from those at the periphery, just as the protocol of a court elevated a king and protected him from the rabble. But there is no such distant power and privilege in Jesus' words and actions. He tells of a lost sheep personally fetched whatever the cost, and of a politically powerless widow who can pester for justice. These are the signs of the kingdom.

There are, however, 'authority figures', to use the current phrase, in Jesus' stories where class distinctions between owners and servants form the background to the tale as they formed part of the society he spoke to. Such stories would be at home among the property-owning middle classes whom Jesus visited and conversed with, for, since he did not observe barriers in society, he was not concerned only with the poor.[1] There are some 'givens' in Jesus' society which he showed no sign of overtly revolutionizing. His mission was to the house of Israel, and only through exceptional efforts by outsiders was he willing to extend it; he did not condemn the tax to Caesar with all its political implications so long as full attention was given to God; he could presume the class-structure and tell his parables within that (although he also told a rich young man that to *follow* him involved giving away all he had to the poor). Possibly his apparent conservatism on these issues was because he believed that time was too short for social upheaval before the great and final Day of the Lord. But it is equally possible that he was instead more fundamentally revolutionary. For his priority was to change perceptions and values, and it is only with renewed hearts and openness in relationship that any really worthwhile change in society can occur.

For this reason I can see no objection to a retelling of the story of the prodigal son which occurs in Graham Greene's *Monsignor Quixote*. One character in the book, a Spanish communist mayor who had been to seminary in his youth, describes the father in the story as a typical capitalist living off the surplus value of his servants. The older son is happy to be part of such class oppression, but the younger is sickened by the notion of unearned wealth. He asks for his share of the inheritance and gives it away to the poor, becoming a peasant on a pig farm. But he wavers in his intention and returns home, where a fatted calf is killed. (What one might call typical capitalist conspicuous consumption, and a meal which, presumably, gave the servants extra work.) But as he lies on his soft bed the prodigal feels again the oppressive atmosphere of bourgeois capitalism.

> After a week of disillusion he leaves home at dawn (a red dawn) to find again the pig farm and the old bearded peasant, determined to play his part in the proletarian struggle. The old bearded peasant sees him coming from a distance, and, running up, he throws his arms around his neck and kisses him, and the Prodigal Son says, 'Father, I have sinned. I am not worthy to be called your son.'[2]

This story may be thought of alongside Jesus' one. It does not supersede it, because the point in both is a quality of forgiveness which is total and without recrimination. To object that the mayor's version moves away from the letter of the original is to put more store by the letter than by the insight it produces. Again, to object that God is rendered by a pig-farming peasant rather than by a rich landowner is to have missed the extent of Jesus' 'tendency to democratize the kingdom', in Vermes' phrase.[3] For instance, in line with the prophets who had seen images of God in potters and washerwomen, Jesus used housewives and shepherds to make his rendering vivid. What may happen, especially among an urban middle class, is that potters or shepherds are romanticized, or at least verbalized, out of the dirt and dust of their working-class realities.

If Jesus wanted his hearers to *hear*, in the full sense which includes self-involvement, he made the setting easy so that they could follow the story. If he told the story of the prodigal and his father to property-owners they would have no trouble with the background, and could concentrate on the surprising freedom the father allowed his son, and the complete forgiveness and reunion with which the story ends. They could then wonder how it affected them. Had Jesus told the story in the terms of the communist mayor they might have been so shocked that they could hear nothing else. Conversely today, when a significant number are concerned about the effects of unequal distribution of wealth, or the disadvantages of patriarchy, they may not be able to *hear* (in Jesus' sense) a story about a rich patriarchal landowner. (Yet it does no one any harm to remember that there are good men who may be landowners or peasants.) There is ample evidence of Jesus' concern for the poor, so his story is just as true, just as revelatory of God's constant relationship with wandering inconstant humanity, if it is told from the other end of the class structure with presuppositions other than bourgeois behind it.

But there is still more to be said about the authority figures which appear in Jesus' parables, especially as these represent God. The role of the authority is to open story after story by taking the risk of delegating so that the interest of the parable lies in what the son, the servants or the stewards do on their own initiative. The authority is there to give freedom; the response to that freedom makes the story. For just as one cannot be moral without sufficient freedom to decide one's actions without coercion, so one cannot have self-changing perceptions without the freedom to assess the past and intend the future. Moreover, when the owner in Jesus' stories does not delegate but remains powerful, surprises still result, for when expected 'suitable' guests fail to respond positively, unexpected and hitherto 'unsuitable' guests are invited. Or the owner of a vineyard who hires workers morning, noon and evening keeps his bargain with all, but shows generosity to those who served him briefly and belatedly. If this is the kingship of God, it is not like that of any recorded king.

Nor does Jesus' account of the kingdom follow the traditional Jewish understanding of God's reign, an image which had been in use at least since David's time. It was an image which had already undergone changes as Israel's own history changed. The Psalms celebrated God's past and present rule over nature and history, but when disaster struck at the exile Isaiah envisioned a peaceful and harmonious rule of God in the future after the desolation (Isa. 24–27). Then, when Jewish history worsened again, with impious invaders who even desecrated the Temple, Isaiah's picture was intensified apocalyptically with fantastic images of warfare and destruction before final triumph (Joel). Some of this remains in Jesus' allusions, especially the expectation of an imminent accounting, as in the parable of the sheep and the goats. But there is radical novelty as well.

The reign of God in the Old Testament was always an exercise of external power directing or consummating the course of history and commanding the forces of nature. Majesty was its principal characteristic, awe and obedience the appropriate attitude of humanity. And in apocalyptic the world is considered unfit to bc the locus of the kingdom until it is renewed. But in contradiction to the glory and externality of most of the tradition and to the apocalyptic despair at the world, Jesus could liken the kingdom to a mustard seed – organic, earthed and tiny in its inception. Rarely do his stories suggest that the kingdom is extra-terrestrial, powerfully manipulative, awesomely majestic or difficult of attainment. To put that positively: the kingdom he spoke of was present in the world, allowed humanity its own determination, drew by attraction (the pearl, the treasure) rather than by force, and was freely available to all.

What, then, is the kingdom? There is a sense in which the kingdom is something which shows itself, which happens in the ordinary world. It is thus always proximate, either happening, or among the possibilities of any situation. It is extraordinarily difficult to define, for it is just what breaks down or transcends all human and historically contingent classification, including the term 'kingdom', and yet relates to all historical contingency. To give an abstract, all-embracing definition does not help, for the point is not so much to know the kingdom in general as to recognize its happening and to enact it. If Jesus, when he was asked 'Who is my neighbour?', had merely answered, 'Everyone is your neighbour', that response, though true, would have been so general as to have lost its compelling and involving character. Instead he told the story of that hyperbolic instance of the neighbour, the good Samaritan. Similarly, the kingdom is better known through perception of and involvement in instances of its occurring than from abstract consideration of its characteristics. Certainly it counts everything as valuable, down to a single lost coin; it gives a quality of joy like good fellowship at a feast; it bubbles through society like leaven; it is as various as a trawl of fish; it happens suddenly as a thief in the night and requires readiness of perception and action like bridesmaids with oil in their lamps. So one could go on, but description is at best stimulus to response.

Because this is the kingdom *of God*, there is more to be said concerning God. Yet awareness of God does not enter into Jesus' parables as a motive for action. So no bounds may be put upon the kingdom's happening by insisting on religious intention or correct doctrine first. In the parable of the sheep and the goats it came as a *surprise* to 'the sheep' that in helping and maintaining relationship with those in trouble they had been acting towards 'the least of these my brethren' (Matt. 25.40) and hence to God. God's presence is everywhere, part of every situation, including the suffering of the sick, the stranger and the imprisoned. Whatever is done, by anyone, which creates relationship and enhances life is a moment of the kingdom, one might say of salvation and of eternal significance.

Awareness of the kingdom, however – and this is one of the things Jesus brings about – makes a radical difference, like being born again or having the doors of perception cleansed. Yet it is the same world into which one is reborn, with all its powers, inequalities, suffering, conflicts, co-operation and occasional goodness; what has changed are one's understanding, values and priorities. Since the kingdom concerns the enactment of relationships in relation to God, there can be no merely instrumental usages of creation, no egocentric manipulation of others, no withdrawing from relationship. Everyone and everything in inter-relationship has intrinsic value by virtue of the relation with God. Even the sparrows have their place within this scheme according to Jesus, and by extension all other apparently negligible creatures matter in their own way to the Father of all, and hence in their relationship with humanity. And as for humans, Jesus told his followers that anger was to find its outcome in reconciliation rather than conflict, that even enemies were to be loved, thereby denying the divisive categories of friend and foe, together with the behaviour thought appropriate for each. 'Judge not, and you will not be judged; condemn not, and you will not be condemned; forgive and you will be forgiven; give and it will be given to you' (Luke 6.37f.).

It is clear, then, that the kingdom, a social metaphor for salvation, consciously comes about in the two related aspects of seeing (or hearing) and doing – catching a vision of the new state of affairs as it affects oneself, one's group, country or the whole world, and acting on that. Seeing is not enough, but the doing will not take place without it. And it is possible to look without 'seeing' at all. Jesus asked what people had seen when they went to look at John the Baptist – a reed swaying in the wind? a man wearing fine clothes? (Matt. 11.8). This is irony bordering on sarcasm, since John 'wore a garment of camel's hair, and a leathern girdle about his waist; and his food was locusts and wild honey' (Matt. 3.4). John's clothing and food were those of the traditional prophet, but they were also outward symbols of the austerity of his call to repent. But, Jesus asked, did you see this, or only the rare spectacle of a prophet one could view for its novelty and frisson of excitement without being touched by the message? In what is also the traditional warning of the prophets: 'He who has ears to hear, let him hear' (Matt. 11.15). Then he continues the indictment of blindness and deafness with his own case. The ascetic John was rejected as a man possessed; Jesus, open to everyone, eating and drinking with rich and poor alike, was called a glutton and a drunkard, and thus summarily dismissed as not worth taking seriously. To those who will not see or hear there is always an excuse masquerading as sufficient reason for withholding from engagement. 'But to what shall I compare this generation? It is like children sitting in the market place and calling to their playmates, "We piped to you and you did not dance; we wailed to you and you did not mourn"' (Matt. 11.17). The uninvolved can see that there are games going on, but they will not join the play no matter how the game is presented. They have chosen to be left out.

To Jesus it was a deadly thing not to respond, like the fate of the servant who wrapped up and buried his talent, and the responsibility lay with the person concerned. Yet Matthew includes in his account of Jesus' protest against inertia the verse: 'No one knows the Father except the Son and anyone to whom the Son chooses to reveal him' (Matt. 11.27). This appears to put all the responsibility on Jesus: those whom he chooses see; those whom he does not choose remain blind. Certainly this notion of election, of being chosen by God, runs like a strong thread through Old and New Testaments, and is a natural way of expressing surprise and gratitude at newness of life.

There is a sense that something marvellous has been achieved which one could not have achieved oneself. But when God's choice is made to account also for the blindness of others (and that is a natural extension of the notion of divine choice), a very different picture of God emerges from those of the father whose prodigal son made his own choice to come back, or the shepherd so concerned for the entire flock that he did not simply dismiss the lost sheep as blind, but searched for it. Again the bridegroom did not decide which bridesmaids were wise, and which foolish, for their wisdom and folly emerged from what they did or failed to do. An effort must be made to do justice to the sense of specialness and divine effectiveness involved in the notion of God's choice, while still allowing for Jesus' practice of calling on people to choose whether or not they would hear. For that the whole picture of God's constant presence and relation with creation has to be borne in mind. The divine presence and initiative are prevenient, already there at all times and places. God therefore chooses all, making such relationship possible by that choice. But that again is a general statement which is not compelling until we ourselves *see* and find God's choice, which is open to everyone, actually alighting on *us* in a special instance, a fullness of time. Yet human seeing is a response, made intermittently and imperfectly but made by creation. And it is possible that God's lure to see and enact the kingdom, with loving, forgiving companionship through the attempt, may be missed out of inattention or unwillingness.

As well as personal failures there are stumbling-blocks which social institutions can raise. The principal one Jesus encountered was the religious establishment, especially as represented by the Pharisees. The Gospels, in fact, take a fairly limited and negative view of the Pharisees, since for the evangelists these represent the intransigence of the religious *status quo* towards Jesus and the later church. The Pharisees already had their viewpoint and their way of life, putting into practice the belief that the way to please God was to keep the whole law in all its minutiae. In terms of the children in the market place they were playing a different game from Jesus, but theirs was a difficult game, impossible for ordinary people to join, and that was what Jesus objected to. The Pharisees incarnated that rule-like conception of law whose demands were numerous, time-consuming and cumulatively impossible for any who could not spend their whole lives on it. So others were excluded from the game by its difficulty, not from choice. The Pharisees' self-discipline and devotion were exemplary, but in the Gospels they represent a whole programme of doing without seeing, without the vision Jesus had of God closely involved, accessible to all, calling for response but infinitely forgiving, a vision which changes all life and relationship.

So Jesus told a story about a tax collector (and by any standards that was an unsavoury occupation), whose relationship with God was more effective through his immediate humble asking of God's mercy than that of a carefully-tithing Pharisee, who was proud of having erected the law into a barrier which only the elite could cross. Pharisees divided the world and its contents into the clean and the unclean, but that is just the kind of opposition which is broken down in the kingdom: 'Give for alms those things which are within; and behold, everything is clean for you' (Luke 11.41). Just as the children in the market-place become symbolic of the uninvolved of all ages, so the Pharisees symbolize all later religious institutions who trust to their observances to confer righteousness, and whose understanding of God is so fixed that they have no place for the surprising enactment of the kingdom.

Other institutions, however, may be at least as rigid and blinkering. Cultural assumptions and categories, styles of education and business methods, are these days far more potent providers of constraints on imagination and conscience, curtailers of vision and patterners of conduct whose result, if absorbed without question, can render the kingdom invisible. Even then, in human relationships, in occasional perceptions unclassifiable in commonsense categories, its unidentified shadow may persist. Francis Hope expresses such a sense in *Instead of a Poet*:[4]

There were no dragons in his dreams,
No armies wheeling in the sky.
To his exact and conscious eye
The world remained the thing it seems.

The flat and documentary truth
Clung to him like a nagging wife,
Complaining of the wretched life
Her narrow vision gave them both.

But sometimes winter mornings brought –
Frost-sharp, ice-clear – the feeling of
A wider certainty of love
Colouring the outlines of his thought.

And foreign towns could sometimes chase
Routine like clouds away, and yield
Visions of otherness revealed
In the exactitudes of place.

At times like these, he cried aloud
That not to be a poet is
The worst of all our miseries,
That silence choked him like a shroud;

And scribbled lines like fallen hopes
On backs of tattered envelopes.

Thus dissatisfaction or sorrow at things as they are may open one's eyes, especially when the world is diminished or relationships disrupted or denied. In the Gospels, that feeling, when it becomes effective, is called repentance, which is not emotion alone, but a change of mind, heart and direction. Such active repentance is itself a sign of the presence of the kingdom rather than a precondition for entering it, for by the time one *repents*, the change has already taken place. A parable of Jesus tells how a man asked his two sons to work in his vineyard, and a vineyard was the symbol of Israel under the care of God. Here God, as usual with Jesus, allows humanity to make up its mind. One son said he would go, but defaulted. The other refused at first but later *repented* and went. Jesus acts on the presumption that it is never too late to change direction. Past failure in seeing what the kingdom is about does not debar anyone at any time, unless that failure is embraced as worldly success, or at least as *normality*. Optimism about human capacity to change even settled ways of being and thinking, to transcend group clannishness or the self-preservation and advancement of individuals, underlies Jesus' whole approach to people in spite of his frustration at their lack of response.

Moreover, an urgency was imparted to his message by his sense of crisis and the coming end of things as they are. Like death, these ideas concentrate the mind wonderfully. In its final fullness, which Jesus believed God would bring about, the kingdom is joy, fellowship and well-being, symbolized by a banquet. But he could also tell stories of judgment, and of what is not the kingdom being eternally lost. If humanity is free at every moment to enact the kingdom, it is also free to fail. The rich man in Jesus' story who had no concern for the beggar at his gate had no share in the kingdom because he had never done anything which brought it about. The kingdom and the salvation it stands for is something which happens in the interrelationship of creation, not something which exists wholly independently. Its content from the human and temporal point of view is the accumulation of all the diverse moments of its coming to pass, which become part of the eternal divine presence. So what people do to each other and to the rest of creation either is or is not the kingdom; there is nothing else here and now. What is lost is lost both to the individual and to the kingdom, for it means there has been no response to God. But can anyone be completely lost? God is loving, forgiving and completely understanding of human circumscribed and fallible lives. But God has also given humanity a freedom which is real freedom. So, if it can indeed be that someone who has been able to exercise freedom of choice has *never* participated, however briefly, in an open, loving and thoughtful relationship, that is, has never enacted, and would by preference never enact, the kingdom in word or deed, he or she cannot, as it were, contribute later, whatever else may happen after death. Jesus foresaw a great accounting day in the near future, in line with apocalyptic thinking. His near future has passed, but the now-or-never time of the kingdom remains.

So this is the kingdom begun, continued and ended in God. Writing of the Jewish use of the phrase, C. H. Dodd observed that 'the substantive conception . . . is the idea of God, and the term "kingdom" indicates that specific aspect, attribute or activity of God in which he is revealed as king or sovereign Lord of his people, or of the universe which he has created.'[5] Jesus democratized the kingdom and did not present God as sovereign although he kept the term which had that connotation and saw God as the final assessor. There remains, however, the 'substantive conception', that understanding of God which includes God in a parable, even when the name is not mentioned. Parables are arresting instances of life and values in God's presence, given in narrative mode. Something may perhaps be said of Jesus' 'substantive conception'. He called God 'Father' in his prayers, and was so certain of God's love that he forgave sins and told stories of forgiveness. Moreover, God had drawn Jesus from home, work and family to a ministry with no human safeguards. This is an unsettling, stirring, but always loving and supporting God. Such a conception is certainly consonant with a God who gives creation freedom to develop and have its own life, accompanying it in love and yearning for response. With such a God, humanity is free to respond or to remain unaffected, and God is free to judge as well as to comfort, attract, energize and companion. All life is lived in the presence of God, and parables of the kingdom are clues to what this might mean.

Entr'acte: Jesus and the Grand Inquisitor

In *The Brothers Karamazov* Dostoevsky puts into the mouth of Ivan, the socialist, a story of the return of Jesus to mediaeval Seville where he is healing, reviving and blessing when he is taken into custody by the Grand Inquisitor, fresh from the burning of heretics.[6] The Grand Inquisitor justifies his methods as those of real, practical love by condemning those of Jesus as impossible, hence unloving. Jesus is indicted for offering humanity a freedom and responsibility of which it is not capable. If the Pharisees appeared to have made things too difficult with their rules, the Grand Inquisitor condemns Jesus for having made things too difficult by dispensing with rules: 'You wanted man's free love so that he should follow you freely, fascinated and captivated by you. Instead of the ancient strict law, man had in future to decide for himself with a free heart what is good and what is evil, having only your image before him for guidance' (p.299).

That indictment might appear to carry no weight since it is made by a Grand Inquisitor, a type who has become one of the 'villains' of church history. Yet what Ivan/Dostoevsky has done, like Jesus in his use of the hyperbolic instance, has been to take an extreme case of alternative views in action which includes within it all lesser examples of those concerned to control humanity for their own good. Just as Jesus' stories aim to shake up the settled expectations of his listeners, so the story of the Grand Inquisitor appears to recommend settled expectations so that people know where they are. The literary excerpt is familiar, yet it is worth rehearsing again, since Dostoevsky's character is not merely fictional but is the encapsulation of the most serious and total questioning of Jesus' approach to men and women as displayed in the Gospels. It offers a recognizable alternative with cogent reasons and practical methods.

Dostoevsky focusses the complaint against Jesus on his rejection of mystery, miracle and authority in his temptations according to Luke's circumstantial rendering (4.1–12). First Jesus was tempted to turn the stones of the desert into bread and win people to his cause by providing for their material needs. 'But you did not want to deprive man of freedom and rejected the offer for, you thought, what sort of freedom is it if obedience is bought with loaves of bread?' (p.294). Thus the Inquisitor understands what he is opposing, but immediately counters with a different picture. People need bread, and they are unable in the individual freedom Jesus proposes to see that each has a fair share, so the weak among them need the strong to look after their physical well-being. The weak, therefore, are willing to enslave themselves to the strong in return for bread, easing their conscience from Jesus' demand on them and yielding their intolerable and unworkable freedom.

Likewise Jesus refused to allow humanity to be enslaved by the miracle of casting himself down safely from the pinnacle of the Temple. But, says the worldly-wise Inquisitor, 'what man seeks is not so much God as miracles', especially 'at the most fearful moments of life, the moments of his most fearful, fundamental and agonizing spiritual problems' (p.300). That is to say, what people actually want is rescue when necessary and not the trouble of transformation. A God who can save from a tight corner is useful, but a God who desires self-involving response is asking too much. Again Jesus has estimated humanity too highly: 'Had you respected him less, you would have asked less of him, and that would have been more like love, for his burden would have been lighter.' Again, only the strong can cope: 'Why is the weak soul to blame for being unable to receive gifts so terrible?' (p.301). The church's duty in that case is to relieve the feeble and ignoble of a responsibility so impossible that it had lost the character of love. 'Tell me – did we not love mankind when we admitted so humbly its impotence and lovingly lightened its burden and allowed man's weak nature to sin, so long as it was with our permission?'

Again, Jesus was tempted by being shown all the kingdoms of the world and offered their domination if he would worship the devil. He was mistaken to refuse, argues the Inquisitor, since he could thereby have brought about universal peace. By default the church has to pursue this path: 'For who is to wield dominion over men if not those who have taken possession of their consciences and in whose hands is their bread?' To control them the church will show people 'that they are weak, that they are mere pitiable children' (p.304) and will take on its ministers the responsibility, the judgment of parents and directors. But, since they have made people happy, 'Judge us if you can and if you dare!' (p.305). Jesus' only response is to kiss the Grand Inquisitor and depart.

The Grand Inquisitor is a haunting figure, whose paternalism persists in many ecclesiastical and political movements. Moreover he cannot be said to be entirely wrong. Feeding the hungry, caring for the weak, rescuing those *in extremis* and exercising wise rule may be admirable concerns in church and politics, and they are actions attributed to God. Yet there are different ways of engaging in these efforts, depending on the assumptions concerning power which lie behind them. On the one hand power may be retained by its possessors in order to make and repeat the gesture *de haut en bas*; on the other it may be used in such a way as to empower others so that rescue turns into transformation. The

Grand Inquisitor, for instance, insists that people need bread, which is true while there are still famines in the world which require an organized response of rescue. But there is a difference between a project which simply continues to hand out bread, thereby retaining and exercising power, and one which endeavours to encourage local agriculture, milling and baking, thereby spreading power and responsibility in the community. Western aid agencies are aware of this and have moved from the paternalistic to the enabling mode. Likewise, liberation theology insists that salvation includes this-worldly relief from oppression and exploitation by those who keep the power of (bread) distribution to themselves.

Inherent in both liberation theology and the change in aid agencies is an optimistic view of what humanity is capable of, such that once people are given the condition in which response is possible they will respond. Of course there will be some who remain helpless or apathetic and some who use enabling to create their own domination. But these negative reactions do not invalidate the aim to empower the physically, materially, or politically weak. Such hopefulness, or at least the refusal to despair, has more in common with Jesus than with the Grand Inquisitor who declared: 'I swear man has been created a weaker and baser creature than you thought him to be' (p.300). Everything the Grand Inquisitor does is predicated on that judgment which allows him and the few others he designates 'strong' to govern the weak for their own good.

As a description of society at large, however, such pessimism is surely wrong – more convenient for the ideology of the strong than an accurate estimate. Such division is made by those who have the power to define themselves as strong, and they are confirmed in their superiority by defining others as weak. Once defined the groups are looked to, treated as, and expected to behave as, the strong or the weak. It is, for instance, the classic protest of women against male power that the entire sex was once defined by men as weak – an ontological definition of their being-as-such which allowed of no diversity and no change.

Jesus, however, required no weak group to make him strong, so when categories like these created difficulties for people in their relation with others or with their access to God, Jesus opposed and disregarded them in order to draw strength from unlikely people. Certainly he could be disappointed, misunderstood and rejected, but these look like risks he took in persuading people to see for themselves. Moreover the God whom Jesus called Father was not strong at the expense of humanity, but strong to strengthen humanity as the man Jesus was strengthened, drawing by a love which elicits response and growth from the other rather than a love which swaddles and keeps the loved one childlike. Some humans need a child to remain child out of their own inadequacy in coping with adult offspring, but that can hardly be attributed to God. The Grand Inquisitor is therefore partly right in that there are weak souls who cannot manage responsibility but wrong in making that the norm of expectation.

The Grand Inquisitor claims that all humanity wants is a little divine help when required. Again he is not entirely wrong. People who thought themselves entirely secular may call on God when all other power fails. But once more he has taken as the norm the lowest of possible common denominators, a crudely instrumental and temporary appeal to God. It is perceptible that the Inquisitor also despises those whom he does love in his paternalistic way. He has the same condescension as newspaper proprietors who believe that popular taste is so low that one cannot underestimate it. The Grand Inquisitor might regard their papers' circulation successes as vindication, arguing that if Christianity is to have mass appeal it may not aim higher than sensation and rescue – preferably dramatic. But Jesus was looking for something much more profound. In the story of the ten lepers cleansed (Luke 17. 11–19), a story which could make banner headlines, the nine who were simply rescued appear to be a kind of failure (theirs, not Jesus'), whereas the Samaritan who returned to praise God and give thanks was commended for his faith. Readers of the tabloid press are as capable of that response as anyone else. Jesus sought out the worth in people individually, their intrinsic value despite society's manipulation of them and their own failings. Therefore, however much it was a long way round and fraught with the possibilities of disappointment, Jesus did not seek easy and instant illumination, but the diffusion of light from person to person. The freedom the Grand Inquisitor so dislikes and fears remains.

But his question also remains. Is Jesus' unorganized offer of the kingdom with no detailed provision for its interpretation and living really workable – either in terms of the possibility of the diverse ways people would in fact put it into practice, some of them horrendous, or in terms of the possibility of any ordinary person keeping up with the call of God, however lovingly supported? There is a sense in which all churches have taken their stand with the Grand Inquisitor here, for they have produced creeds, catechisms and confessions, that is, statements intended to communicate and teach *the* faith rather than parables to elicit *a* faith. Such statements become directives: 'Believe this way', rather than Jesus' question: 'What do you think?' Moreover, when subscription to such documents is used to define 'who's in, who's out' in any sense, they oppose Jesus, for the whole tenor of his approach was to break down such divisions with his belief that the most surprising people (surprising to the orthodox) might be part of the kingdom: 'the tax collectors and the harlots go into the kingdom before you' (Matt. 21.31).

Yet the development of definition is inevitable and need not in itself be vicious in a Grand Inquisitorial manner. For if belief (in Jesus, as it developed, rather than in the kingdom he parabled) is to be communicated or even expressed, some closure of understanding has to be made. So, in time, statements and doctrine accumulate and organization takes place. Paul, for instance, for all his metaphors, did not tell parables, and chided the Corinthian church for being positively opaque in its diversity. Indeed part of the burden of a later chapter is that *any* presentation of Jesus, including that of the evangelists, will have to select, organize and harmonize. But Jesus is the disturber of those at ease in Zion. His demand for vision here, now, of God in relation to the world stands over against any statement whatsoever which may be merely inherited passively. The same is true for his reminder that the sabbath and all organized religious institutions were made for men and women in their diversity, of whose capacity to respond he had a high estimate. If, therefore, in the process of credal statement and ecclesiastical organization the freedom of people to see the kingdom for themselves and to enact it in love in their own circumstances is lost, then the church owes more to the Grand Inquisitor than to Jesus.

It is probably empirically true that there are some weak people, that there are people who want God only in emergencies, that there are people who are happiest when they have no need to think, respond or involve themselves. It is also probably empirically true that counter examples exist in every case. But the Grand Inquisitor was not just arguing from an empirical basis. His ideology of the strong had divine legitimation for he believed humanity was *created* base and weak. That belief has informed christologies and church organization. But it is not a belief one would arrive at from the Gospels. Paul's 'For all have sinned and fall short of the glory of God' (Rom. 3.23) is undoubtedly true. But to make that the only relevant theological or ecclesiastical observation on humanity is to miss the way Jesus expected people to see, to understand to some extent and to shape their lives accordingly. Dostoevsky has noticed what many theologians down the ages have missed, that if one begins with Jesus' own behaviour one has to have a hopeful opinion of humanity. It was not that Jesus sentimentally overlooked faults. Rather it was in spite of his frustration at the irresponsive, his criticism of impossible religious requirements, his perception of Herod as 'that fox' (Luke 13.32), in spite of his rejection by his own family and locality that he continued to offer stories for discernment, and teaching for the transvaluation of values.

Doctrinally one could call this a 'high anthropology'. Jesus acted on the assumption that humanity remains lovable to God. And if Jesus is the revelation of God, then God too is everlastingly optimistic. Hope springs eternal in the *divine* heart in spite of the continuing contrary sinful indications which normally provide the staple of soteriological patterns. Thus instead of counting the weaknesses, crimes, follies and omissions of humanity as the final estimate of the worth of human creation, God suffers these as negative moments in the continual process of seeking and stirring up the good in the sense of what is of the kingdom. Humanity remains able to respond and to align itself with the divine purpose by enacting the divine kingdom in its behaviour. Humanity thus remains worth the freedom which it can also use to produce misery. God's compassion is aroused by the curtailment of that freedom, by what cripples life and blocks responsiveness. It is only selfish indifference which brings about judgment.

It is certainly a real question whether Jesus (and thus God) does not ask too much of humanity, and the darker side of church history must give one pause. It would be interesting to know too, for instance, how Zacchaeus was doing six months on. A liberation theologian, who has utopia among his ideals, admits: 'Realistically one can only struggle for a type of sociability in which love will be less difficult, and where power and participation will have better distribution.'[7] It is not surprising that efforts to contain rather than transform men and women came into being. Yet when all has been said of weakness and sinfulness there remains this surprising, unquenchable divine hopefulness, a presence in the world seeking and stirring up vision and action and a love which forgives failure. For if humanity has the freedom it needs to respond in love it has also the concomitant freedom to fail.

There are probably far more moments of the kingdom going on in the inter-relationships of earth than are noticed: it is, after all, seed growing secretly. But there are also failures, acknowledged failures of love and failures to 'see' which may not even be recognized. Yet here comes a point which the Grand Inquisitor never mentions – the reality of the forgiveness of God. However much has been missed or failed, repentance is always possible, and God's presence is constant. 'How often should I forgive?' asked Peter, and Jesus' answer was 'Seventy times seven', a notional number which has no end (Matt. 18.22). To this extent we are forgiven, and are called on to forgive, while forgiveness makes the continuation of relationship possible. So the undoubted failures of humanity do not remove the high estimation Jesus had of their continuous capacity to respond to God and their fellow creatures, and thus to enact the kingdom in their lives.

Life and death

Thus far this chapter has concentrated rather more on the invitation of the kingdom than on the circumstances of Jesus who made that invitation his whole life. That course has been in keeping with Jesus' own practice, for he consistently tried to avoid being tied down by classification. 'He sighed deeply in his spirit and said, "Why does this generation seek a sign? Truly I say to you, no sign shall be given"' (Mark 8.12). 'And a ruler asked him, "Good Teacher, what shall I do to inherit eternal life?" And Jesus said to him, "Why do you call me good? No one is good but God alone"' (Luke 18.18). These sayings do not represent the attitude of a man who wanted to draw attention to the self who was saying and doing what he did. If Peter called Jesus 'Messiah', that was something he had arrived at by his own perception, not through instruction. Jesus made no issue of the name, brushing away its use by neither accepting nor rejecting it (Mark 8.29f). Freedom for Jesus from the closure of classification would mean also freedom from preconceived expectations so that he could travel, heal, relate, challenge and forgive with the accessibility and untrammelled openness he ascribed to God.

He was much more concerned to point to God than to dwell on his own role. 'One has the impression that Jesus wanted to highlight the essential point. People were to pay attention to God and not to him, but the God they were to heed was God as Jesus experienced and proclaimed him, the God who was deeply concerned with everyone's happiness.'[8] Jesus experienced God in prayer and life as the loving Father who sought the response of love in the actions of his creation, so he spoke for God with certainty and acted with decisiveness the intention of God in healing and exorcism. Such authority derived from Jesus' own certainty of his understanding of his Father and his total self-giving to that proclamation. It followed, therefore, that the reaction of his hearers to Jesus was at the same time their reaction to the God and Father for whom he spoke. To follow Jesus was itself to engage with the God whose message he carried, while to reject Jesus was to exclude oneself from his vision of the transformation of life in God's presence. So even while he rejected classification and sought no personal prominence, Jesus simultaneously commanded attention and evoked response.

He certainly attracted attention by exorcism and miracles, although in neither was he unique in his time (cf. Matt. 27). Such acts might then be expected of holy men, sometimes as a demonstration and guarantee of their holiness, and are not distinctive to Jesus. Some onlookers could even attribute Jesus' miracles to the power of the devil, so as contemporary events these actions as such did not prove anything. But since his parables are permeated with a sense of the kingdom, his actions must surely share in this totality of understanding too. With the concern for creation's well-being which was part of the experience of the kingdom, the expulsion of demons and disease would not be mere tools of the trade, nor self-advertisement, but an expression of the intention of God for humanity.

Thus the healing of the sick in the Gospels is paradigmatic of what was going on in Jesus' ministry. The understanding which gives the action its point is God's desire for and encouragement of wholeness, while the physical and mental illnesses represent the counter-forces to God, warping and diminishing possibilities of life and relationship. Against this background of divine involvement there are two actors, Jesus and the sick person, each with a role to play, or, more particularly, a response to make. Jesus did not conduct a healing mission as such, but responded in compassion to those who sought him out. This response enacted the response of God. And those who came were told time and again, 'Your faith has saved you', for their very coming (or being brought) was a response of tentative faith and hope that things might be better. This is a response of faith as the opposite of fatalism: 'Fatalism is the prevailing attitude of most people, most of the time. It finds expression in statements like "Nothing can be done about it"; "You can't change the world"; "You must be practical and realistic"; "There is no hope".'[9] Such fatalism can do nothing and go nowhere; it is ideologically unresponsive to possibility, while possibility is God's creative gift. But when the sick responded to the infectiousness of Jesus' convictions and actions, they were also responding to God whose desire for healing Jesus put into practice. In this way the Gospels present interlocking perceptions, responses and actions giving rise to healing in the same relationship as brought about 'seeing'. Vision and health are two aspects of the same thing, which Jesus called the kingdom, and which can also be called salvation. In the Gospels people are always healed, for Jesus is the door to the kingdom *par excellence*.

Jesus' life put into action the nature of the kingdom he preached by his openness and spontaneity towards others of all kinds, by his compassion and forgiveness and the creative storytelling which brought religious perception into everyday living. Had Jesus remained a healer, exorcist, teacher and parabler, especially in rural Galilee, he would not have been put to death. Certainly some people might have been offended at his arrogation of authority in speaking for God, and at his inclusion of sinners in the care and benefits of God without reference to the law. But these were not capital offences. The real confrontation with religious and political authority came in Jerusalem, the place for a prophet to be, the place to bring his mission to a head. In Galilee every moment was a possible instance of the kingdom which God would finally bring to completion, but although that made the message urgent it did not make it abrupt. In Jerusalem, however, as if he saw that his time, and hence the time for heralding the kingdom, was short, his message and his method became starker, more concerned to make a statement than to interact with others. The comparatively leisurely appeal of 'What do you think?' has gone.

That change is visible in his overturning of some money-changers' tables in an outer court of the Temple, and driving away both sellers and buyers of animals. This was the symbolic act of a prophet alone on centre stage. His action was probably not so much a comment on the purity of the religion being practised there as a gesture that the end of such sacrifice was at hand. Certainly there were animals in the outer courtyard and money-changers for the Temple coinage. But sacrifice was commanded of Jews in the Mosaic law, so animals guaranteed 'without blemish' would have to be available for pilgrims at the one place where sacrifice could be made. And it was reasonable that the Temple authorities would not wish to deal in a coinage which bore the image of a temporal ruler.[10] The arrangements may have been abused sometimes – most arrangements are – but this was far from the 'robbers' cave' of Mark's description. As in his declaration that 'there will not be left here one stone upon another' (Mark 13.2) Jesus was forecasting and symbolically anticipating the destruction of the Temple. His belief in the nearness of the fulfilment of the kingdom of God led him to this apparently impious warning as a prelude to the foundation of a new and perfect Temple. The end of things as they are, including the Temple, the very heart of religious things as they are, was at hand. Jesus' action, and the general distrust of popular preachers, gave the authorities sufficient reason to bring a charge against him.

Before the net closed, however, he celebrated the Passover with his disciples. So his desire was not for the overthrowing of Judaism as such, but for a recognition of the new thing he believed God was about to do, whose news he brought and embodied. The Passover is celebrated by a meal, and this was the culmination of a whole history of meals Jesus had shared with his disciples, friends and enquirers. He came 'eating and drinking' (Matt. 11.19), enjoying the fellowship engendered by eating together as an instance and foretaste of the banquet of the kingdom. Such meals 'were the sacrament of the reign of God, for sacrament . . . is a ritual which effects what it symbolizes'.[11] If that is true of all meals, it is particularly true of the last Passover supper. At the Passover Israel's history with God is remembered: not only the salvation from the Egyptians, but also other occasions like the deliverance of the Jews from Sennacharib and the victory of the Maccabees. Remembrance of the past and expectation of the future create the mood of the week: 'the Passover hope of approaching redemption, the dream of victory over death, the comforting Psalms of the Hallel and Ezekiel's vision of the resuscitation and resurrection of the dead bones'.[12] In that context Jesus shared the Passover meal, blessing the bread of affliction, breaking, eating, distributing; taking up the cup of blessing. But he gave it all the focus of his imminent death: 'This (bread of affliction) is my body: this (cup of blessing) is my blood.' Remembrance and hope were concentrated at that moment into Jesus' action and self-giving – the sacrament of the reign of God indeed. Then, when they had sung the psalms, they went out into the dark.

Jesus' agony in the garden of Gethsemane, which followed immediately upon his solemn self-dedication at the supper, is the paradigm of his humanness. The energy, love and availability of God whom he called Father characterized his actions, but were not a divine addition to his humanity. It was only through his constant openness to God, in prayer alone and as he contemplated his people, that these divine traits marked his words and actions. He chose to live this kind of life, he chose at the time of his temptations how he would proceed, but it was a choice which had to be renewed at every moment. He did not go ironclad in divine security through his ministry to his death, but maintained the openness which mediated God to others in a vulnerable life which included fatigue, loneliness, irritation and doubt.

Thus at any moment Jesus could have chosen to abandon his mission. He was as free to see and choose as his audience in Galilee. There was no compulsion other than his trust in and response to God to keep him faithful. His mission, however, was not a duty to God to be performed but a relationship which so engaged his being as to define all his thoughts and actions. Equally he experienced no sense of duty to the people of Palestine, but a burning compassion and desire that they should know and enjoy what he knew. Fidelity in all these relationships kept him on course. He was a man going to a slow death for his beliefs, and whatever he hoped about his kingdom of God he did not know the future. His agony in the garden was real agony: 'Let this cup pass from me' (Matt. 26.39). But his trust still held.

Jesus was examined by the Jewish religious authorities on a charge of blasphemy and handed over to the Romans as a dangerous evildoer. The background to this is the following Jesus attracted and his presumption to speak for God, both of which would have contributed to the religious irritation and political nervousness of the Jewish leaders, anxious to keep the peace with no Roman reprisals. But in the foreground is Jesus' forecast of the destruction and rebuilding of the Temple, and more especially the disturbance he raised in the Temple itself. This 'would certainly have been seen as hostile . . . arrogant and wicked'.[13] Considering the holiness of the Temple in the Jews' religion the action 'would have been offensive to most Jews. The gesture, even if it did not raise much tumult, could readily have led the Romans to think that Jesus was a threat to public order. In particular the *physical demonstration* against the Temple by one who had a *noticeable following* looms as so obvious an occasion of the execution that we need look no further.'[14]

So Jesus was condemned for reasons of religious affront and political good order, and died by the 'leisurely cruelty' of crucifixion.[15] Quite apart from the pain of the death, this presents a picture of defeat, failure, abandonment and curse. The one who had preached the accessibility of God's love and care hung rejected by his people. His belief in the immediate coming of the kingdom was not justified. His disciples were scattered. No one saw any meaning in his dying, they caught no vision of God through it. Jesus, who in his life had been like an open door to that vision, now seemed like a door which had been closed. Everyone was again an onlooker. No one 'saw', not even Jesus: 'My God, my God, why have you forsaken me?' (Mark 15.34). Crucifixion was the unholy death of a blasphemer. But this was also the death of a man faithful to his twin loyalties – his Father and his people. He died for the love of God, since God had called him to his work, and he died for love of the people, for whose wholeness of being and seeing he had expended himself. But for him these causes were one, since creation and Creator were intimately related, like father and son, or like a mother hen and her brood. From that point of view, in rejecting Jesus creation displayed its freedom to reject the relationship, and by killing him tried to put it at an end.

Death is the end of a personal biography. But life, as they say, goes on. To find meaning in a death it has to be put into a larger context, where it takes its place as a moment in a continuum rather than being the end of the story. And that, according to the disciples, was what the death of Jesus became – part of a continuum. In the Gospels the disciples are notable chiefly for their incomprehension. In Mark, for instance, just as the Pharisees become the stock characters of the opposition, so the disciples appear in a role like the stock 'straight man' or 'feed' of a comedy partnership. The straight man is both a foil and an audience for the comedian, just as the disciples are a foil for Jesus' perception and wisdom. They are also the askers of pertinent questions (from the evangelists' point of view) and an audience for Jesus' explanations. This is an editorial device, although no doubt it was difficult to understand Jesus from scratch, as it were, in spite of an upbringing in Judaism. But during his ministry the disciples had invested all their time, energy and understanding of God and humanity in Jesus. It is not possible that they had not grasped his message of God's nearness and his concern for wholeness and reconciliation of relationship. They had themselves been sent teaching and exorcising, entrusted with both speaking and acting the message of the kingdom of God (Matthew 10).

The death of Jesus ended all that at the time, but proved in fact to be an intermission and a refocussing of the same concerns. What gave the continuity was that Jesus, who had led and instructed and inspired them in his life, became after his death what Paul called 'a life-giving spirit' (I Cor. 15.45). Something happened so that the emptiness of the disciples was filled, their disorientation was turned to direction, their inactivity to mission and their fear to boldness. This is clearly an expression of thorough integration and invigoration – a *life-giving* spirit indeed. Their sense of the presence of Jesus, individually or collectively at their common meal, was so strong that they expressed it by saying that God had raised him from the dead. That belief echoes the hope of the time in a general resurrection of the dead on the last day, but sharpens and particularizes it into the claim that this man had been raised now.

The spirit in the New Testament is the enlightening and effective power and presence of God. Such power and presence Jesus had known, taught and enacted in his lifetime. The disciples, though not, of course, Paul, had come to know of this stirring, caring relationship through Jesus. Now, after Jesus' death, that part of the pattern remained the same: the disciples knew for themselves God's presence and power through an intuition of Jesus. Without the previous experience this one would not have been seen in this light, and indeed no one who did not share the disciples' faith encountered Jesus 'risen' – except Paul, belatedly and blindingly struck by the conviction. Another way of putting it which would include Paul and members of the infant church was that Jesus was experienced with a power which could come only from God.

In that case, Jesus who had died for the God who companioned him and for the people whom he companioned was affirmed, shown to be right. Love had been shown to have no end to its self-giving, to have met rejection and not been extinguished. God had not been absent at the cross with its brutality and torture, but had suffered it all as the embodiment, the enactment of opposition to his love disclosed in Jesus, yet had continued to love and desire the well-being of creation. And as for the people who had trusted Jesus' message of the love and healing of the kingdom, they too were shown to be right, since his death and resurrection showed that *nothing* could separate any particle of creation from the love of God. The resurrection was therefore an endorsement by God of all that had gone before and an affirmation of its truth.

It was also a commissioning, for the disciples themselves were now to be engaged in Jesus' mission with the power of his (God's) spirit. The concerns were to be the same – God's offer of healing and saving relationship – but the message was not identical, for Jesus himself became the key instance of love and salvation. To express this new aspect of the communication the disciples searched their scriptures, exploded in metaphor and constructed arguments. The process continues to this day. It is a proceeding fraught with insight (or distortion) and irony, for the 'seeing' of Jesus, that involvement which has to be expressed, lived and communicated, leads also to the encapsulation in language of the man who never wrote anything, and who rejected classification.

PART TWO
The Form of the Given

3 · *The Imaginative Construal of God*

This is not an easy time in which to write a christology. Perhaps every age has had its difficulties, but at present there is not a single aspect of the endeavour which escapes doubt and controversy. A herd of wild bulls has trampled through the orderly china shop of traditional christological belief with its expression and rationale.[1] Areas of difficulty include uncertainty concerning the history of Jesus; the relation of history to theology; the enormous variety of Christs (many of them incompatible with each other) described in Christian tradition; the attribution of divinity; the finality of Christ in relation to other religions. Such problems have to be faced if a christology is to be both honest and faithful. For it is not only a matter of intellectual integrity that difficulties be not shirked, it is also a matter of faith. If we believe we have 'the light of the knowledge of the glory of God in the face of Christ' (II Cor. 4.6), accumulated problems cannot be allowed to hide that light under their bushel. The endeavour to maintain belief in its traditional modes while being aware of the difficulties is reminiscent of Victorian attempts to adhere to traditional beliefs in creation in spite of discoveries concerning the age of fossils. Just as fossils had eventually to be accommodated within Christian belief, changing but not ending the doctrine of creation, so the problems facing a christology have to be assessed and changes allowed so that the doctrine may continue to flourish vividly. What follows is one attempt to face the problems and also to explore new possibilities in understanding what is being affirmed in saying 'in Christ God was reconciling the world to himself' (II Cor. 5.19).

The first matter to affect the shape of this, or any, christology concerns what has been called comprehensively 'the given' or 'the given upon which the discipline operates'.[2] The word is misleading if it suggests that in total independence of the theologian there exists fully fashioned timeless material 'out there' only waiting assembly like kitchen units in a do-it-yourself supermarket. Instead, whatever is to count as 'the given' is (and always has been) given only in the process of being understood, selected and shaped by theologians in their own time and place, influenced by their own character, society, language, philosophy, imagination and commitment. 'The things concerning Jesus' are not just 'given' and 'received' as straightforward revelation models suggest, for the reception is at the same time a shaping of form and content into comprehensibility and value.

To hold this view of the given is to subscribe to some form of relativity in knowledge, but it does not involve capitulation to relativism of the kind which believes that if there is no objective truth independent of humanity then all is opinion, none more justifiable than any other. Certainly I believe that everything in this world is in process of change and is for ever being reinterpreted; that this is a world which is seen by everyone from an individual or group point of view; and that therefore there can be no timeless knowledge and no singularity in human truth.[3] Even in science which for so long was thought to be clinically neutral it is recognized that the values, interest and method of the current scientific paradigm shape questions and observations which are made in its terms. So knowledge, in theology as elsewhere, derives formally both from what is external and from simultaneous finitely-conditioned processing of the intuitions. But that need not lead to a paralysis of relativism, which is an impractical over-reaction to the loss of truth as an objective absolute. Rather, it leads to the realization that humans are no more like gods in knowledge than in any other aspect of their humanity. (One might have expected relative knowledge to have occasioned no difficulty to theology where human fallibility and finiteness are presuppositions. But such has not proved the case.)

What is still possible, indeed to be welcomed, is what I have elsewhere called *relativity* as opposed to impotent *relativism* which can only catalogue variety but give no direction among it for lack of absolute criteria. Relativity acknowledges the relationship the knower has with the known to produce knowledge, but also 'sees variety and change as a call to judgment among possibilities and the justifying of one's option'.[4] Options thus are still justified by criteria deemed appropriate, and the demand is that 'one choose the best one knows (intellectually, morally and so forth), although there is no absolute justification for any one choice'. This book is written from such choice and embodies its relative justification.

The given starting point of a christology generally dictates the entire shape of what follows, and when that starting point is too limited it creates an imbalance in the whole structure. Up to the nineteenth century traditional types of christology gave such prominence to God's being and activity that the humanity of Jesus in its freedom and individuality was depreciated. Such christologies 'from above' were always in danger of producing a docetic Christ, divinity in human appearance. Since the rise of historical consciousness and of interest in the individual much more allowance has been made for the human, historical nature of Jesus. But christologies which begin 'from below' have difficulties not only in retrieving the history of Jesus, but also in making attributions of divinity, for once a human man in action has been described it is not clear in what his divinity consists (or subsists). This opacity is increased when the christology contains no description of God or of how God relates to the world. It is wrongly assumed that that is not a contentious matter. What may happen in that case is that after a description of Jesus God is brought in at the end almost *ex machina* to account for this man. Divinity is then claimed to be implicit in the career of Jesus in a vague way without the totality of claims traditionally made for the Christ. Such a procedure avoids the problems of offering models for the humanity and divinity of Christ, although such models are central to christological understanding and the classical versions are now in disarray.

Christologies 'from above' and 'from below' each have a one-sidedness which takes the other side too much on trust in the sense that it is not given individual description and discussion. To recover a balance the given starting point has to be dual, concerning *both* God *and* Jesus called the Christ, neither of whom may be taken as already existing clear and distinct ideas.

Here I have to discuss God and Christ one after the other because a book follows a sequential line, but in the end the accounts have to be able to be held together if christological affirmations and constructions are to be made.

God is as much a presupposition for christological thought as anything concerning Jesus. More specifically, belief about the nature of God in relation with the world is presupposed. Two objections might be raised here: first, that belief in divine involvement is made too easy if God is treated as part of the given, especially if God and Jesus Christ are to be smoothly aligned at this stage; secondly, that for Christians beliefs about God come through an understanding of Christ and therefore should not be part of the *given* but rather the *conclusion* of a christology. To argue in this manner, however, is to treat beliefs about God's nature and connection with Jesus as if they were deductions from a supposedly belief-free appraisal of Jesus in the way that scientists used to think that their hypotheses emerged from cumulative value-free observations. As that account of scientific procedure has been discredited, it should not be continued in christology, where in fact it rarely worked, since premises concerning God were continually smuggled into the so-called 'historical' accounts of Jesus. Instead of that, to keep the parallel with current conceptions in the sciences, belief in God is to the understanding of Jesus Christ much the same as a scientific hypothesis is to the understanding of observations; that is, it gives direction to the study and provides categories and values in which to express the findings. The shaping of the alignment between God and Christ has to be imaginatively presented and argued for, but christologies do presuppose some belief in God and are not the place for foundational arguments.

There is always the danger of a safe circularity in, as it were, reading God off from Jesus Christ and then finding that God mirrored in Jesus Christ, and after two thousand years of Christian tradition some of that circularity is bound to remain. But the circularity is not vicious because, on the one hand, beliefs about God are not arrived at through Jesus alone (without, for instance, input from the Old Testament or present circumstances such as the ecological crisis), and on the other hand what happened at the beginning was that the God of Israel, already believed in, was *recognized* in the activity of Jesus' career. Belief in God was thus the prior feature. It could not be dispensed with *then* as the prior comparator. Nor may it be dispensed with *now*. Christocentrism is possible only by taking for granted a doctrine of God. This point also illustrates the purely logical matter that only what is known can be recognized, so if the reality of God is not entertained at least as a possibility, Jesus Christ will not disclose God, for in that case there will be nothing to disclose. There are plenty of instances of people with no belief in God finding in Jesus only 'a completely secular figure, a *man* called Jesus of Nazareth with a brilliant gift for metaphor, for creating a personal mythology, for acting on his beliefs'.[5]

Those who first believed, however, believed precisely because they saw the God they worshipped at work in Jesus. The movement was from belief in God to recognition of the divine spirit in Jesus – the movement which, I believe, still holds in christology. Christ was never held to reveal a totally different God from the one known in the Jewish tradition (except by Marcion, whose views were ruled out). The whole burden of the stories of Christ's pre-existence, and his image as God's eternal wisdom and word is that this was no new change of direction or character on God's behalf. When Paul or the evangelists wrote of Jesus, their beliefs about God were not overturned or even radically changed, for they searched their scriptures to gain understanding. What they found was a new demonstration of the same God which focussed their prior beliefs and made them more vivid and urgent.[6] The same is true of christology today, which will not prove the existence of God to the sceptical. But to those who believe, however vaguely or residually, Jesus can make all the difference by illuminating, defining, focussing (it is impossible to avoid metaphors) within human conditions what God is like from everlasting to everlasting. So one part of the christological given has to be how God is now believed to be from everlasting to everlasting.

A further important reason for finding God part of the given rather than the conclusion of a christology is that there is more to belief in God than comes through Christ, particularly belief in creation. A concentration on Jesus Christ alone as the given removes salvation too far from creation in both time and doctrine, making them entirely separate actions of God. Thus the shape of belief has been that God created a good world, then humanity sinned and all creation fell from goodness; thereafter, in the fullness of time, God sent his Son to save what was lost. This belief, although aesthetically balanced, and whole within itself, providing an account faith could once give of God's dealings with the world, has a number of negative effects which make it hard to sustain now. For instance, it turns the history of God's presence with Israel into 'promise' alone (a view only slightly ameliorated by seeing Christ's death having retroactive effect); it has nothing to say about the presence of God outside the Judaeo-Christian line, and it cannot be held together with any account of evolution – this is not a good world fallen. It attributes to God a fragile creative action which was at least vulnerable to the entrance of evil (wherever that originated) and to the damage of sin, a creation which had to be rescued. The only logical way to preserve the Godness of God in face of the failure of creation was the supralapsarian view that God had intended the fall with all its consequent misery from the beginning. It could even be argued that all the suffering, grief and death in the world was the result of a *felix culpa*, a happy fault, since in time it produced so great a redeemer.

Against all that division of time and exclusiveness of belief creation and salvation have to be kept together as the way of God with all the world from the beginning. (Admittedly this still uses categories of Christian doctrine, but these are necessary to explicate Christian faith. I shall consider the relation with other faiths in Chapter 7.) Creation comes into being and continues because God freely lets it be, while salvation is continually offered through God's loving companionship of all that is. God's freedom and love are distinguishable but not separable, for it is unselfish love which lets be, and it is the freedom to judge with perfect understanding all that is going on which enables loving forgiveness, since there is no forgiveness without judgment, wthout taking seriously the better and worse of life on earth. On the human side God-given freedom is a necessary condition for free response, while divine love grounds that response in confidence and hope. The situation is like a parent giving a child space to develop while continuing to cherish it.

So, having given creation freedom, God seeks response in the use of freedom within the conditions of the multiple world. Humans are capable of love and of enlarging the capacity for free response in others, and that is the form of their possible response to the omnipresent God, who is involved in every situation. It is from an unfree and unloving life that men and women are to be saved. Jesus Christ, in whom Christians see salvation enacted, is also an image of the gift of freedom to creation in that there is no overwhelming of others in his words and deeds. People were free to see for themselves what this man might mean and respond to him in the faith which makes whole. Jesus is thus the particular and contingent enactment in time of God's eternal relationship with creation.

To represent God as creating the world in freedom and accompanying it in love is to encapsulate in imagery parts of scripture and tradition on the one hand, and personal and social experience on the other. The picture is both the end-product of theological thought and a way to understand and relate to God in belief and life. It serves also as a criterion by which to judge other accounts of God. It is thus an 'imaginative construal' of God of the kind David Kelsey discerned lying behind a theologian's use of scripture.[7] Kelsey traced how a number of theologians actually used the Bible, whatever theoretical views they might have held, and discovered great variety even among contemporaries. His conclusion was that the diversity arose fundamentally from different 'imaginative construals' of the mode of God's presence *pro nobis*.

> At the root of a theological position there is an imaginative act in which a theologian tries to catch up in a single metaphorical judgment the full complexity of God's presence in, through and over against the activities comprising the church's common life and which, in turn, both provides the *discrimen* against which theology criticizes the church's current forms of speech and life, and determines the peculiar 'shape' of the 'position'.[8]

It should not cause difficulty that this construal (a word which bridges analysis and interpretation) is called 'imaginative'. The imagination is precisely what is perceptive and integrative in our interaction with the world.[9] It need have nothing to do with fantasy, and everything to do with what gives rationality or belief its direction, character and deep appeal. Such imaginative construal of God probably underlies *all* theological thinking, and should not be absent as a *discrimen* for the christological tradition, since what is to be said about Jesus is said in its light. But since it is so powerful, the imaginative construal should not remain unconscious, tacit or taken on trust.

There are features of the picture I have drawn in Chapter 1 which act as a *discrimen* in relation to other christologies and as a basis for this. The characteristics of freedom and love are two to which I shall return, and two more come from the insistence on the *presence* of God in *relationship*. Thus, first, the omnipresence of God is fundamental, so that God is part of every situation, whether recognized and acknowledged or not. The whole vertical axis of God above and humanity below, although it is so frequent in the tradition, is here replaced by the horizontal axis of God accompanying creation, vividly expressed in the fire and smoke which companioned the Israelites in the wilderness. There are therefore no 'sending' motifs in this christology, at least as far as pre-existence and descent are concerned, although Jesus, like the prophets, was called or sent by God. 'Sending' as it was developed in christology implies God's distance and absence from the world, whereas God, our companion, is always Immanuel, God *with* us. This means that instead of Christ mediating between creation and its distant creator, Christ becomes the visibility in human conditions of the here, now, but invisible God through which Christians understand the character of God's constant presence.

Moreover this is not the presence of a divine voyeur or spy, but a presence *with* or alongside creation in companionship. Many soteriologies are based on the notion that sin has ruptured the divine-human relationship which has to be won back, and that a great gulf exists between God and humanity which only the death of Christ could bridge. This view couches God's dealings with humanity in abstract terms of morality and justice rather than in the terms of relationship. It does not seem to me to be possible to adhere to that version and simultaneously to affirm that God is love, for love has its very existence in relationship – a matter to which I shall return. Love may be vulnerable to inattention or violence, but it does not on that account surrender its own side of the relationship; not at least if it remains love:

> Love is not love
> Which alters when it alteration finds,
> Or bends with the remover to remove:[10]

Nor does love preclude judgment in the sense of a clear-eyed awareness of what the other is like. But it does preclude distance and unforgivingness. So the relationship remains in place on God's side, as Jesus' life of accessibility to all portrays.

Much of this discussion will be taken further in the following chapters, but the imaginative construal of the relationship with God as I understand it may perhaps be made more clear here by brief comparison and contrast with the description given by Karl Barth, who also represented freedom and love as the pre-eminent characteristics of God.[11] In this respect there is some change in Barth's later writings, for at first he saw nothing which could be called a relationship between sinful humanity and the 'wholly other' God whose action of revelation, judgment and mercy was always 'perpendicularly from above'. Thus in the 1930s Barth could write: 'Knowledge of revelation can and must mean, then, a knowledge of a far away, strange and holy God. It prohibits the useless and dangerous thought that, in meeting God, man can appear and co-operate as God's partner, as if he were filled and endowed with a capacity and good will for God.'[12] But in the 1950s Barth signalled a change of emphasis which had already been forming in his work. He now stressed the freedom of God *for* humanity which meant that God was not, as it were, shut up in deity, but was free to bend down and love humanity with all its blemishes. 'He wants in his freedom actually not to be without man but *with* him and in the same freedom not against him but *for* him, and that apart or even counter to what man deserves.'[13] Again, 'he is *man's* God, not only as Lord but as father, brother, friend; and this relationship implies neither a diminution nor in any way a denial, but, instead, a confirmation and display of his divine essence itself'.[14]

In these latter quotations Barth is describing what he calls the humanity of God, that is, God's openness to and affirmation of humanity. Yet for Barth God never loses his transcendent majesty. He is 'the sovereign Lord of the amazing relationship'.[15] Thus the vertical axis remains in place. Barth uses the term 'partnership', but it is one where God gives, speaks and orders while humanity receives, hears and obeys. On the human side Barth is not concerned with freedom in general, which would be too like a basis in natural theology outside the sphere of revelation for which he had no patience. He sets up an opposition of slavery and sin outside revelation to freedom and obedience within it. 'It would be a strange freedom which would leave man neutral, able equally to choose, decide and act rightly or wrongly! . . . Man becomes free and is free by choosing, deciding and determining himself in accordance with the freedom of God.'[16] There is still nothing worthy in humanity itself except that God in freedom has chosen to affirm it, and God grants the possibility of obedience which frees humanity from the agony of continuous deciding. For when the decision for God is made 'the reign of chance and ambiguity is excluded'.[17]

One way to describe the difference between Barth's account and my own briefer effort can be taken from Otto's description of religious experience as that of a *mysterium tremendum et fascinans*, a mystery which arouses both awe and attraction.[18] On the one hand there is the sense of the littleness of humanity physically, morally and spiritually before the greatness of God, and on the other this mystery is attractive, drawing the self on to engage with it. That God is God, both mystery and the 'that than which nothing greater can be thought' of Anselm's phrase, is not at issue. But Barth's account of the *relationship* between this God and humanity is overwhelmingly in terms of the *tremendum*, imaged as the condescension of a majesty which still rules, sovereign, in the relationship. What there is in Barth of the *fascinans*, the attraction of God, is wrapped within the *tremendum* and takes its character from the emphasis on majesty. In my own account (partly from scripture and its implications, but also from my experience, beliefs and reading of the contemporary world) God is first of all *fascinans*, one who draws people to attend to the divine presence, which is neither remote nor condescending but alongside, imaged in terms of companionship. The *tremendum* is not absent, but is discovered within the *fascinans*, for this companion is also and simultaneously creator and saviour. At times that majestic otherness may be experienced as compellingly as in Barth's account, but in theology and in life the priority of the *fascinans* in companionship alters the tone of the other term, making it warmer and more approachable, just as the sense of otherness in a companion is different from the sense of otherness in a sovereign. Yet that sense of otherness remains a necessary perception in using companionship as the model for God's relationship. Divine companionship could easily be sentimentalized into a friendly neighbourhood deity, with all the emphasis on God's support and comfort but none on God's independence for assessing, enjoying or judging with complete understanding everything that happens. Just as in Barth's description God's freedom enables him not to be remote in heaven, so in my description divine freedom keeps God from being domesticated for human ease.

If God is known in relationship, conceptions of what makes a good relationship enter in here. What is not at issue in this case is that any relationship at all is possible only through the prior love of God directed towards creation. For Barth a good relationship is one where the senior member has knowledge and power whose benefits he conveys to a receptive junior. It is like a teaching relationship conceived in terms of instructor and instructed, while the growth of the junior partner is in obedience rather than maturity. 'Human freedom is the God-given freedom to obey . . . Love is the obedience of the witness who is summoned to announce this transition (from sin to righteousness).'[19]

Barth is describing a relationship on the vertical axis *de haut en bas* not too dissimilar from the general pattern practised by the Grand Inquisitor. But such relationship among humans has become suspect. It is widely perceived among Christians of very different theological standpoints that vertical relationships of command and obedience make possible oppression, dehumanization or at least perpetual immaturity. Therefore social concern is expressed and social action taken to enable people to take responsibility for their own lives. Social workers of all kinds, for instance, do not provide blueprints and demand obedience to their commands, but work *with* the disadvantaged who participate in the process. Equally, the healing which people experience through consulting a counsellor comes from working *with* him or her on their personal histories. These seem to me much more appropriate models for the divine relationship than old-fashioned classroom instruction. Modern teaching is equally concerned with the participation of the student. 'With' is a word which has vast theological potential: 'In or into company of, or relation to, among, beside' (*Concise Oxford Dictionary*). But that potential will not be realized while the benefits of *human* horizontal relationships (with) are affirmed but the relationship with *God* continues to be expressed and proclaimed on the vertical axis.

The move to the horizontal axis does not make for equality or symmetry of relationship. That state is rare in human relations, where one has often more to contribute than the other, and clearly does not obtain in relationship with God. Yet many of the features which make a good horizontal relationship have a place in the divine companionship.

First of all, a good relationship is entered on freely by both, not like a contract but as people are drawn to each other. In this case God establishes the relationship through free initiative and humans freely enter into it as they respond to the attraction of God.

Secondly, each member contributes what he or she has in sensitivity, humour, dependability and love to the relationship which encompasses them both. This is one area where there cannot be symmetry in companionship with God, yet humans do contribute to God's experience of relationship with creation. God does gain something 'existential' from the relationship which is not otherwise procurable.

Thirdly, respect and enjoyment of the other are characteristics of a good relationship in which each has independence enough to remain him- or herself while being open to the influence, change or even transformation which an unoppressive, enriching relationship brings about. Divine respect for the otherness of humanity shows in God's refusal to dominate, and while this independence allows divine judgment it also allows divine enjoyment. If there were nothing to enjoy in creation it would be the failure which traditional accounts of the Fall imply. Clearly relationship with God's love can bring about transformation in humanity, but what changes *in God* through divine openness is the cumulative experience of joy, pain and suffering through a relation with finite creation. This could come to God only through actual relationship.

Fourthly, no relationship would endure unless values, aims and experiences were shared. Humanity aligns itself with its perception of divine values and conducts life in terms of the relationship (thereby doing what was called 'serving' in the vertical model). On the divine side God shares in the frustrations and difficulties of finite and fallible creatures endeavouring to implement the values of love in a complex and changing world.

Fifthly and finally, no mutual relationship happens or continues effortlessly. It requires attention and commitment.

None of this account of relationship with God denies the reality or weightiness of sin. But sin should not be measured primarily in abstract moral terms. As I shall be describing later, sin is a failure in relationship or a failure to relate at all, like Luther's man *incurvatus in se*, a being curved in on the self. Justice in that case is not a moral ideal, but a matter of fair relations actually obtaining in society, and the sin of injustice occurs through a failure of fair relations. Similarly, goodness is less a matter of individual virtue than the enabling, enjoying and enhancing of good relationships on the model of divine companionship personally and in society generally. The evils in society from child abuse to war may be seen in terms of warped relationships or the deliberate withdrawal of relationship so that the other may be less than a fellow human. So good may also be described in terms of what is better in any kind of relationship. Freedom and love are not abstract ideas either, for freedom is visible in the openness of relationships it leads to and love in the quality of these relationships. As the omnipresent God is part of *every* situation, failure/guilt/wrongdoing in *any* situation also takes on the specifically religious aspect of sin in relation to God. What we do to our neighbours we do also to God, whose concern is for the well-being of every part of creation in its interrelationship. Yet out of the perfect freedom and love of God's relating the divine relationship is not closed or diminished on account of failure.

Human relations, whether with other humans or with nature, are in fact mixed, containing in different proportions elements which are both good and bad for those who participate in them, elements which may change with time and circumstance. Therefore although sin is always serious, it is not always easily isolatable for facile condemnation. Sin is much more an insidious aspect of finitude and selfishness which pervades relationships throughout the world. I therefore differ from Barth in his absolute division between slavery and sin outside revelation, and freedom and obedience, which excludes all ambiguity, within it. There are two questions here, one concerning the sphere of revelation, the other its effects. Barth was considering mainly the effects *on the believer*, who, from being undecided and confused in not knowing what to believe, became integrated in a firm orientation towards God, which God enabled: an experience like coming out of a fog into clear air. Much Christian testimony bears witness to this account.

There is, however, a danger in over-simplifying Christian life (not that Barth always does that), for the world and all its relationships, including one's own relationships, remain as manifold, as open to various interpretation and as changing after decision as they were before. And for many there is never a moment in their lives which could be clearly defined as 'decision'. The move, therefore, is not as complete as that from slavery to freedom. Rather, the discovery of relationship with God leads people to recognize and respond to the presence of God within the ambiguity inherent in the multiplicity and finitude of the world. This response may sometimes be better (or more effective) and sometimes worse. So while people may undoubtedly be changed and transformed by the relationship, the lines are much more blurred than Barth's before and after division suggests.

The same is true for Barth's separation between the sphere of revelation and the darkness beyond. Barth is well known not only for a 'positivism of revelation' but also for an exclusivism of revelation (however much in some statements he appears universalist).[20] Sin is certainly everywhere in the whole world, but the presence of God is confined by Barth to the revelation in Jesus Christ, which is by no means identical with the Christian religion, but is certainly not to be found in any other. What for Barth differentiates Christianity from other religions is not its practices, devotion or any righteousness of its own but its connection with Christ, or more exactly, Christ's giving of himself to the Church. Where there is no connection with Christ there is no revelation. Barth never really moved from this point of particularity. Although in his later writing Barth could assess creation-as-such to be the external ground of the covenant of salvation and write of 'lights' in other religions, Paul Knitter is right to conclude that he continued 'to affirm that such positive content in other religions can be known and assume its value *only* in and after the revelation of Christ'.[21]

In contradistinction to all of that, I do not believe that God's freedom and love are so restricted. It sits oddly with Barth's view of God as sovereign that this Lord has chosen to illuminate only part of his dominions. In my belief, the presence of God is everywhere, as fully in, for instance, Mars or Ethiopia as in Rome or Geneva. Nor does that presence change its quality or its characteristics in different locations.God is always the God who in freedom allows creation its independence and who in love forgives, nourishes and draws creation on. There is the same companionship seeking such response as the varieties in all creation are capable of, at its most developed a response consciously reciprocal to God and to the rest of creation, whatever frameworks of belief may be in place. (In relation to this totality my own framework of belief is just as relative, but since nothing at all can be said if there is no point of perspective and belief, I must write from within my understanding of the Christian faith with its imagery and categories.) Since creation and salvation are not two separate activities of God, but two aspects of the one relationship, there is no room for a doctrine of general revelation open to all but falling short of the special saving revelation available only through Christ. All revelation of God has salvific possibility, to continue the description in Christian categories, although the significance may be differently rendered in other faiths.

Revelation in this account is not the occasional self-disclosure of God breaking into human concerns from outside, but rather human awareness of God's presence and call which are always there but are often discovered with a suddenness which makes them revelatory. The world is seen in the larger context of its relation to God in the midst of things as they are, and God is known not as an abstract possibility but in relation to some part of creation and its circumstances. Even so, however, the demarcation Barth drew between what happens within revelation and what happens outside is not wholly lost. The difference does not come about through God's selectivity (since God is available to all), but is a difference between humans who are aware of and attentive to the presence of God and those who are oblivious to its attraction and effect. That difference is not between two well-defined groups, even in a country with a Christian tradition, for in a second- or third-generation secular society there may be those who respond to God without knowing or using religious terms, while there may be others who know the traditional words (like 'salvation') and use them in place of making an actual response. And it is probable that most of the people who acknowledge God's salvation move in and out of responsiveness.

Responsiveness has to do with freedom (openness) and love (enjoyment and concern for the well-being of the other) in relationships. Revelation may concern the state of one's personal relationship with God or the state of relationships within the world which demonstrate or deny freedom and love to the participants. To work for better relationships personally, locally, socially or globally is to respond to God who gave the world its possibility of being, even if God is not known as God. Awareness of God, however, gives ultimate purpose to all quest for creation's well-being. It is the undergirding and forgiving support for such action and the lure to leave unfree, unloving self-sufficiency for the delight and risk of the undertaking. Jesus Christ both expresses such salvation in his life and promotes it among his followers.

Awareness of this kind requires what Simone Weil called 'attention', and in French the connection between *attente* (waiting on God) and *attention* (directing consciousness towards God) is clearer. Yet to illustrate attention which is not at first obvious as attention to God, Weil uses the parable of the Good Samaritan.

> Those who pass by this thing ('a little piece of flesh, naked, inert and bleeding beside a ditch') scarcely notice it and a few

> minutes afterwards do not even know that they saw it. Only one stops and turns his attention towards it. The actions that follow are just the automatic effect of this moment of attention. The attention is creative. But at that moment when it is engaged it is a renunciation.[22]

To give attention like this is to be sufficiently open to observe and imaginatively comprehend the other: the renunciation is renunciation of self-interest. The move from imaginative understanding to action may not be as automatic as Weil suggests, and indeed may not be a simple process, but it will not occur without the initial attention. No relationship, with God, humans, or any other part of creation may be formed without such creative attention, which in the chapter on Jesus I called simply 'seeing'.

Jesus lamented its absence with the image of children in the market-place who would not join in any game, who would not 'see' what they were looking at. The failure to 'see' is the failure to attend creatively and make relationship possible – with God or with others. It is a prior and more serious failure than failure *in* relationships. From that point of view the notion of sin as separation from God which humanity brings upon itself takes on a new poignancy, since God is not distant, but present with each one. Separation from God becomes ignorance of or inattention to what is *there*, as men and women may share a house and be ignorant of each other through preoccupation with their own concerns. In Weil's terms, there is no renunciation of their own self-absorption. Salvation is the breaking down of such isolation, forgiveness for the hurt it has caused, the acknowledgment of relationship with God encompassing within it all other relationships, whose flourishing gives human and divine pleasure, and whose feebleness and intermittent character are judged, forgiven and forgotten.

The theology in this section and indeed throughout this book is both continuous and discontinuous with Christian tradition. Freedom of response and expression extends to a theologian's relation with tradition, although that freedom is tempered and directed by love of God. Barth would have agreed with this principle, although he would have spoken of obedience and witness as the fruits of freedom. He wrote a description of the 'free theologian' which is almost an *apologia pro theologia sua*, not for the content of his theology, but for the manner of his theologizing. It will be clear from what has gone before that I cannot follow his emphases entirely, yet there is much in what he says to give encouragement to other theologians conscious of their departures from tradition, even when these departures are different from his own.

> A free theologian . . . will be found ready, willing and able always to begin his thinking *at the beginning* . . . he will always first proceed from God's relationship to man and only then will he continue with man's relationship to God . . . A free theologian starts steadily and happily with the Bible . . . not because some old or new orthodoxy knocked it into him . . . He starts with the Bible because in the Bible he learns about the free God and the free man, and as a disciple of the Bible he may himself become a witness to the divine and human freedom . . . Does this imply his speaking in direct quotation and interpretation of the Biblical texts and contexts? Maybe often, maybe not always. The freedom bestowed on him by the origin, object and content of the Biblical testimony can and must be asserted through his attempt to think and to relate in his own terms what he heard in the Bible . . . A free theologian does not deny, nor is he ashamed of, his indebtedness to a particular philosophy or ontology, to ways of thought and speech . . . No one speaks exclusively in Biblical terms . . . he speaks from within his philosophical skill, speaks in his own cumbersome vernacular which is certainly not identical with the tongues of angels, although the angels may utilize him at times . . . A free theologian thinks and speaks within the church, within the communion of saints, whose ordinary members happen to be not just himself and his closest theological friends . . . He is free . . . to say in his own terms what (the Confessions) have already said . . . The Christian community, its gathering, nurture and mission in the world are at stake, and the free theologian knows this . . . A free theologian works in communications with other theologians . . . He knows that the

self-same problems with which he is preoccupied may be seen and dealt with in a way different from his own way . . . He believes in the forgiveness of both his theological sins and theirs.[23]

4 · *The Imaginative Construal of Jesus*

The title of this chapter may seem surprising, since so much christology written after the development of historical consciousness has begun by inquiring what may be known historically about Jesus, with the presumption that there should be a 'foundation' of historical information beyond the vagaries of imagination and construal upon which everything else may be built. It could be argued that it might be acceptable to speak of the 'imaginative construal' of *God*, since God is ultimately beyond all human speech and has always been described in imaginative metaphors like rock or shepherd. But Jesus was a man at a specific time and place in history, and that ought to make a difference. And it does make a difference, but only to the ingredients of the imaginative construal. The results of historical study are not timelessly true, securely objective facts, as the metaphor of 'foundation' suggests. But even if they were, it is not clear how such putatively value-free information could be embodied in a value-laden elaboration without losing the objective character which made it desirable in the first place. In what follows I shall rehearse a number of practical and theoretical difficulties in the path of historical assurance before coming to consider what may then he said of the historical input to the imaginative construal of Jesus of Nazareth.

Practical difficulties immediately confront anyone who wishes to use the results of New Testament scholarship in arriving at a portrait of Jesus, for there is great diversity within that scholarship. As John Bowden has observed, it often happens that when one reads books by two different, equally reputable scholars, each with its own evidence and coherence, 'confusion begins'.

'What is taken as assured by one author may well be put in question by the second, and vice versa.'[1] The confusion is compounded the more widely one reads. Bowden's conclusion seems likely: 'There is a good deal we probably do know about Jesus; the trouble is that we can rarely, if ever, be sure precisely what it is.'[2] Two examples will illustrate this clearly, one concerning the speech, the other an action of Jesus.

In a number of books Joachim Jeremias propounded the thesis of the uniqueness, centrality and continuing importance throughout the New Testament of Jesus' use of 'Abba' to address God.[3] 'Abba', according to Jeremias, was a child's term for Father in Aramaic, and as a form of address to God was practically unknown in Jewish sources. But it was the form Jesus always used in complete distinction from Old Testament and contemporary tradition, so here we are in touch with the very words of Jesus and may be sure of the special relationship they imply. '*Abba* as a form of address to God expresses the ultimate mystery of the mission of Jesus.'[4] Jeremias used a considerable linguistic survey in support of his conclusion, but other, equally considerable linguistic surveys now call it into question.[5] James Barr, for instance, concludes: 'There is no evidence that the "Abba" of Paul is dependent on the "Abba" of Jesus; it cannot be proved that Jesus used "Abba" only and always in all his addresses to his Father; it is likely that he used other terms which specified "my" or "our" Father; and, above all, the nuance of "Abba" was not at all the nuance of childish prattle, but the nuance of solemn and responsible adult speech.'[6] Jeremias' conclusions about 'Abba' were accessible and congenial to non-New Testament specialists, so that sermons, lectures (including my own!) and christologies expatiated on the Jesus who was so uniquely intimate with God that he alone always addressed him as 'Abba'. Now it seems all that may have been overstated. It remains highly likely that Jesus called God 'Father', but that is scarcely unique. The point is not that Jeremias is no longer to be trusted, but that his conclusions, like all others in this field, are *always* open to the possibility of revision, no matter whether they are congenial or distasteful to Christians for dogmatic reasons.

This is a particular instance of the general point that accounts given by historians have a provisional character and are always revizable. New sources may be discovered which cast a different light on past events; different historians may evaluate what sources there are differently; a changed perspective on the part of historians may give rise to revision of earlier accounts. This provisionality is well expressed in Collingwood's definition of a historical 'fact':

> All that a historian means when he describes certain facts as his data is that for the purpose of a particular piece of work there are certain historical problems which for the moment he proposes to treat as settled: though if they are settled, it is only because historical thinking has settled them in the past, *and they remain settled only until he or someone else decides to open them.*[7]

What Collingwood envisaged and what the example of 'Abba' illustrated was a linear provisionality whereby later thinking upsets earlier. But this is only part of the problem with New Testament interpretation. As change takes place often slowly and piecemeal, there may be relatively contemporary diversity. It would be hard to say, for instance, what the scholarly 'consensus' is at the moment on the part played by fulfilment of prophecy in *creating* events recounted in history-like narrative in the Gospels. One instance of this variety which concerns not only prophecy but other patterns of narrative in the ancient world is the 'triumphal entry' of Jesus into Jerusalem. One manner of interpretation may be represented by C. F. D. Moule in his volume on Mark in the *Cambridge Bible Commentary*, in which he presents the entire episode of Mark 11.1–11 as a deliberate action of Jesus to have himself proclaimed Messiah or King of Israel. 'It might seem as if Jesus was deliberately asking for trouble: after keeping his position so secret for so long, he now does something calculated to touch off a nationalist explosion.'[8] Yet it all ends quietly because, Moule suggests, Jesus led the crowd who followed him to the Temple. Thus for him the action of Jesus was the original datum and the use by Matthew and John of Zechariah 9.9 is the subsequent application of an appropriate prophecy. 'Jesus seemed to his friends, as they recollected the scene, to have ridden into Jerusalem like that.'[9]

One of the problems in taking the triumphal entry as historical is the question why the crowd, so raised in religious and nationalist acclamation, dispersed with so little turbulence that the authorities were not alerted immediately to action. Moule solves this by having Jesus lead the crowd to the Temple, an action which is not in the text and one which might not have guaranteed instant quiet if the crowd really understood the Messiah to have come. D. E. Nineham in his *Pelican Gospel Commentary* on Mark solves the difficulty differently. He does not attempt to state the intention of Jesus and finds that the whole incident was much smaller – possibly a spontaneous demonstration by the disciples as they reached Jerusalem with the leafy branches gathered ready for the Feast of Dedication. Before this, however, Nineham has suggested the situation of the original readers of the gospel, for whom Jerusalem was both the holy city and the city which slew Jesus. They would be familiar with the prophecies of Zechariah 9.9 and 14.4, and with the popular belief that the Messiah would come from the Mount of Olives. So the opening of the story 'will already have told them in principle what they wanted to know. Jesus' entry into Jerusalem was the entry of the Messiah, in full conformity with Old Testament prophecy and Jewish expectation'.[10] Thus while Nineham certainly believes *something* happened on the way into Jerusalem, he gives a greater role than Moule to the power of belief and prophecy to shape the telling of the event.

Many variations on these positions could be adduced – and discussed in much more detail. But to give a sense of the range of possible interpretation, an example may be taken from the opposite end of the present spectrum. David Catchpole, in an article on the 'triumphal' entry, believes, like Nineham, that if there was any action at the entry it must have been small, since there was no arrest.[11] But he is less ready to affirm any such event: 'Whether (Jesus) was greeted like all other pilgrims with the words of Psalm 118. 25f., and/or whether an intensity of expectation of the kingdom of God was apparent in his companions must remain speculative and uncertain'.[12] Catchpole believes that Jesus' arrival in Jerusalem has been expanded with Messianic emphasis to make a fitting introduction to his action in the Temple. He has analysed how closely the account of the entry conforms to 'a family of stories detailing the celebratory entry to a city by a hero figure who has previously achieved his triumph' (as for Mark Jesus had achieved his triumph in the resurrection).[13] Such stories were common currency and appear in Josephus and I Maccabees, while a partially similar form is observable in I Kings 1.32–40. The standard features of these stories as Catchpole enumerates them are: victory is already achieved and the hero's status is already recognized (in this case that involves not only the resurrection but also the naming of Jesus as Son of David by blind Bartimaeus, Mark 10.47f.); a formal ceremonial entry; greetings, acclamations and invocations of God; an entry into the Temple as climax; then cultic activity which may be sacrifice or the purifying of the Temple from uncleanness. The form certainly appears to fit. So while Jesus must have entered Jerusalem somehow, Catchpole is suggesting that the incidents and emphasis of the story were created (created, not influenced) by the belief of the writer in Jesus' messianic status finding expression in the kind of story which to the ancient world demonstrated that kind of status.

Catchpole's essay shows an emphasis on Mark as a theologian in his own right working within a framework of belief in Jesus as Messiah, and equally within a framework of thought and expression typical of his time. This illustrates a move in New Testament interpretation away from the pattern of historical fact (foundation) and secondary Old Testament commentary (part of the superstructure) which is visible in Moule's commentary. There is therefore at the moment a range of proffered interpretation for this, as for almost any other part of the gospels. My interest lies in what a christologian is to do in face of this diversity which, I repeat, is present for every possible feature of a portrait of Jesus. In this case, once Catchpole's account, supported with evidence and coherent argument, has been produced it is no longer possible to be *innocent* in including the triumphal entry as historical, as if there were no dubiety concerning its historicity. Whatever the final decision of the christologian may be on its character, it will be provisional not only because later scholarship may overturn it, but also because at the moment there are other scholarly ways of accounting for what is in the text.

This example begins to illustrate what a historian's account can and cannot do. (I am not concerned with those who affirm the historical fidelity of the Gospels quite independently of scholarly inquiry. If people can affirm that, they can affirm anything!) The naive view (or hope) is that a historically based account will *correspond* materially to 'what happened' in the time of Jesus, or to 'what Jesus was like'. New Testament scholars themselves are aware of the complexity of the process, but the widely-felt desire for a *historical* portrayal of Jesus is based on the notion of the truth and possibility of correspondence. Truth in that view is said to be the correspondence or match between what is said and the state of affairs it describes. But notions of correspondence between historical accounts and whatever happened have many difficulties and always have to be used with extreme caution. Correspondence is the truth of commonsense, which is both its attraction and its limitation. It works very well in delimited circumstances where the perspective, content and values of commonsense are shared, even over time. But when circumstances are complicated, diverse, extending over centuries and across cultures it becomes steadily less operable, or, better, it becomes less clear where it can operate straightforwardly. In this case it may be that contemporary commonsense, which includes a high valuation of history as the way in which to know the past, has been imposed on the biblical texts in ways which are not always appropriate because in those days other ways of relating to and finding significance in the past obtained. Yet if we find that our present values are not always appropriate, it will be because historical study itself has moved on to demonstrate this.

The point is worth dwelling on, for it becomes increasingly likely that some material in the Gospels evolved out of memories of Jesus and that some other material evolved out of the searching of scripture by those who responded to Jesus using the methods of their time. Evolution (so long as that does not have overtones of smooth quasi-inevitable development) is an important term in both cases, but particularly for the way in which earlier scripture was selectively developed by being applied to Jesus. Thus in a simple instance Hosea could create a prophecy out of a verse in Exodus and Matthew could create a journey to Egypt to fulfil Hosea (Ex. 4.22; Hos. 11.1; Matt. 2.15). This reworking has nothing to do with falsehood or deliberate fabrication, but is part of a variously developing account as God's relationship with Israel continued through generations and different circumstances, coming to its climax and fulfilment for the evangelists in Jesus. The truth they may wish to convey is that this life, death and resurrection belongs with the tradition as well as giving that tradition new features.

The same could be said of that Jewish meditation on the past called *midrash*, a symbolic or poetic commentary on scripture. Neusner comments on the parabolic force of midrash: 'The basic principle here is that things are never what they seem to be. Israel's reality is not conveyed either by the simple sense of Scripture or by the obvious realities of the perceived world. A deeper meaning in Scripture preserves the more profound meaning of the everyday world of Israel even now.'[14] With the same desire to express realities beyond those of the perceived world, first-century Jews meditated on the Hebrew scriptures in order to tell a story concerning the significance of Jesus. The birth narratives of Jesus appear to be of this kind, giving a significance far beyond any ordinary birth.[15]

So also are nature miracles such as the Feeding of the Five Thousand, which follow the pattern of helplessness overcome by some wonder performed by Jesus as the provider of fullness or the master over chaos and evil. The story of feeding with loaves and fish caught up into the present of the infant church echoes Jewish memories of the abundant provision of manna and quail in the wilderness by God for his people (Ex. 16; Num. 11) and the distribution by Elisha of twenty loaves and some fresh grain among one hundred men (II Kings 4.42–44). Moses represented the law and Elisha the prophets. What the evangelists appear to be saying is that Jesus is greater than the law and the prophets. Blended in with that are later notions of the messianic banquet in the fullness of God's kingdom and the breaking of bread in the church's eucharist, a church which was on its way through a wilderness of misunderstanding and persecution. 'Such midrash presupposes belief in the continuing relevance of Old Testament texts, a relevance that is brought out by remodelling them, and setting them in a new narrative context, where they will enhance the truth and power of the doctrines shared by the writer and his audience.'[16] In all such cases, to be historical is to set the text and its writer in their own time rather than to demand latter-day 'historicity' or nothing. 'If an author wrote within both the constraints and liberty of current idiom and genre, then we do him most respect when we hear him in those terms.'[17]

But why should such fulfilment, commentary and meditation take the form of telling history-like stories with characters and action? Robert Alter, examining equally rounded and history-like accounts in the Hebrew Scriptures, such as the Davidic cycle of stories, argues that Hebrew monotheism, in contradistinction to the circumambient polytheism, provided the pressure to begin the tradition: 'The implicit theology of the Hebrew Bible dictates a complex moral and psychological realism in biblical narrative because God's purposes are always entrammelled in history, dependent on the acts of individual men and women for their continuing realization.'[18] Thus if God is seen to be involved in shaping Israel's life and history, that involvement is recorded by means of stories which also record the complexity and ambivalence of humanity even in relationship with God. In the Gospels the involvement of God is given in stories full of action and character which display the messianic nature of Jesus. The continuing involvement of God rather than historical accuracy as we know it seems to be the overriding consideration.

Thus too simple notions of correspondence between Gospel accounts and twentieth-century notions of historical precision and fidelity cannot be maintained, because the past is in some respects genuinely different. Further, they cannot be maintained, because the past is not one single clear-cut set of events with one single meaning. As the quotation given earlier from Collingwood made clear, there are no raw uninterpreted 'facts' in history. 'Reality' is not an independently subsisting world with its own singular meaning only awaiting inspection and true reportage, but is rather the conglomerate of the-world-as-experienced, while experience, and thus the world it describes, will be different on account of individual and social differences and change. So the life of Jesus is not, and never was, 'an independently subsisting world with its own singular meaning only awaiting inspection and true reportage', but always something variously experienced and described. We cannot get behind 'accounts of Jesus' to some timeless *je ne sais quoi* lying behind the accounts, for every endeavour will produce only another 'account'. What we have in the Gospels which derives from memories of Jesus has come from the experience of believers (never, seriously, from non-believers) interpreted as it was experienced and subsequently reflected on.

After considerable time some such experiences were reworked into four Gospels by writers each of whom had his own theological understanding of Jesus' reality and was addressing his own church.

We have come, therefore, past the practical difficulties of seeking the historical Jesus by means of the results of New Testament investigation to the theoretical difficulties which lie behind the practical, including the complexity of giving an account of the past when that past is a multiplicity of experience often differently expressed and evaluated from present norms. Another, equally pervasive complication in giving an account of Jesus is that any rendering is written by someone who does not cease to be the person she/he is in the process. It is a twentieth-century discovery that a historian's 'personal imprint is as evident in a monograph as it is in a literary masterpiece'.[19] Historical discipline may curb the most wayward subjectivity, but the point to which I keep returning in the relativity of knowledge is that a *complete* disjunction cannot be made between knower and known such that the 'known' is totally unaffected by the knower. The history of the writing of lives of Jesus may be seen as the prolonged attempt at objectivity always being shaped in fact by input from the interpreter. This is a point worth considering more fully, for the difficulties are as great whether it is a 'portrait', a 'sketch' or a 'life' of Jesus which is attempted.

There is a double point to be made here. First, an account of Jesus is a *presentation* which may use the results of New Testament criticism but goes far beyond them in making a whole coherent picture which will have its own values, emphasis, texture, metaphors and so forth, a matter to which I shall return. Secondly, within the Christian church where Jesus is the icon of God, there is no point in describing him unless that description illustrates the highest values. But, one may ask, whose highest values? Not someone else's, for that would yield a second-hand kind of religion. Therefore these values must be one's own highest values derived from the church-in-society and from society itself. (That is to say, everyone's values are socially as well as religiously derived.) Where and when these highest values are widely shared, they appear to readers to be self-evidently right and objective. But where they are not shared it is clear to the critic that the writer has embodied his/her own values in the account. This is not because the critic is value-free, but because the critic has different values. And as values continue to change, so the process moves on.

The Liberal Protestants, therefore, so roundly criticized by Schweitzer and Tyrrell at the beginning of this century, have had an unduly bad press, as if they alone were guilty of subjectivity, whereas in fact they were the people among whom the universal problem first surfaced and who were therefore least conscious of the danger. Of early rationalism Schweitzer wrote:

> The problem of the life of Jesus is solved the moment it succeeds in bringing Jesus nearer to its own time, in portraying him as the great teacher of virtue and showing that his teaching is identical with the intellectual truth which rationalism deifies.[20]

Tyrrell likewise inveighed against 'this almost miraculous modernity' which Harnack and Bousset were finding in Christ.

> They wanted to bring Jesus into the nineteenth century as the incarnation of the ideal of divine righteousness, that is, of all the highest aspirations that ensure the healthy progress of civilization . . . With eyes thus preoccupied they could only find the German in the Jew; a moralist in a visionary; a professor in a prophet; the nineteenth century in the first; the natural in the supernatural.[21]

Such modernizations continue because it cannot be otherwise, and may be observed in any rendering of Jesus. Thus Tillich, although he places so little value on the historical, yet describes a Jesus according to his own values who is existential man *par excellence* in all but estrangement from God. He is homeless, misunderstood and anxious about death.[22] An example of a very different kind occurs when James Barr, examining the fundamentalists' conception of Jesus, comments:

> Now according to this approach Jesus becomes a little like a 'Bible teacher' himself. He 'taught, held views, claimed' in the manner of such Christians today. Even Jesus' approach to the Old Testament is rendered as that of a 'straight biblicist'.[23]

Because Jesus is seen to express Christian values and is himself of value to Christians, and because Christians have been and are diverse, it is only to be expected that there will be many accounts of Jesus which express that diversity, indeed incompatibility of values, however objective the intent. In theological terms, even when God's revelation and initiative are affirmed, that revelation occurs within the constrictions not only of time and space, but also those of human languages and values.

The development of general interest in the individual life of Jesus is closely paralleled by the rise of a biography- and novel-reading public. It is significant that both the increasing impulse to write lives of Jesus and the market for the results flourished in the same century as the realistic novel with its recognizable characters in action, and biography written as the story of a hero. To such readership Jesus could not seem less 'real' than the characters of Scott, nor less inspiring than the heroes of Carlyle. Indeed, away from the stratospheric levels of literary criticism this demand for realism still exists. But the example of realistic novelists is instructive. Zola was the most determined and programmatic of naturalistic writers. He proclaimed: 'The study of abstract, metaphysical man is replaced by the study of natural man, subject to physico-chemical laws and determined by the effects of his milieu'[24] That was precisely the intention of those who set off on the quest of the historical Jesus: the metaphysical Christ of the dogmas was to be replaced by the natural man of Galilee and Jerusalem.

In pursuit of the last word in realism Zola went down a coal mine before writing *Germinal* on the life of miners. He collected his facts assiduously, then put them into a narrative, just like those who think that a rendering of Jesus is entirely the collection of historical facts subsequently expressed in narrative form. Yet Zola himself realized in a frank moment that what he so meticulously observed was '*vu à travers un tempérament*'.[25] But Zola's temperament or character dictated more than he was aware of:

> Underneath the trappings of scientific objectivity Zola structured his tales much as novelists have always done, using myths,

> archetypes, value-judgments. He faced and made moral judgments which no amount of fact could resolve for him . . . His books, far from being the clinical observations of a technician, were the creation of a complex mind and imagination.[26]

This quotation may again be transferred wholesale to the questers and their successors. *Any* presentation of Jesus, even if *per impossibile* there were a myriad stable 'assured results' of biblical criticism, would equally have the structure of a story and be 'the creation of a complex mind and imagination'.

Once this point is conceded, however, it is possible to raise again the role of New Testament scholarship, and further to ask whether any values at all may be expressed through the medium of a representation of Jesus. Barth claimed the freedom to express in his own terms what he heard in the Bible. He had his own form of faithfulness, which produced a christology vivid enough to catch the imagination of many, although it was little concerned with New Testament historical investigation. Yet history, for all its difficulties and impossibility of certainty, is the way in which contemporary society relates to the past, so if the intention is still to describe 'Jesus' for today with today's values, attention has to be paid to such matters as the differences in character between Mark's Gospel and John's, or the current consensus that the parables are characteristic of the style and content of Jesus' communication. Accounts may be compared, contrasted and weighed as sensitively as possible. Yet even when all that has been done, just as for theology there is one coherent imaginative picture of God which shapes and informs all that is said, so for a christologian there is one coherent, imaginative picture of Jesus which will shape the use made of the New Testament, and to this extent christologians are like Barth.

The process of arriving at this picture is more like baking a cake than weaving with always separable textile strands or building with one kind of foundation and another kind of superstructure. Many of the ingredients of the cake are provided out of the interpretation of the New Testament, however provisional that may be. But the selection of these ingredients and their amounts are influenced by other matters such as the conceptions of incarnation, salvation and the action of God which are held and which will reflect that particular christologian's values. These conceptions in turn have been influenced by the New Testament as well as later doctrine and present circumstance, but in the *presentation* of Jesus, where salvation is the underlying theme, they become decisive for choice and emphasis among the rich variety of the New Testament. The entire mixture is then blended and baked into a new whole which will be different from past accounts. From the time of the gospels such a process has been under way, but in the last hundred and fifty years 'historical' ingredients have had such a high social valuation that they have been thought to be quite different from and superior to all other components. Indeed, some accounts of Jesus have been so tentative because their writers wished to maintain historical integrity that they have failed to convey as attractive Jesus concerning whom the question of salvation might be asked.

There will, therefore, be values blended in with other materials including historical matters for the imaginative construal of Jesus. But now the question arises whether any values at all may be expressed in Jesus' figure. History has been thought to provide a curb on the excessive subjectivity of values, but at best that is a partial, provisional curb for those prepared to take New Testament scholarship seriously. It is easy to be critical of values one does not share, and for this reason nineteenth-century lives of Jesus are unlikely to appeal today being for the most part either tediously pedantic, heavily moral, or (to our taste) cloying in their romanticism. It is easy to mock simply by quotation, as in this excerpt from Renan's romantic picture:

> The beautiful climate of Galilee made the life of these honest fishermen a perpetual delight. They truly preluded the kingdom of God – simple, good and happy – rocked gently on their delightful little sea, or at night sleeping on its shores.[27]

In the same way we may (or may not) find Dean Farrer slightly ludicrous when he commends Jesus for having all the remnants of bread gathered up after feeding the five thousand, since that shows he was a tidy man.[28] Variation in values may thus give some grounds for rejection. On the other hand it is equally possible that the values perceived in a christology may enlarge or criticize one's own values. Thus the strong emphasis on Jesus' concern for the poor expressed in liberation christology has offered a critique of the unconsciously bourgeois values of the European-American tradition.

This matter of critique points to the one thing which should be built into every imaginative construal of Jesus so that the values expressed do not simply domesticate his figure within the current social consensus. The danger of a Jesus who is only relevant and is not free to judge and transcend the values of an age can be shown by the extreme example of the Jesus of the German Christians, people who supported the Nazi ideology of Aryan racial superiority and required a Jesus to cohere with that. Here is the description given by Houston Stewart Chamberlain, 'as successful as anyone in inculcating pro-Germanic and antisemitic sentiments within the educated middle classes in Germany, including many churchmen':[29]

> We need to tear away the foreign rags and tatters that still hang upon our Christianity as the trappings of slavish hypocrisy: we need the creative power to construct out of the words and the spectacle of the crucified Son of Man a perfect religion fitting the truth of our nature, our capacities, and our present culture – a religion so directly convincing, so enchantingly beautiful, so present, so plastic, so eternally true, and yet so new, that we must give ourselves to it as a maid to her lover, without questioning, happy, enraptured, a religion so exactly suited to our highly gifted but delicate, easily injured, peculiar Teutonic nature, that it shall have the power to master our inmost souls.[30]

One immediate objection to this particular hi-jacking of Jesus for ideological ends is that Jesus was a Jew, one of the despised race, not an Aryan. History does in that case appear to provide a criterion. Yet in a day when the *European* character of countless less objectionable pictures of Jesus is recognized, and when Indians, Africans, Japanese and Koreans among others are developing their own christologies in their own situations, the fact of Jesus' Jewishness cannot be the deciding factor in the critique of the German Christians. There is much to learn from the Jewishness of Jesus in terms of continuity with the Old Testament, for instance, and the emphasis may restrain antisemitism. But for Jesus to be saviour (however that is understood), he is saviour in the circumstances in which people find themselves, not in abstract nor in general, and to that salvation the Jewishness of Jesus may be irrelevant. What the hitherto unconscious practice of linking Jesus to one's society involved, then, was the recognition of Jesus as salvific within the society. Criticism will have more to do with the kind of values expressed than with the relation of Jesus to the society.

To maintain the connection between Jesus and the society within which he is proclaimed as saviour, yet to avoid the total enculturation of Jesus demonstrated by the German Christians, the freedom of Jesus to confront, criticize and transvalue all values has to be built into the picture. One of the features of an ideology is that nothing is allowed to count as effective criticism of the beliefs involved. When Jesus is harnessed to such self-righteousness the result, as in the Teutonic Christ, is his domestication to powerlessness within the culture. He becomes the legitimation and religious sanction of the *status quo*. Instead of that, the presentation of Jesus has to include the summons to look critically at the social and spiritual *status quo* ('Woe to you . . . hypocrites'; 'You have heard it said . . . but I say to you . . .'; 'You have a fine way of rejecting the commandment of God, in order to keep your tradition'). In the terms I have used this is the summons to 'see' where freedom and love are lacking or diminished in society and the church. In today's parlance Jesus offers '*critical* solidarity'; which includes an aspect of protest at things as they are as well as positive relationship. Values in a presentation of Jesus or a christology which have no room for this protest, which consider themselves in effect to have arrived, are open to criticism. This is an equivalent in terms of the picture of Jesus to the freedom of God to judge which goes along with the divine loving companionship, and that keeps the unavoidable element of historically-conditioned value in the presentation from being dangerously complacent.

With that proviso, the multiplicity of renderings of Jesus, due as often to changing values as to changes in New Testament scholarship, may be seen not to be vicious. Yet the fact of multiplicity has been disturbing to many. In the sensitive introduction to his own *Jesus of Nazareth*, Günther Bornkamm lists 'now the "enlightened" teacher of God, virtue and immortality, now the religious genius of the Romantics, now the teacher of ethics in Kant's sense, now the protagonist of social theory', and comments that it is 'alarmingly and terrifying evident how inevitably each author brought the spirit of his own age into his presentation of the figure of Jesus'.[31] Moltmann is equally dismissive: 'An analysis of the changing ideas of Christ and portraits of Jesus in history shows that they correspond so much to the needs of their age, place of origin and intended purpose, that one cannot avoid the suspicion that they are illusory and artificial.'[32]

Yet from all the argument in this chapter so far it should be clear that there is no escaping the effects of finitude, even in picturing Jesus. *Of course* Jesus the saviour will correspond to the needs of an age. He will not be perceived as salvific unless he is perceived to respond to what people need to be saved from in their own particular time. Yet these needs still have to be critically examined and confronted. What is illusory and artificial is the notion that a particular, value-filled rendering of Jesus will somehow transcend human limitation and, in the hope of von Ranke long since departed from, describe things 'as they really were'. Multiplicity in the making of portraits is written into the whole exercise undertaken by individual people in time and not in some Platonic timeless reality, and diversity will not be transcended by either historical or devotional means.

Further, as Don Cupitt once noted: 'Jesus has been declared to be a model for hermits, peasants, gentlemen, revolutionaries, pacifists, feudal lords, soldiers and others.'[33] This is a small selection from the actual variety of Christians, worthy of the name, among whom different understanding and emphases are bound to be found, even if they chorused in unison down the ages, 'Jesus is Lord'. Identity of language is no guarantee of identity of understanding. But such variety is just what one would expect to develop concerning someone whose importance transcends the particularities of his original time and place. The difference since the rise of historical consciousness has been the expectation of arriving at one historically guaranteed portrait owing nothing to the imagination and giving a basis outside faith for faith itself. That expectation has to be set aside, although history remains an important ingredient.

Moreover, every sketch, picture or life of Jesus is a presentation in *narrative* form, and the exigencies of narrative are only beginning to be understood. For one thing, language is neither plastic under a writer's skill nor a pellucid conveyer of intended meaning. It is not a clear and distinct medium totally at the disposal of the articulate. Language does not simply *refer* to extra-linguistic realities, mirroring them in the manner of the correspondence theory of truth. Nor does it give a limpidly clear presentation of a point of view, which would be correspondence of a narrower variety. Deconstructionists have shown that the concepts in even the most staid or technical prose function as rhetorical devices like metaphor, whose effect is to persuade rather than demonstrate, and whose meaning is elastic or, in one of the current terminologies, has 'a surplus of signifiers'.[34] For this reason no one is in total control of language and texts are always open to deconstruction from the avowed intention of their authors. This account goes further than Wittgenstein's description of language as a collection of tiny, overlapping games, for that metaphor led to the notion of meaning being determined by the way language is used.[35] Certainly there are varieties of language games, and if you understand the game you will follow the use, but what deconstruction plays with is the excess and difference of meaning among the omnipresent metaphors which make nonsense of the notion of rules (for a game) and outrun every stable meaning. Texts are in transit along with the rest of the changing world, so no final meaning may be attributed to any, whether it is a canonical Gospel or a pedantic nineteenth-century life of Jesus (which no doubt did not seem pedantic to its author, and may come to be seen to have the virtue of *gravitas* again).

Thus, just as in the field of science can be found the impish scientific relativism of Feyerabend, who continually discloses the unprovable assumptions on which research proceeds, so in the field of language there is the playful deconstruction of texts by Derrida and others, in a process of endlessly undermining and displacing meaning.[36] Feyerabend and Derrida successfully dismantle the attempts of others to employ or express correspondence with reality as truth, but avoid any solution themselves to the problem of what in that case is to be done, except to convey the implicit conclusion that there is no solution. Their work is a corrective to older certainties and simplicities, but offers no help to those who actually wish to make decisions, take action and live out their beliefs.

In this connection the comment of the literary theorist Terry Eagleton becomes important. Eagleton is a Marxist, and Marxists, like Christians, have things to do in the world and cannot for ever entertain indeterminacy of meaning. Relativity (which here means the relative and provisional closure of meaning) rather than relativism which makes no closure is the result. Eagleton writes:

> Meaning may well be ultimately undecidable if we view language contemplatively, as a chain of signifiers on a page: it becomes 'decidable' and words like 'truth', 'reality', 'knowledge' and 'certainty' have something of their force restored to them when we think of language as something we do, as indissociably interwoven with our practical forms of life. It is not, of course, that language then becomes fixed and luminous: on the contrary it becomes even more fraught and conflictual than the most 'deconstructed' literary text. It is just that we are then able to see, in a practical rather than an academicist way, what would *count* as deciding, determining, persuading, certainty, being truthful, falsifying and the rest – and see, moreover, what beyond language itself is *involved* in such definitions![37]

Eagleton's suggestion is not without its difficulties. But it does point to the practical possibility of a middle way between the extremes of the older certainties of meaning and truth on the one hand, and the realization of the impossibility of final truth expressed in language on the other. If anything is to be done (even in ordinary living, let alone commitment to a cause), some closure of meaning is necessary 'to get on with it' as it were. The effect of finitude upon knowing can be admitted in the revisibility of all meaning, yet the discovery of personal and interpersonal meaning may still elicit commitment and permit praxis of all kinds, even though such language will continue to be 'fraught and conflictual', as every theological or political argument demonstrates.

Any portrait of Jesus Christ, therefore, and any christology, is an instance of the use of language for commitment and praxis which will be deconstructible like any text, and hence provisional, and may well be conflictual as well. Yet if this were recognized, it might become possible to *enjoy* multiplicity, as the excess of meaning in the Gospels is worked and reworked into new presentations of Jesus. Moreover, although none of the portraits will be final, it is possible that one of them, or parts from many of them, may so vividly express one's commitment to God in Christ that it gives contemporary meaning and direction to our lives, lives which, after all, are also contingent and provisional.

It becomes clear, therefore, that a description of Jesus like that in Chapter 2 of this book comes from both an imaginative and a historically-aware reading of scripture on the part of an author whose interests and sensitivities affect the final text, whose language is open to interpretation and reinterpretation, and whose offering will be variously received. In the process of giving the whole picture a coherence expressive of its theme in contemporary time and space some matters will be emphasized and enlarged while others are played down. In my own account, for instance, I have made little mention of eschatology, that sense of the nearness of God's kingdom arriving to end or to renew the world which characterizes Jesus in the Synoptic Gospels. Certainly today there is a secularly-based doom-laden fear of nuclear destruction or climatic disruption, and to that extent eschatological themes may be relevant. Yet I agree with Boff:

> We must take due account of the difference between Jesus' situation and our own. In his day there was an apocalyptic atmosphere and people were looking for the immediate breakthrough of the kingdom. In our eyes the parousia has been held up and history still has a future. Hence there must be differences in the way we organize love and justice in society.[38]

Boff's point of the organization of love and justice points to Christian responsibility *now* in the presence of God, an emphasis which may be lost if too much weight is given to a future (even imminent) end. Present human response was an important theme in my description of Jesus, found in the Gospel descriptions, and it will reappear in the christological model to follow, where on this point I shall be echoing John rather than Mark, seeking the decisive presence of God in Jesus (realized eschatology) rather than looking beyond present horizons to a future eschatology.

Everything consciously included in or omitted from my description of Jesus could be justified in a similar way by reference to New Testament scholarship on both the historical and the literary character of the Gospels, and to the coherence of my own developing picture of Jesus, in which the freedom and love of Jesus in relation to God and to his fellow men and women have been the dominant traits. To give the background to all of it would be too long, but my treatment of the resurrection may require more explicit justification, since it is at once so central and so contentious an issue. Clearly this cannot be a full discussion, which would take volumes on its own, but it is intended as a defence of taking Paul's phrase in I Cor. 15.45, that Jesus became a 'life-giving spirit', as the central motif.

What is the resurrection? For many reasons it is very difficult to say. There is no account in the New Testament of its actual happening and what is recounted are its effects. Even the effects so far as they refer to a continuing Jesus are differently described, with, one might say, varying degrees of solidity. Paul in the same chapter in I Cor. seems to presume a spiritual body like those he expected in the resurrection of believers – and Paul is the only writer in the New Testament who declared himself to have seen the Lord. But Luke's account in 24.36–43 argues for something considerably more solid, even to the eating of broiled fish. Yet, as Norman Perrin points out, there may well have been an apologetic purpose in Luke's description. In the Hellenistic world for whom Luke was writing 'it was widely assumed that a religious hero overcame death by being transformed into a spiritual being who no longer had any contact with the essentially unreal world of flesh, blood and bodies . . . Jesus would thereby have joined a pantheon of religious heroes in which there was always room for one more'.[39] But, as Luke may have been emphasizing, the resurrection, whatever it was, was not an *escape* from the world of flesh and bodies, which in any case had higher value in the Jewish tradition, and the resurrection was the occasion of sending others out to mission *in the world*. Moreover

Jesus was not one of a pantheon, and was not to be made to seem like any other current religious hero. So the heavily emphasized solidity of Luke's picture may have more to do with 'the increasing threat of absorption into the vast and multitudinous world of Hellenistic religiosity' than with what one might call 'historical solidity'.[40]

If Perrin is right, however, it means that in Luke's accounts he was acting, with good reason and effectively, as a theological author rather than a historical recorder. A further instance of authorship, also from Luke, is his concentration of the appearance of the risen Christ in and around Jerusalem, rather than in Galilee. Jerusalem was the *holy* city (which was no mere phrase), but by the time Luke wrote it had fallen to the Romans. On a theological understanding it had rejected Jesus and was therefore itself rejected by God. But Jerusalem was likewise the place of God's new beginning with humanity, where Jesus' passion culminated in resurrection. It was therefore theologically important that the appearances should be in Jerusalem and that the Christian movement should begin in Jerusalem before moving out as Luke portrays in Acts to another symbolic centre, Rome. There is a wealth of symbolism here after the style of the Jewish midrash which would resonate among Luke's hearers, but which can be entirely missed if the only question is whether this is historical, or how it can be harmonized with Matthew's account of an appearance in Galilee.

For Matthew has equally created his own theological rendering of the resurrection. Indeed, after examining all the Gospels on the resurrection, and finding behind them all the conviction that Jesus of Nazareth 'continues to be and to operate', C. F. Evans concludes:

> Each of these is complete in itself; each has developed along its own line so as to serve in the end as a proper conclusion for an evangelist of his own particular version of the gospel . . . Each evangelist gives his own version as a total version, which was not intended to stand up only if it stood alongside another, or was supplemented by another.[41]

A Gospel description of the risen Jesus, therefore, is another instance of every account of Jesus having its own coherence which comes from theological values and imaginative recounting as well as remembrance of things past.

There are few Old Testament verses affecting descriptions of the effects of the resurrection. What may have been more influential were various speculative ideas of the time, such as the resurrection of martyrs described in II Maccabees. Indeed 'this combination of ideas of martyrdom, expiation and hope for the future may have had more influence on New Testament thought than has been recognized'.[42] Other versions of resurrection belief more or less current at the time included a general resurrection followed by judgment and resurrection followed by some form of immortality in joy or suffering conferred by God. What is possible is that some forms of some of these beliefs which were speculative and diffuse expressed for Paul and others the action of God they felt themselves part of, and which they applied to the particularity of Jesus, making the beliefs concentrated and increasingly definite in the process of describing Jesus' resurrection and exaltation, his 'entering into his glory'.

These two motifs of resurrection and exaltation, together with the impartation of the Spirit, have a different relationship in the New Testament from the one the church has become accustomed to in the liturgical calendar, which follows Luke's strung-out sequence in Acts (not in his Gospel), where resurrection is followed by ascension and then Pentecost. In the New Testament, resurrection and exaltation are like two aspects of, or two ways of giving a context to, the post-mortem impact of Jesus. The Letter to the Hebrews, for instance, hardly mentions resurrection but is based on the exalted Jesus being at the right hand of God. And for Paul: 'The resurrection was conceived not as the return of Jesus after his death on the cross to earthly life, but as his elevation into his position of power *in heaven* as the Son of God to whom all powers had been delegated.'[43]

Evans suggests that the accounts of appearances in the Gospels, which are later than Paul, may represent the teasing out of the notion of exaltation, since exaltation must presuppose resurrection. The latter would then express the time of the first encounter with the life-giving power and the receiving of the summons to act in its name. Yet whether exaltation or resurrection is described, each is a context, a dramatic vehicle for the impartation of the

Spirit and the empowering for mission. The vehicle is not neutral, of course, because it comes from the tradition of God's relationship with Israel (enthronement, kingship, Son of God), fused or varied with the forms the tradition was taking at the time (resurrection, post-mortem existence decreed by God, final judgment). Without the whole complex of beliefs in God's involvement there would have been no belief in resurrection or exaltation nor in the impartation of spirit which these themes make possible. In John's Gospel, Jesus, who as the incarnate word of God is always in control, himself breathes the spirit on the disciples (John 20.22). In Matthew (28.20) the whole force of the resurrection appearance is the commissioning to go teaching (a very Matthean emphasis) into all the world 'and lo I am with you always, to the close of the age' (i.e., to the parousia and final judgment). The risen Jesus in Luke promises 'power from on high' (24.29), while in Mark 14.28 and 16.7 Jesus is said to be going before his disciples into Galilee (symbolic of the Gentile mission). Thus Jesus integrates and equips for witnessing, teaching, suffering.

In that respect Paul is not significantly different. He asks 'Am I not an apostle? Have I not seen the Lord?' (I Cor. 9.1), although he gives little indication of what 'seeing the Lord' was. The accounts in Acts are Lukan and may or may not derive from Paul. What the seeing did, however, was to commission Paul to apostleship, carrying the message to the Gentiles, counting everything else worthless 'that I may know him and the power of his resurrection, becoming like him in his death, that if possible I may attain the resurrection of the dead' (Phil. 3.10f.). James Mackey sums up Paul's understanding of the resurrection (apart from the exaltation of Jesus) thus:

> He understands the resurrection to mean, not primarily an event in the personal destiny of Jesus himself, not primarily what we have called the personal resurrection of Jesus, but that Jesus is a power or spirit in our lives, enabling us to overcome destructive evil, enhancing our lives with faith and love and a hope that defies death.[44]

And, as Mackey comments, if that is denied, then faith is indeed made void.

I wrote at the beginning of this discussion that the New Testament does not describe the resurrection but its effects. The clearest and most widespread effect is the power, hope and faith which comes from the spirit of God through Jesus (that is, experienced as Jesus-shaped) and which continues – as in the quotation from Mackey it is 'our' lives which are enhanced. To know that life-giving spirit is to 'encounter the risen Jesus' or be saved by the power of God. But such encounters do not happen outside a context, and the variety of descriptions throughout the New Testament of resurrection, corporeal or spiritual, of exaltation, of ascension and the pentecostal gift of the Spirit are the dramatic ways, full of theological depth and apologetic intent, of rendering the context in which the continuing relationship between God and humanity given shape and direction through Jesus is powerfully experienced after Jesus' death.

The reality of the life-giving Spirit is shown by the change in the disciples.

> Unless something extraordinary happened to convince them that against all their expectations God had reversed his verdict on Jesus, I cannot imagine that they would later on have taken immense risks to assert in public that a man who had been condemned and hanged was no less than God's Messiah.[45]

One person who has challenged this reading is Don Cupitt in *Christ and the Hiddenness of God*, objecting to the 'beaten men' argument that 'any sociologist could reply, it is precisely among the powerless that such beliefs begin'.[46] There is point in the observation, even though beaten men often remain only beaten men, but with hindsight Cupitt's parallels such as Che Guavara (Che lives!) are not convincing. Twenty years on, Che is not the cause he was in Britain in the 1960s – whatever other sociological factors have to be taken into account and whatever memories remain in Cuba or Bolivia. The spirit which drove Paul round the known world and persuaded Peter to eat Gentile meat, which the Corinthian church enjoyed in their undisciplined way and the Galatians nearly lost through a relapse into law, which has gone its way through the chequered history of the church and beyond, had and has, *at the very least*, a vivacity and durability, even a capacity for recrudescence which is striking. That does not of course prove that it is God's Spirit, for nothing will. What the apostolic age shows is the force of the experience: 'Paul's life was not turned upside down because he reflected on the value of Jesus' life and decided that goodness, even in defeat, is a more potent force than triumphant evil.'[47] It was Paul, never one of the 'beaten men', who asked, 'Am I not an apostle? Have I not seen the Lord?'

The existence of God and the long relationship between God and Israel are the (often silent) presuppositions of the Gospels, just as they inform Paul's wrestling with his new beliefs. Everything that happened in Jesus' career as it was happening or as it was reflected on later was referred to this relationship with a naturalness which is quite hard to recapture in a secular age, even for Christians. But in that way Jesus' life, death and resurrection came to be interpreted vividly but variously in terms of this relationship, and the relationship itself in terms of its fulfilment or new creation in Christ. It is always possible and often fruitful to winnow New Testament accounts for their historical residue in a twentieth-century manner. But that may not be where they have their value. In one sense one may say of the resurrection, 'By its spirit you shall know it', but that spirit itself is one which in the hope and stimulus and life it gives goes on to produce fruit: 'By their fruits you shall know them.'

In this section I have been arguing that history is only one of the variables taken up and worked with into a presentation of Jesus. It remains important for this society, since for us this is a primary source of knowledge and significance concerning the past. Yet the history is always selective and compounded with other values and concerns to make what is, finally, a literary and imaginative presentation. Yet there remains a historical crux for any christology, any rendering of the relationship between God and humanity given point and shape through Jesus called the Christ. The point is that the response to Jesus, so varied in the New Testament and beyond, was a response to a man in history, in ordinary time and space with all the difficulties and conditions that implies. As I should express it, there was in history a man whose effect on many (not all) who met him was such that they saw in him the enactment of relationship between God and humanity.

Words like 'enactment' and 'relationship' betray the modernness of the account. People would not have put it like that in the first century – nor in many others when 'relationship' was not an important issue. But they did associate God with what they saw in Jesus. It is important to call this affirmation historical, not in order to retain an unassailable area of security, which no verbal formulation could give, but in order to distinguish it from the ideal, such as that envisioned by Kant of a 'person morally well-pleasing to God' who could be an archetype of the consciousness and need never have existed.[48] Relationship with God can take place only among people who live and die. Such relationship might possibly be based on an ideal case, and certainly has been based in practice on a wide variety of interpretations of Jesus. But because relationship with God is a lived experience, an *Erlebnis*, Christian faith would become hollow and questionable if it did not take its rise in response to a man's own *Erlebnis* under ordinary historical conditions.

Something like this is reflected in Gregory of Nazianzus' christological criterion 'What is not assumed is not healed', except that it expresses in classical ontological terms what I am saying about relationship.[49] Gregory was objecting to a concentration on the divine nature of Christ to the point where the human nature was nugatory, or, in Apollinarius' case, to the point of denial that Christ had a rational human soul. The force of Gregory's apothegm is that the need for salvation lies in the human and in the 'rational human soul'. If there is no such soul in Christ then that need has not been met. Within a very different framework of thought I have been arguing that relationship with God is something which happens in a human life. If what has shaped Christian human lives within that relationship was not itself a human relationship with God, then the whole movement rests on a theoretical base and the possibility may not be realizable.

The importance of this point is quite independent of the variety of actual response, for what it concerns is the historical trigger to that response. It was possible for a human life under human conditions to be seen as revelatory of the connection with God or, as I would put it, of the nature and possibility of the divine-human relationship. At present there seems little doubt concerning Jesus' historical existence, but precisely because that is a historical affirmation it shares in the vulnerability of all things historical. Given that actualized human historical possibility, however, the multifariousness in time and through time of people and societies with their different values, metaphors, needs and systems of thought come into play, so that any presentation of the historical actuality will be humanly, finitely and contingently mediated.[50]

In theological terms that represents the freedom God has given the created world. But God also accompanies the world, and one of the ways of expressing that is to speak of the spirit of the risen Jesus, without which reflection and presentation would never have taken place. To know the presence of God (or the Spirit) in its openness, forgiveness and love is salvation. That puts the humanity of all expression into the larger context of belief in God, but because God respects the freedom of creation it does not make that expression any less human. Therefore, again from a theological point of view, it has to be said that incarnation (however understood) is *thorough* incarnation, so that there are no safe areas of language or thought for divinity to protect it from the variety and change of humanity, let alone from its self-centredness. Variety of belief and expression is thus what one should expect theologically and not just historically.

Knowledge of variety, a knowledge anyone can have from the history of christology, does not preclude conviction and commitment with relative closure on the meaning of Jesus in the New Testament. Such closure is necessary if anything is to be believed or done, and it may be final for our own understanding or following of Jesus. What has to be recognized is that this is a relative finality for us, while the text and the world may go on to generate other meanings, which is in its way another form of the belief that there is yet more light to break forth from God's word. What Frank Kermode writes about the literary classic as a work of art can be applied to scripture as a sacred text:

> In fact the only works we value enough to call classic are those which, and they demonstrate by surviving, are complex and indeterminate enough to allow us our necessary pluralities . . . It is in the nature of works of art to be open, in so far as they are

> 'good'; though it is in the nature of authors, and of readers, to close them.[51]

The openness occurs when 'the constraints of a period or culture dissolve (and) generic presumptions which concealed gaps disappear' creating a 'hermeneutic gap in which the reader's imagination must operate'. We are practically in this situation, with the collapse of the notion of historical foundations discoverable in the Gospels and the discovery of the creative power of strange midrash. This imaginative operation in the 'gap' between text and meaning is the reader's response to Virgil, to Cervantes and to scripture, and for this reason scripture, including the New Testament descriptions of Jesus, like 'King Lear, underlying a thousand dispositions, subsists in change, prevails by being patient of interpretation'.[52]

There is a useful German word which could apply to such interpretations and to much else: *dauerprovisorisch*, meaning provisional permanence or enduring provisionality. It is said, for instance, of a temporary bridge which continues to be used when there is no hope of money for something more permanent, or when road works have not been completed, but traffic is allowed to continue on the temporary lines as if they were permanent. That seems to me to be an image of most human undertakings, and certainly of expressions of belief which allow the traffic of faith to run on them while having only provisional permanence. Some may have more *Dauer*, more permanence, than others, but all remain qualified by the *provisorisch*.

When theologians recognize the role of imaginative construal in their descriptions of Jesus and the provisionality which make them address present circumstances with present historical knowledge, it may be that more effort could be expended on presenting the attractiveness and challenge of Jesus. There seems little point in proceeding to christological and soteriological questions unless the Jesus portrayed actually *does* draw people to him and to the relationship with God he represents, and unless the description is actually stimulating to Christian belief, life and devotion. (That point remains, whether or not I have succeeded.) Jesus was believed to be and was preached as saviour, and I believe that this description should be shaped in such a way as to make that at least a question to be taken further, because it can no longer be taken for granted that christologies have only a dogmatic role. I realize the dangers of such freedom of description, but these exist in any case, whether or not responsible theologians take to endeavouring to make their descriptions attractive. If theologians do not enter this field, it is left clear for those who have little sense of biblical criticism or the history of doctrine.

I have found in the Gospels and set in the foreground a Jesus who was free to respond to God and to his fellow men and women, free from class constraints and from the restraints of custom and law when these cut people off from God; moreover a Jesus who wished this freedom for all, so unlike the Grand Inquisitor. But such freedom is only productive when it is fuelled by love, love for God and the neighbour, a love which will not override freedom, but is always accessible and knows no end to its self-offering; again this is a love to which those who are drawn to Jesus in their freedom are called. Freedom and love are equally the characteristics of God in creation and salvation. The rest of this book is concerned with a model for moving from the two descriptions of God and of Jesus to talk of the incarnation of God in Christ and of salvation through Christ.

PART THREE

The Christological Model

5 · *The Dramaturgical Prototype*

It is a commonplace of Christian rhetoric to speak of the 'drama of salvation', whereby God, Christ and humanity are seen to be vividly caught up in action and interaction the end of which is salvation, however the action or the salvation is understood. The metaphor is apt, for it emphasizes that salvation and the transformation it brings are not a natural state of things as they are for people, but rather something enacted and accomplished in the midst of things as they are. Salvation may be reflected on, but it is neither given nor received through *theoria*, which is mental contemplation or the viewing of a spectacle. Instead, it comes about through *praxis* and *drama*, involvement in an action. Drama, indeed, is derived from the Greek verb *dran*, to do or to accomplish, the equivalent in Doric dialect to the Attic *prattein*, whence *praxis*.[1] While there are evident differences in emphases in our present use of these nouns, there is no absolute line of demarcation between the action we call praxis and the action we call drama. Thus, for instance, a procession in which churches demonstrate their desire for peace and justice is both praxis and drama.

> For the fact is that the art, activity, human craving or instinct which embodies itself in drama is so deeply enmeshed in human nature itself, and in a multitude of human pursuits, that it is wellnigh impossible to draw the exact dividing line between where one kind of more general activity stops and drama proper starts.[2]

There is another aspect of drama which makes it congenial to the theological tradition in that it can be a form of thought, a cognitive process by which abstract concepts can be worked out or realized in human situations in interaction. Witness, for instance, the current use of 'scenario' for thinking through the implications of a decision. Drama is, in Martin Esslin's phrase, 'a form of philosophizing . . . in existential terms'.[3] He points out that Sartre, an existential philosopher, felt compelled to write plays as well as novels to work out the concrete implications of his abstract thought. 'Salvation' is an abstract term. It can certainly be explained by further general terms, but it can also be shown, and the Christian claim is that it was first shown and then told.[4] Even the showing was human, however, and in the Gospels which preserve the emphasis on showing there are moments of 'telling' like any omniscient narrator. ('He proceeded to tell a parable because he was near to Jerusalem and because they supposed that the kingdom of God was to appear immediately', Luke 19.11.)

Conversely, however, as I shall argue, even the most abstract and metaphysical account of Christ has not departed totally from dramatic action. Drama thus straddles thought and practice, embodying the abstract in the particular and the metaphysical in a pattern of relationships in such a way that the audience becomes involved in the action. Drama certainly came to mean something done within a frame, such as a raised stage or particularly a proscenium arch, and that action could be passively contemplated. But even in that case there is a difference between attendance at a drama which is a mere 'looking', an uninvolved observation of the surface, and the openness of 'seeing' in the sense of discerning and wrestling with what is going on through the visible gestures and audible speech.

The dramatic metaphor is thus capable of being much more than rhetorical embellishment. It can bear the weight of serving as a model for both christology and soteriology, with action and relationship as its primary characteristics, rather than putting ontology in the forefront. Some metaphors (for instance 'ransom' in atonement theory, Mark 10.45) work only as surprising, suggestive figures of speech and cannot take the strain of having their implications teased out in the extension of a model (to whom was the ransom paid?). But drama, which concerns action and relationship through time, has already proved fruitful enough for social psychologists to use it as a model for all interaction in the serious play which is human life. It is equally serviceable for the action of salvation and the person of the saviour. Both sociological and more strictly dramaturgical aspects will come into play in this model. But it will remain a model: that is to say that sets of relationships in a known sphere (drama, society) will be used to illuminate relationships in another (God, Christ, humanity) to assist comprehension and action. Models are human and finite *ways* of understanding which work when they are appropriate to their subject-matter and fruitful in practice.

Any drama is more than the sum of its components, yet in the putting together of a model the making of a play is as important as the experiencing of its production, and in that case components have to be considered in outline, at least. Aristotle in his passionless analysis gave first place to the plot, 'the arrangement of the incidents', which had to have a beginning, a middle and an end and represent one whole coherent action.[5] So far as that goes there is not much difficulty in observing the plot of 'the drama of salvation' either in the evangelists' variously coherent accounts or in polished later doctrine. I shall return to consider the evangelists more particularly in the next chapter. Yet there are features of dramatic action which Aristotle could not have observed, which become clear only from the whole history of drama, namely that the kind of action deemed possible, or the conventions for drama, change in a way related to changes in the society of the playwright, director and audience.

> For a convention is not just a method: an arbitrary and voluntary technical choice. It embodies in itself these emphases, omissions, valuations, interests, indifferences, which compose a way of seeing life, and drama as part of life.[6]

Raymond Williams illustrates this, beginning with Sophocles' *Antigone*, a play of acted speech and sculptured scenes whose 'design, in the open theatre as in the experience of the writing, referred the audience outwards, to an accessible order'.[7] *Antigone* shares with the mediaeval *Everyman* a setting of human action within divine reality such that drama could without difficulty express both divine and human action, but as naturalism increased, so dramatic action became the activity of humans in human terms. The stage was closed in and soon represented a room in a private house, for it was no longer at courts and on battle-fields that important bourgeois reality took place.[8] First it appeared that humanity in almost all its naturalness could be reproduced on stage, but then came an emphasis on private, opaque, complex internal experience and the stage was cleared of its mimetic room. And so the process goes on. For action to convey dramatic experience through its plot, therefore, it has to connect with some present way of seeing life. Older drama, however vividly communicative in its day, becomes literature (worth study, certainly, but a minority occupation) unless its excess of meaning survives through time, like the classic, to make new connections and generate new meanings. A similar process is equally visible in the history of christologies from the breadth of classical doctrine with its unproblematic account of the divine to the humanly naturalistic Jesus of the nineteenth and twentieth centuries where the divine is not obvious. Thus again even in a christology, philosophical and social conventions have embodied, in Williams' words, 'these emphases, omissions, valuations, interests, indifferences, which compose a way of seeing life'.

Coherence was an important element to Aristotle, and the coherence of a plot is largely gained by the unifying vision, idea or theme of a play embodied in the action. Even in plays which make their point through deliberate incoherence themes such as the futility of life underlie the unpredictability of events or the suspension of action. In performance a theme is inseparable from its enactment, yet it is the perception, however fragmentary, of a theme which allows an audience to 'see' what a play is about, to grasp as a whole some meaning beyond the succession of incidents. By reflection a theme may be extracted from a play apart from its performance, although all vividness, suggestiveness and particularity are thereby drained from it, leaving a disembodied abstract, a general statement, not necessarily profound or new, about the human condition. Thus one might perhaps say that a deducible theme from Macbeth is that ambition may undo a man, although that statement is a poor substitute for watching Macbeth's dissolution. Themes other than the one the dramatist intended may of course be found in a play, giving different resonances in different societies. It is true of drama (as indeed it is of the New Testament) that 'the meaning of a work of art is not exhausted by, or even equivalent to, its intention'.[9] I am more concerned with theme as an opening on to meaning than with asserting a single meaning for a play. Yet since drama is serving as a model for the construction of a christology, an author's intention has more relevance that it sometimes has in literary criticism.

Therefore, just as it was not enough to remain with the formal definition of plot as a series of incidents, so it is not enough to say that an author's theme guides the subject matter of a play. For as Raymond Williams pointed to the social earthing of the dramatic experience conveyed by the action, so Ronald Gaskell argues that the nature of a theme and the way it is presented arise from a writer's 'vision of reality', however amorphous or unconscious that may be. He takes the phrase from a letter of Yeats to his father: 'I think with you that the poet seeks truth, not abstract truth, but a kind of vision of reality which satisfies the whole being.'[10] Gaskell explores drama since Ibsen and concludes:

> A theme takes shape in the mind of the writer who sees the world in his own way. To Brecht man is a political animal, to Eliot a spirit capable of salvation, to Beckett a useless passion. Theme, at its very roots is fed by a personal vision of this kind – which is not just a way of looking, but a way of thinking and feeling. And from this it follows that the action of a play (structure, character, speech, etc.) does more than explore and clarify a particular theme. It also expresses and defines a distinctive vision of human life.[11]

This observation suggests some important points for a christology. For instance, if the theme in the prototypical Gospels may be said to be 'salvation is here' embodied in the action of Jesus, it is nevertheless expressed differently in each according to the difference in visions of reality, that is, what the human condition is and requires. Moreover, this may serve as a reminder that all christology 'at its very roots is fed by a vision of this kind' apart from which there is no point to a description of Christ and his benefits.

Thus a play consists of dramatic action (the plot) embodying an underlying theme, and characterization has to fit into the scheme by advancing the action coherently. No matter how fully a playwright may have conceived a character, nor how curious an audience may be to know him or her more fully, a dramatic *persona* can be presented only as psychologically or morally appropriate for and contributing to the action. As the Swiss dramatist Friedrich Dürrenmatt commented:

> In contrast to the epic, which can describe human beings as they are, the drama unavoidably limits and therefore stylizes them. This limitation is inherent in the art form itself.[12]

The relationship between character and plot is well described by Martin Esslin:

> Only what characters *do* tells the audience what they are like. Thus it must be the action of people within the plot which develops character, while that character of the individuals involved in turn *motivates* the action and makes the plot interesting to follow.[13]

Thus in drama a character is understood by the decoding and evaluating of his/her actions in a manner like ordinary human interaction, but quite unlike the novel, where a narrator can give expansive and intimate descriptions of character apart from action. In this respect also the Gospels are very like dramas, for they *show* Jesus in action far more than they *tell* what he was like.

Yet, as Dürrenmatt observed, character conveyed by action for the audience to understand as the play proceeds is more limited, more stylized (and hence more symbolic) than someone in real life or a character in a novel. A good positive account of this limitation is given by Harold Rosenberg in *The Tradition of the New*.[14] He begins by distinguishing between the conception of a person as an individual with a biography, psychology and biology, living freely and erratically but recognizable in the continuity of his being, and the conception of a person accused in a court of law, defined by a series of overt acts leading to the fact which has brought him for judgment. In the latter case character is of importance only in relation to these acts and only information relevant and material to the legal cause of action may be introduced. Such a character, defined by a central fact (the charge which brought him to court) and the coherence of other acts with that fact, Rosenberg calls an 'identity':

> Representing the human individual as an actor, the term stands against the biological or historical organism-concept, which visualizes action as a mere attribute of, or clue to, a being who can be known only through an intuition.'[15]

From this distinction he proceeds to another:

> The characters of biography and the novel are persons with histories, but in the drama the characters are identities with roles.[16]

Biography aims to picture a life as fully and precisely as possible, but the dramatist leaves aside personalities with their growth and variable peculiarities to concentrate on coherence of action dominated by the relation of the identity to the central motif of the play, the 'fact'. Rosenberg, pursuing the forensic analogy, finds judgment implicit in the way the action terminates. For there are ethical overtones in drama sometimes intended by the dramatist but always present in the approval or disapproval a play arouses in the audience.

He makes his point clear by taking Hamlet as an example of the transformation of a personality into a dramatic identity. In the first part of the play appears the argumentative, self-analytical Hamlet of 'non-action', who uses his introspective speech as a substitute for deeds and compares himself disadvantageously with Laertes or the players who are all ready in their own way to act. At this stage Hamlet has no real role to perform in the furtherance of the play. 'It is not a weakness of personality that impedes his action, but the fact that he is a personality.'[17] For the play to become a tragedy with a plot and not a series of episodes exposing psychological layers, Hamlet must be given an identity. Rosenberg is impressed by the religious conception of achieving new life by dying to the old and finds a symbolic death in Hamlet's narrow escape from pirates on the voyage to England with his own death warrant. Now he has a role of self-purifying vengeance and his action drives the play to its tragic close. 'Transformed from the image of a personality into that of a dramatic identity, he has found at last his place in the play.'[18]

It will be my contention that the Jesus of the Gospels, of Paul and all subsequent christology is, in Rosenberg's terms, an identity, whatever historical memories may be present. Only what coheres with his significance and advances the action is described while the whole presentation elicits the judgment of the hearers. Rosenberg's summary of his point fits Jesus presented as Messiah:

> Individuals are conceived as identities in systems whose subject matter is action and the judgment of actions. In this realm the multiple incidents in the life of an individual may be synthesized, by the choice of the individual himself or by the decision of others, into a scheme that pivots on a single fact central to the individual's existence and which, controlling his behaviour and deciding his fate, becomes his visible definition.[19]

In this brief survey of those features of play-writing relevant to christologizing my emphasis is on the fabrication of plays, and I cannot begin to do justice to the complicated and never-completed transactions between author, text, actors and audience perceived by modern critics, especially of the 'post-structuralist' persuasion. Yet I have emphasized what I take to be their main contribution, namely that there is no one determinate meaning in a text. It will not come as a surprise to anyone who has preached a sermon and received some feedback that there is no assured fit between utterance and hearing, or even between intention and utterance. Yet, though a text is not determinate it is determinable; a meaning may be found, a voice heard, or even deconstructionists would cease writing. I do not share in, for instance, Derrida's objection to a 'metaphysics of presence' through texts, for although language precedes anyone's use of it, or (since language is not a pure instrument) anyone's being caught in its web, it can still be used differently with perceptibly different points of view, as Beckett differs from Eliot. That is not to say that the 'authentic' Beckett or Eliot is smoothly communicated in the text, let alone in a performance, but that is not a new perception. Eliot himself, writing of poetic 'experience', could have been writing of drama or the Gospels:

> What we experience as readers is never exactly what the poet experienced, nor would there be any point in its being, though certainly it has some relation to the poet's experience. What the poet experienced was not poetry but poetic material; the writing of the poetry is a fresh 'experience' for him and the reading of it, by the author or anyone else, is another thing still.[20]

To return to plays for some final characteristics which have a bearing on what follows. Plays take place in a perpetual present tense no matter in what period they are set, and they happen through present time. To watch a play unfold is to watch present choices, deeds, quarrels and reconciliations. A novel can never capture this degree of immediacy, partly because it is not visually presented, but also because novels require a story-teller, or at least some comment on the inward motives and reflections of the characters. We are instructed by a narrator, but a drama 'makes us see the action as though it were an objective presence, something that occurs spontaneously before us and that we have to observe to evaluate it, form an opinion as to what it is and what it means. The audience in drama, whether they want it or not, are compelled to arrive at their own interpretation.'[21] In the same way, as the theologians of crisis maintained, there has to be an evaluation and response to Jesus in the presentness of the presentation.

Naturally, however, response will vary among an audience, whether to Jesus or to a play. T. S. Eliot analyses the possibilities of response sensitively. The second part of the quotation is important, for plays are not necessarily élite productions for the educated bourgeoisie. I have attended a play in the grounds of a castle beside a housing scheme which enacted its history, with the difference between rich and poor heavily underlined. There was no doubt that the local audience perceived a meaning!

> For the simplest auditors there is a plot, for the more thoughtful the character and conflict of character, for the more literary the words and phrasing, for the more musically

> sensitive rhythm, and for the auditors of greater sensitiveness and understanding a meaning which reveals itself gradually. And I do not believe that the classification of audience is so clear cut as this; but rather that the sensitiveness of every auditor is acted upon by all these elements at once, though in different degrees of consciousness.[22]

Some members of an audience, however, react to a play as if it were real life. Such response is probably most pronounced with continuing radio and television serials where people feel they 'know' the characters and may, for instance, send flowers to the studio when a character is represented as ill. To dramatic critics this is a bad thing, for the precisely *dramatic* experience is aesthetic and includes knowing the difference between a play and lived reality. In that case, if the play illuminates life, it is not through the identification of the one with the other by the spectator, but through the enlargement of understanding or the effect of catharsis brought about by the play. With drama as the model for the saviour and salvation, however, the situation is rather different.

Although there have been many accounts of Jesus, so that no one version can be identified with Jesus' reality, which was not in any case a single simple thing, this is an instance where the signified (salvation, which can come only from God since it is not a human possibility) is meant to be aligned with the signifier (Jesus in action), so that the signifier is identified with the reality behind it in the belief of Christians. Moreover, 'saviour' however dramatically presented, is in the end a social rather than a dramatic role, and is thus something to respond to as one person to another. To put that another way: as far as the *presentation* of Jesus goes the dramaturgical model is enlightening; but for salvation as a *lived experience* the social aspect of roles comes into play. It is not the case in the presentation of Jesus that a world is created which has no existence at all outside the text.

To complete the general considerations of drama with which this chapter is concerned I wish to apply them to Robert Bolt's *A Man for All Seasons* by way of an example. I chose this play partly because it is a historical drama concerning Thomas More and this introduces questions of historicity which have not yet been addressed. I chose it also because it was the modern dramatic text set for the senior pupils I was teaching in a small town in New Zealand before studying theology. New Zealanders of that age quite naturally have not grown up with a sense of the past reaching to the sixteenth century and have not studied much English history. It was therefore hard work for all to cover the historical background which British audiences could take for granted. In the process I discovered that historical dramas are not 'about' history and that the history is there, like the proscenium arch, as framework. A fortnight after the university entrance examination the excellent film version with Paul Scofield as More at last arrived in town. While the pupils had of course been well prepared by our discussion of the text, they all reported far greater imaginative grasp and understanding of the play's resonances from watching it unfold. Just so, I shall argue, to watch Jesus in action gave a 'far greater imaginative grasp and understanding' of God's offer of salvation than the study of even a sacred text.

In his preface to the play Bolt explains its underlying theme as he intends it. The modern person, he finds, has no firm conception of selfhood, so that the self becomes an ever more equivocal commodity apart from the description of one's occupation. 'Both socially and individually it is with us as it is with our cities – an accelerating flight to the periphery, leaving a centre which is empty when the hours of business are over.'[23] Bolt is not a Catholic and disclaims being a Christian 'in the meaningful sense', but he found in More 'a man with an adamantine sense of his own self'.[24] More could yield to the encroachment of friends and enemies, but in Bolt's view he was finally asked to retreat from the area in which he located his self. 'And there this supple, humorous, unassuming and sophisticated person set like metal, was overtaken by an absolutely primitive rigour, and could no more be budged than a cliff.'[25] Bolt does allow that 'it may be that a clear sense of the self can *only* crystallize around something transcendental, in which case,' he continues, 'our prospects look poor, for we are rightly committed to the rational.'[26] Whatever one may make of the latter part of that sentence, Bolt's play does allow for a spectator committed to 'something transcendental' to see similar commitment involved in what finally makes it impossible to wheel and deal for ever, with expediency the only criterion.

Bolt thus intends to portray a modern malaise, but takes a historical character as the vehicle for discussing it. The events of More's life are well known: his rise to the Chancellorship of England; his refusal to support Henry VIII's break with Rome and marriage to Anne Boleyn or Henry's becoming Head of the Church in England; his imprisonment and final execution under the Act of Succession and Treason. Bolt could not have altered these without losing credibility. His play had to be poured into the mould of given events, but these, to change metaphors, could be telescoped for dramatic effect or selectively portrayed according to what the theme demanded. History is not *recorded* by playwrights but *used* to enact something they wish to say. The results may not necessarily please historians, and I shall return to that, but unless it jars too irritatingly with general historical knowledge, the historical vehicle serves only as a framework for the interesting construction of human relationships in the play. I shall argue later that the evangelists likewise do not *record* history but *use* it with all the freedom of dramatists.

Clearly the play revolves around More as the principal character who promotes the action and symbolizes selfhood. Even when More maintains silence on the Act making Henry Supreme Head of the Church, that silence provokes action among his enemies, and this propels the plot. More is seen with royalty, family, friends, servants and enemies, while everyone else is seen only in relation to More, who is both the centre and the criterion, like Jesus in the Gospels. And yet a handful of adjectives would describe the More of the play – able, judicious, witty, devout, friendly and humble – all of which go together to make a coherent character. There is only a moment's suggestion of harshness, quickly repented of. But what of the 'historical' More? David Knowles teases out some of the complexity:

> Sir Thomas More . . . might at first sight seem a fairly simple subject: the text books agree on his personal candour and integrity, and historians at least since the days of Addison have been all but unanimous as to his intellectual power, his charm and his courage. Yet More is not quite the simple subject that

> he looks. We may consider that Chambers has eliminated the charge of harshness to heretics, but what of his asperity in controversy, his unchivalrous treatment of the fallen Wolsey, his occasional coarseness of language and the manner of his two marriages, seen in relation to his own hesitations and to a cheeky ambiguous phrase of Erasmus?[27]

A. G. Dickens' comment on the pamphlet war between More and Tyndal is more trenchant:

> On both sides there looms not only the closed mind, a refusal to admit any legitimate differences of doctrinal viewpoint, but a personal uncharity so bitter that it seems to blunt the weapons of controversy themselves.[28]

That aspect of More is absent in the play for the sake of coherence, just as the facts that Alice is his second wife and that he had more children than Margaret are omitted for dramatic economy.

Not only was More, like all men, not all of a piece, he was:

> a personality that developed very markedly under the stress of renunciation and hardship and physical and spiritual solitude. A man who has moved away from and beyond all his friends, who has chosen to abandon all his interests rather than compromise with what he sees as evil: who has known illness, treachery, the threat of a disgraceful death and the ultimate solitude of misunderstanding from those he loved most – this is not the same man as the friend of Erasmus and the centre of Holbein's family group.[29]

What Knowles is stressing here is that people as *personalities* vary, develop and change, but this can only be hinted at in dramatic *identities* with the symbolic weight they bear in a short action on stage. Bolt has breathed fresh life into the traditional, somewhat stereotyped picture well expressed in the words of Robert Whittinton which provides his title:

> More is a man of angel's wit and singular learning – I know not his fellow. For where is the man of that gentleness, lowliness and affability? And as time requireth a man of marvellous

mirth and pastimes; and sometimes of as sad gravity; a man for all seasons.

The identity, then, is not all there is to More, but a significant and well-known side of his character.

Thomas Cromwell and Richard Rich are foils to the good and steadfast More of the play, the one a Macchiavellian 'Renaissance bully' and the other a weak character, originally vacillating, who becomes Cromwell's tool, created Attorney-General for Wales for perjuring himself to secure More's conviction.

> More: For Wales? Why, Richard, it profits a man nothing to give his soul for the whole world . . . But for Wales – ![30]

Again Bolt has particularized a once general view of Cromwell, which enables him to show a man with no area of selfhood, so that there is no compromise he cannot make. Yet the historical Cromwell, again a complex character, appears in a better light than that. G. R. Elton in particular has come to have a high regard for him.[31] He was a man of considerable learning who could on occasion outargue More, as he is never allowed to do in the play. He was evangelically inclined and had a sincere desire for reform although also a practical realization of how far he could go politically in that direction. He was certainly pragmatic, but appears to owe more to Marsiglio of Padua than to Macchiavelli. It may be said in Bolt's defence that a more unkind picture of Cromwell has been given by historians in the past, since historical judgments are always revisable. Moreover an identity such as Bolt has given Cromwell is demanded by the exigencies of the play. It would, for instance, be beyond the scope of the play's short duration to show that More and Cromwell were once friends. If that were shown then their falling out would have to find a place and a reason within the action and would overload the plot line. Moreover, because a drama cannot reason out its theme it has to adopt other means, and a presentation through conflicting characters can make the issue plain to the audience. Bolt has achieved this by taking the worst in Cromwell's traditional picture and playing it off against the best in More's.

If Cromwell is diminished, Cranmer is positively shrunk in his peripheral role as Henry's and Cromwell's ecclesiastical rubber stamp. But he has very little to do, and that little is dictated by the rush of events to the close of the action, so again the play is not overloaded by developing his role. On the other hand there is a universal character threaded through the play (and absent from the film), the Common Man (common meaning average, not vulgar, perhaps Everyman) who survives by cutting his coat according to whatever cloth is presented to him. He is More's steward who is paid to spy on him, the boatman who will not take the fallen More back to Chelsea, the jailer who is only doing his job, a member of the jury who condemns More, the executioner who beheads him and thereafter walks off to continue his life. As Bolt notes wryly, this character was criticized from different angles, but what these criticisms had in common 'is that they thought of him as somebody else',[32] and that probably demonstrates his effectiveness as the pragmatic transhistorical survivor. In his case a historical point is being made, but it is not one concerned with origins.

What this discussion has demonstrated is the way in which a dramatist with something to say and a historical instance as symbol uses that period of history. Although Jesus is the source rather than the instance-as-symbol of the 'something to say' which is christology, history is *used* in the same way to present him. Bolt as a twentieth-century dramatist would research the period for a play before an audience imbued with historical consciousness, for whom history is a background to the aesthetic experience. In this he is unlike the evangelists who, although they used events from Jesus' life, expressed significance through midrash and the fulfilment of prophecy, since that was the background to contemporary understanding. But even in Bolt's case history is telescoped and character shaped to fit a theme with its vision of reality to which it is always subservient. Events and parties to the conflict are imaginatively presented within the exigencies of the genre to be imaginatively received. The people least pleased with the result may well be professional historians specializing in sixteenth-century England, who though they may not always agree among themselves might wish to qualify or elaborate time and again. (The relations of theologian and New

Testament specialists are distinctly similar!) Against that judgment of specialists (Kähler's 'papacy of scholars' which becomes a papacy only when the usefulness of New Testament scholarship is mistaken for the last infallible word) it may be said first, that so far as historians use *narrative*, they also give a direction, coherence and order to the past which was not there in its experiencing and which is a configuration (a plot) imaginatively arrived at. So the distinction between artistic and historical form is not absolute. Secondly, nuanced qualifications and balancing of evidence will never achieve the vivid communication of a play. Theology, I believe, is in the service of communication as well as thought.

Two possible metaphors for the way in which we may relate to the past are the window and the stage. Historians make primary use of the window, cleaning it in their research and looking on the past as past, although the glass itself may be cloudy or crazed and they remain men and women of their own time as they look through it. For all its ambiguities this is a useful pursuit which has rid us of many a foolish notion. Historical narration, relating to the past as stage, is secondary tidying up for communication which justifies the research and is justified by the research. The emphasis is different with dramatists who, having used the window and absorbed what they needed from the long view, *stage* the past, bringing ancient conflicts and tensions into present experience, intending first and foremost to comment on the human condition and being justified by the extent to which they are felt and thought to have succeeded. Yet the action, if it is to be a credible vehicle for today, has to maintain a historically acceptable story-line (unless, of course, the design is to shock).[33] For two hundred years history has functioned in theology primarily as a window through which we endeavour to look at Jesus. But although that attitude remains worthwhile and useful, I wish to suggest that theologians relinquish the situation of onlookers and the more rarefied reaches of scholarly nuance and variety to present Jesus as the dramatic signifier of salvation. For that was the practice of the evangelists.

6 · *The Presentation of Jesus*

There are indications in the Gospels that Jesus resisted categorization, self-explanation or advertisement, being more concerned with the kingdom of God than with his own status. John, even with his lofty christology, expresses that: 'My food is to do the will of him who sent me and to accomplish his work' (John 4.34). This is an important matter for a christology in the relationship between Christ and God, and I shall be returning to it. But Jesus' concern that he should not be typecast went along with his focussed action indicative of the kingdom, so what he left behind, instead of a body of teaching, were memories of his kind of action which had been so revelatory of the love of God, and a sense of mission so that such action with the same purpose should continue and spread.

> The focus of the new faith was in concrete human relationships and encounters. Therefore the new community, living out a new kind of human and divine relationship, naturally rehearsed models of Jesus' actions and interactions, since it was through these that the saving work of God had initiated its course . . . Exemplary stories about Jesus' ministry were repeated because they applied just as well to his followers after his departure as they still apply to his hearers today.[1]

Moreover these stories of Jesus were *preached* as well as told. The preaching would bring out the theme of the stories but would also affect how they were told. A story preached has present vividness, no extraneous details and a pointedness of symbolic concentration – very like a dramatic performance. And to judge from the plethora of metaphors and images in the New Testament, the style of preaching was histrionic. In John Knox's words:

> The early preachers would have dealt with the crucifixion, or for that matter with any other incident in the life of Jesus, not in manner of historians, but in the manner of dramatists.[2]

Paul reminded the Galatian Christians how he had 'placarded' or 'publicly portrayed' the cricifixion of Jesus (Gal. 3.1). The New English Bible translation draws attention to the vividness of the verb: 'before whose eyes Jesus Christ was openly displayed on his cross'. Knox continues:

> The crucifixion had to be *pictured.* Men must see and feel it, imaginatively entering into the sufferings of Christ and sensing the awful significance of what happened on Calvary. The story of the passion must be told in such a fashion that the stark reality of it be felt and the full redemptive meaning of it be realized.

Further, one of the characteristics of the first communities was a vivid sense of the presence of the divine Spirit (called both the spirit of God and the spirit of Christ), a sense which could be nurtured and given content by the preaching. A group thus addressed would find itself 'not only within reach of Jesus' voice, but in fateful give and take with him'.[3] Just as watching a play is to watch *present* action in progress, and to make evaluative judgments on that action, so in the present created by the Spirit and the preaching, with the dramatic exposition framed in the space given to the preacher and received by the infant church as a group, people were not concerned to distinguish between the pastness of events and the presentness of presentation. Knowing this was the Risen Lord, they could rejoice in Jesus' triumph over the scribes in debate, share Jesus' frustration at the incomprehension of the disciples or shudder in pity and fear at the passion. Thus they shared personally in the drama of Jesus' life and death. A hymn which retains even today something of that vividness and involvement is 'My song is love unknown':

> They rise and needs will have
> My dear Lord made away
> A murderer they save
> The Prince of life they slay.

Amos Wilder has commented on 'how large a place the dramatic mode has in the faith of the Bible and in its forms of expression, even though we find no theatre-art as we know it in the Bible or among early believers'.[4] There must always have been dramatic possibilities in the breaking of bread – that time when the sense of Jesus resurrected was so strong – but theatre-art in a more conscious sense came later in liturgy and ritual. 'Theatre-art as we know it' tends to be visual, but it makes no difference to my argument that preaching is not visual drama for, in the obvious modern analogy, radio drama also lacks a given visual dimension.

> Yet experience . . . shows that even this dimension is present, simply because the performance in time and acoustic space very strongly conjures up visual images. It has been argued that in this respect radio drama is even more satisfying than those forms of drama that contain palpable visuals. If the heroine of a play is described as the most beautiful woman who ever lived, each listener produces his own ideal image – something that no actress physically present could do for all spectators.[5]

This particular way of suggesting the visual element may well have assisted the move of the gospel from one culture to another, as each could imagine Jesus in its own terms and the physical particularities of the first century Jew could be transcended. That makes a virtue out of the lack of any physical description of Jesus, for the saviour could be visually grounded in the society of the congregation.

The Synoptic Gospels

In the move from what Wilder calls the 'incandescent period' of the spirit-filled, parousia-expecting first communities to the churches out of which the Gospels came and to which they were addressed, some changes appear to have taken place.[6] For one thing, time went on without Jesus' return, and while the Spirit remained vivid, there was the process sociologists call 'routinizing the charisma'; in other words, control developed. Possibly for those reasons, or because there had been time to search the Hebrew scriptures and meditate on the significance of Jesus, the stories came to be told more for the light they shed on Jesus' role.

In Mark the eschatological note is still urgent; in Luke-Acts the whole process has become more gradual. Another change was that there had been time for differences to grow within a community or for problems to be confronting it. The Gospels could by their depiction of Jesus recall people to the 'true' faith, or show how a problem, such as persecution or Jewish intransigence, had been dealt with by the Lord.[7]

Thus the whole story was reshaped to fit current circumstances in order that it might continue to be effective in these circumstances. This is an important point, for it justifies the existence of later and present change. In terms of dramaturgy the abstract *theme* remains the same, while the action and characterization are adapted so that the theme can be communicated in the situation in which it has to be heard. Without that capacity for adaptation shown from the beginning, Christianity would not be a living religion but the subject of religious archaeology. A similar point concerning the presentness of presentation is made by Chilton and McDonald who, in a book on *Jesus and the Ethics of the Kingdom*, light on 'performance' as the key to ethics, performance being 'the enactment of possibilities' which is itself a response to performance.[8] What Christians have always responded to ethically was 'the dynamic operation of the kingdom' in Jesus' actions and parables. To the point that the parables in the Gospels have frequently been recast they offer an alternative to the hunt for the earliest version presumed to be the purest:

> The reason for the recasting of the parables in the early church was precisely to *preserve* their performative character. The representation recognized the immediacy of the message of the kingdom for the new hearers. It combined freedom to adapt the parabolic materials with respect for the essential motifs and above all for the parabolic dynamics, and it became counterproductive only when these features were lost.[9]

I do not wish to equate the Gospels structurally with drama nor the evangelists' conscious intentions with those of dramatists. Narrators' comments, as I have mentioned before, abound in the Gospels as they cannot in a stage performance (except in a Greek chorus), though they are often there to explain an interaction with dialogue, a dramatic vignette. They are more like nudging the audience than taking the limelight. And while the evangelists may not have had any conscious intention of dramatizing Jesus, they inevitably did so because they presented him in action in a role, which is the very stuff of drama.

Clearly much of what I have to say would be the same if I had taken 'story' as the model, and indeed contemporary retellings, like my own in Chapter 2, are more like telling a story or recounting a plot. Yet drama as *model* has the edge in vividness and immediacy, even starkness. It calls forth a personal and moral response just to understand what is going on. Primarily, however, I am using drama because there character is known only through action, while people are 'identities' in Rosenberg's term, with roles as their 'visible definitions'. That seems to me both to fit the evangelists' practice and to make christology possible to a much greater degree than stories, let alone novels. After a century of realistic novels 'stories' tend to be assimilated to them, with expectations of psychological explanation and interaction particular to a time and place. (And, of course, there is criticism today of realistic novels for tidying up reality unrealistically. Much the same could be said of nineteenth century Lives of Jesus.) The way things happen one after another in a story (metonomy) occupies the foreground, although that does not exclude metaphorical overtones. In drama metonymic sequence serves the metaphorical range of the theme. The theatre is one of the last places where today one may encounter and respond to symbolism, for through their limitation dramatic characters carry significant symbolic weight – Hedda Gabler as much as Eliot's Becket, historical characters like More as much as the transhistorical Common Man.[10]

Novels are individually read, stories may be communally told (most often to children in our culture), but plays are certainly communally enacted. This point does not have immediate relevance here for what is, after all, a book likely to be privately read. Yet the dramatic theme may have something to say about the presentation of Christ in society. It is significant that Martin Esslin finds the mediaeval four-fold hierarchy of meaning present in plays: the literal; the allegorical (metaphorical or symbolic); the moral; the anagogical or spiritual.

> This 'anagogical' meaning, which Dante elsewhere (in the *Convivio*) calls '*sovrasenso*' – supreme sense – is the ultimate spiritual meaning that the reader can derive from the scriptures. In our context it is the highest form of spiritual or intellectual insight the spectator of a dramatic performance may experience.[11]

Perhaps in theology and church we have been too leadenly preoccupied with the literal and the moral.

The Gospels are like drama in that their underlying theme is expressed in action through characters who are presented only as they advance and enact the theme. This is an analysis of the order of presentation, not the order of belief, which usually begins from the presented Jesus (just as reception of a play begins from experience of the action and actors). The theme in the Gospels could be given a number of names: life, or eternal life is one (Matt. 19.17; Mark 9.43; Luke 18.30; John 1.4); healing might be another (Matt. 8.16; Luke 9.11); or salvation (Luke 2.30). But the Gospels do not use abstract terms widely, which is understandable, since their presentation is dramatic where theme 'regulates the development of the discourse without being literally present in it'.[12] Metaphors such as the kingdom of God/heaven or the fullness of time also indicate the theme. Salvation may be taken as the umbrella term, simply because it is general enough to cover all the above varieties of meaning and to include such others as Mark's freedom from demons and Matthew's empowering for a moral life in the church. Salvation is life liberated, integrated and concentrated now and hereafter, demonstrated in and inseparable from the presentation of Jesus.

For the evangelists such life could only be the gift of God, for it is part of the vision of reality which they share that the God who had accompanied Israel, God who alone could save, had acted in the situations they presented. So although the presence of God is often understood rather than mentioned, the action the evangelists present is simultaneously the action of God from first to last. This is their way of seeing what happened which they offer to others to persuade them to see it in the same way. But clearly, just as people may attend Marlowe's *Dr Faustus* without a belief in the devil, or Eliot's *Murder in the Cathedral* without a belief in

God, not everyone is going to see what the evangelists intended. For the evangelists, however, a sharing of their perspective, however tentative, is the faith which makes whole, and their Gospels are documents for persuasion.

Each Gospel begins with a prologue which makes God's involvement and the protagonist's character clear, and in which the individual visions of reality are at their most overt. Matthew's first verse, for instance, 'The book of the genealogy of Jesus the Christ, the Son of David, the Son of Abraham', immediately informs the reader that this concerns the Christ, God's anointed one, who is of the royal line, thus fulfiling the promise of II Sam. 7.3, and the son of Abraham fulfilling the promise that in him all the families of the earth would be blessed (Gen. 12; cf. Gal. 5.16). Then follows the genealogy with these pivots of Jewish history: Abraham to David; David to the exile; the exile to the Christ. God, for Matthew, has made himself plain. Luke, the story-teller, after his literary dedication to Theophilus, tells of expectancy and fulfilment: the physical expectancy by Elizabeth and Mary of John the Baptist and Jesus, and the expectancy of Israel whose total fulfilment is announced in Simeon's words 'Mine eyes have seen thy salvation . . . a light for revelation to the Gentiles, and for the glory of thy people Israel' (2.30, 32).

Mark is equally plain on who Jesus is and how he relates to the past. He announces immediately that this is the Gospel of Jesus the Christ, and immediately tells the story of John the Baptist as the forerunner (Mal. 3.1; Isa. 40.3), followed by the baptism in which 'the Messiah stands *with* his people'.[13] Then the heavens open for the descent of the Spirit and God's affirmation of Jesus in terms of the tradition (Ps. 2.7; Isa. 42.1). 'Some will get him right and some will get him wrong, but there can be no argument about the truth of words uttered from heaven.'[14] Thereafter Jesus enters into cosmic battle with Satan, who cannot overpower him. All these events, already dramatic, are set in the wilderness, a barren place of preparation and testing, and the scene of new beginnings.

The effect of these prologues is to give heightened symbolic force to Jesus, and hence to everyone else involved, however 'realistic' the narration thereafter. G. B. Caird has commented:

> If the Hebrews had been given to dramatic production they would have needed a stage with two levels, on which human events could be transacted in the foreground below, while their heavenly counterpart was represented above and behind.[15]

Given the sequential nature of narrative, what the evangelists have achieved has much the same effect, letting their (ideal, implied) readers know the divine import of the following human scenes, keeping Jesus' action and his parables of the kingdom, but putting Jesus also within a frame of divine significance. Moreover, without some contemporary equivalent to the prologues concerning the involvement of God there is still no way of developing a christology from an account of Jesus.

After the prologues salvation is proclaimed not in terms of philosophy or ritual, but through the *action* of the total career of Jesus. Action is often advanced through conflict, like More with Henry VIII and Cromwell. It is possible to see the Gospels as a series of conflicts in which Jesus alone (and there is no one like him nor any dependable partner in this) faces and overcomes all that stands in the way of the kingdom of God. Simultaneously the cosmic battle with Satan is joined: 'I saw Satan fall like lightning from heaven' (Luke 10.18). There are obvious conflicts with stiff-necked authorities in public and uncomprehending disciples in private, conflicts with nature, disease and demons, culminating in the conflict in Jerusalem, first in the Temple, then in the trial and execution which were not the end of the story, even for the abrupt Mark. Conflict is conducted in dialogue, and even in those moments which are not conflict, such as the Last Supper, speech and interaction propel events.

Thus the meaning of salvation is fleshed out rather than conceptually presented, having the impact not of Plato's metaphysics but of Bolt's incarnating his message of selfhood in Thomas More. But just as in a play More could not have been portrayed in all the roundedness of historical life, so Jesus in this *presentation* is not a personality, in Rosenberg's terms, but an identity, in this case the Saviour, the Messiah. Messiahship is the 'fact', the 'visible definition' under which Jesus is represented through a series of overt acts – teaching, parabling, healing, exorcism, conflict, suffering, death and resurrection – which cohere with that fact to produce an identity disclosed in the prologue. The dramatic nature of the presentation is increased by its use of, but difference from, the diffuse messianic expectations of the time, for messiahship comes to be demonstrated only by that particular action, just as Jesus points to his deeds in answer to the inquiry from John the Baptist (Matt. 11.4f.). Moreover the action can be presented rather differently, to underline the particular Messianic character being advanced. Thus in Mark's version of the paralytic who was lowered through a roof a good deal is made of the faith of the bearers who brought him, while Matthew dispenses with the roof and gives more prominence to the authority of Jesus (Mark 2.1–12; Matt. 9.1–8).

Whatever the original provenance and import of the stories the evangelists used, in their Gospels they have the function of showing the Messiah in action. Everything in the Gospels is equally corroboration of identity to the evangelists, whether today we would regard it all as historically likely or not. They draw on all the sources available to present the Messiah, sources which include fragments of the scriptures interpreted as promise or type, and story patterns known to convey what they wanted to say. It was fundamental that the Messiah had actually appeared, that Jesus was a historical man, but their priority was to present his messianic character.

Messiah/Christ, like other appellations given Jesus in the New Testament, such as Son of God, has traditionally been called a title, indeed in Hahn's phrase 'a title of majesty'.[16] But 'title' is both inappropriate for Jesus' practice and too static and fixed a term for what is going on in the Gospels. There Messiah is not so much a title accorded to Jesus as a role seen to be enacted by him, Rosenberg's 'visible definition'. To be the Christ is to act in a certain way which gives immediate content to the traditional imagery. But Jesus' way quite overturns previous notions of 'majesty'. In the process of hearing the Gospels there is a continuing interpretative spiral between the prologues and the story, the images and the action, whereby the first gives the framework of understanding which is reinterpreted by the second. Thus images like Messiah change because of the way the role is enacted, but the portrayed enactment itself has reverberations from the role and the prologue.

Since Jesus as the Messiah is an identity rather than a personality, we are told nothing about him which does not add to the messianic demonstration – even his family is introduced only for this purpose and we have no general information on them, just as there was more to More's family than appeared. Nor do we know whether Jesus was married, and it would be distinctly odd for a Jew of his age not to be married.[17] But whatever his marital status, it was not seen to be germane to his messiahship, so the Gospels are silent on the matter. They consistently distance Jesus from identification with anyone else including family and contemporary movements or groups, so that there is no one like this man. There is historical material on Thomas More independent of Bolt's play by which one could seek More's personality and historical life. But there is none on Jesus. So the twentieth- century desire to know Jesus as one 'knows' a character in a novel, or even in narrative history, full of psychological and physical description and contingency, is to go beyond what is given with dramatic starkness in the Gospels.

The emphasis in presentation naturally differs in each Gospel according to the conception of 'salvation' which coheres with a 'vision of reality', for in each case a rather different saviour will be understood. While being convinced that Jesus was the Messiah and having access to stories and sayings of his, the evangelists shaped the stories to present an identity, as much in the history-like Mark as in the metaphysical John. The messianic secret in Mark, whereby Jesus is shown to endeavour to keep his messiahship secret, has to be read in conjunction with the prologue, where the key to understanding is given to Mark's church. Mark comes up with a saviour who is Son of God, the favoured one who is adopted to work and to suffer to bring in the kingdom. Matthew presents a Lord of the church who teaches a law which out-laws all previous versions. For Luke, Jesus is the saviour of the world, and for John the revealer of God. Whatever in the Gospels is not directly action is editorial comment in support of the identity the evangelist is portraying in his imaginative construal of Jesus.

If one implication of Jesus being an identity in the Gospels is that we know nothing of his 'private life', another is that his actions take on symbolic and moral dimensions. In practice drama is a genre with ethical overtones because of the approval or disapproval a play can arouse in the audience. Thus the self-seeking Richard Rich and the wily Cromwell are played off against the goodness of More. Moreover they represent more than they are, becoming a type of the possibilities open to humanity. In the Gospels, too, where the breadth of the historical person is channelled into the role of Messiah, his actions acquire symbolic depth and ethical overtones with a force they would not have had if life in all its diffuseness and ambiguity had been recorded. The price of symbolic force is starkness of presentation. For this reason also the disciples are portrayed as uncomprehending and the scribes and Pharisees are for the most part wilfully blind. Both groups have symbolic rather than historical force. In ethical matters Jesus' action was the action to be followed both positively and negatively, *for* the good of the kingdom and *against* what stood in its way, however these were perceived.

The Gospels, then, are very similar to plays in the thematic portrayal of action, the constraints of characterization and the impact of presentation. In a sense they resemble historical dramas in that they represent severally an author's response to a set of past circumstances. But it is a response, not a transmission. Nor is theirs the response of a playwright imbued with historical consciousness writing for an audience with a similar sense of the past. Yet the difference between Bolt and the evangelists is one of the degree of historical sophistication, not one of kind. Anyone who had to investigate the historical More only through *A Man for All Seasons* would have the same kind of problems as New Testament exegetes in endeavouring to disentangle Bolt's construction from what a historian might write, and the same is true of any historical play. In every case, from the evangelists to Bolt, history has been *used* rather than recorded, and that is the main point I wish to make about history. The historical investigation of the gospels is justified in its aim and by its results, but for a christologian whose concern, like the evangelists', is messianic presentation with the theme of salvation, the history is there to be used as wisely as one may. From a theological point of view the Gospels and all subsequent presentations should be judged by the way they use their materials to present the Christ.

Paul and John

Clearly Paul is very different from the evangelists and is much more concerned to explain to his churches the significance of Jesus than to rehearse his actions. Abstract nouns like redemption, righteousness, salvation and new creation play a much larger part in what is exposition rather than presentation. Yet there is a dramatic case to be argued for Paul as well, for if Jesus is seen as doing something, or if God is doing something through Christ, then the categories of theme, action and characterization still apply.

> (Jesus') death and resurrection above all, seen as a drama in which God was in action, dealing decisively with him, had been the crisis leading to the transformation which was the centre of Paul's theological awareness.[18]

Paul is in fact a good instance of the extent to which theme influences the other categories. His vision of reality includes hostile, dangerous cosmic principalities and powers, so salvation must be cosmic in scope. This dimension is put into the foreground rather than symbolized as Satan as in the Synoptics: 'When we were children we were slaves to the elemental spirits of the universe' (Gal. 4.3). Therefore the action, while it centres on the death and resurrection of one 'born of woman, born under the law' (Gal. 4.4), takes in also creation, Adam's sin and the rebellion of cosmic powers. The identity fits into this huge framework and becomes the Heavenly Man, the Son of God who shared our condition that we might share his, the second Adam undoing the harm of the first.[19] For Paul especially, Jesus' resurrection is his vindication by God, so that he is established in his cosmic role fulfilling and superseding the law.

It is notorious that Paul's references to Jesus' earthly life are meagre. I suggest that the cosmic theme is so compelling that Paul can use for his christology only that part of Jesus' career which is appropriate for it. Thus not only is history used rather than recorded, the required identity to be effective saviour controls what history is used. It is difficult to believe that Paul in his dealings with the early church would not have encountered stories of Jesus' life. But clearly for him, who never did know Jesus in the flesh, such memories were not of first importance compared to his sense of being 'in Christ'. It was his experience of transformation rather than loyalty to a historical person which was at issue. That phrase 'in Christ' functions for Paul much as 'the kingdom of God' did for Jesus. Both are like a new vision of the present environment through which one walks in communion with God, following (enacting) his way in companionship (the Body of Christ) with others. It takes a cosmic Christ to create this possibility whereby the kingdom becomes Christ-shaped. For Paul things have to be one or another in opposites: either 'in Adam' or 'in Christ', 'according to the flesh' or 'according to the Spirit'. Jesus Christ was serially flesh and spirit (leaving pre-existence aside for the moment); the flesh anchored Jesus symbolically to the tradition of God's dealings with Israel ('descended from David') and was the occasion for God's action (resurrection and endowing with power); but as Christ, the one who saves, he is cosmic spirit.

In all this Paul may seem to have moved quite far from what Jesus said and did, but 'the question we have to ask about Paul is not whether in relation to Jesus he played the role of the plastered cistern, losing not a drop of his master's teaching, but faithfully handing it on, and, in interpreting it, interpreting it only in accordance with the decisions of the Christian Sanhedrin in Jerusalem. We have rather to ask whether in his theology he affords a valid interpretation of the total event of Jesus Christ'.[20] That is the question for all christologies, including the Gospels and present endeavours, but it leaves a question to be addressed later – what would be a 'valid' interpretation?

The same defence with its inherent question could be made of John, who combines a presentation of Jesus akin to the Synoptics with a cosmic understanding of Christ. In this case it is the Logos, the Word of God which is pre-existent, like Wisdom the agent of creation, who then became flesh and dwelt among us. 'Logos' acquired even more philosophical resonance than other pre-existent figures like Wisdom or Torah, especially at the hands of Philo with his Platonic inclinations. For Philo the Logos was the image of God, the heavenly primal man, the transcendent High

Priest (cf. the Letter to the Hebrews). John may not be directly dependent on Philo; indeed C. H. Dodd believes his Logos owes more to the thought of the Stoics (as well, of course, as being the traditional word of God), but such intellectual spiritual ideas had 'entered the texture of thought'.[21]

As with all the Gospels, the clue to the theme of John lies in the highly symbolic prologue which has on the one hand the everlasting, life-giving divine Logos, source of all truth and light, and on the other the darkness of creation. Salvation from darkness is already accomplished by the Logos becoming flesh and bringing light into the world. The Word of God is true and all that comes from it is true, so to know that Word is to know truth and God's own self. Such knowledge is fullness of life here, the quality of eternity experienced in time. To have faith is not to trust, as in Paul, but to know this doctrine (20.31).[22] To be saved is to dwell in the eternal Word, but light also shows up darkness which opposes and indeed does not understand light. So the obverse of salvation is judgment, since light, just by being what it is, condemns darkness.

The action of the Gospel follows from the theme and is the descent of the Logos, its dwelling as Jesus among humans, which is not humiliation, but the bringing of glory into the world, and his ascent to God in the full splendour of the cross. What happens *en route* is a series of exemplary episodes which give rise to discourses. There is intermittent drama which often begins as if it were the realistic variety of the Synoptics, but turns into a much more symbolic enactment of a transcendent truth. The raising of Lazarus, for instance, is the enactment of John 5.21: 'For as the Father raises the dead and gives them life, so also the Son gives life to whom he will.' Once more a two-level drama in process has been discerned in such stories as the healing of the blind man: one level concerning the action and situation of Jesus, the other that of the church at the time of the Gospel.[23] The concern is to see present truth enacted *then*. So in a more pronounced way than the earlier Gospels the action collapses together the time of Jesus and that of the church, carrying its symbolic overtones with it. Where there are no stories, the large symbols of the Gospel like vine and bread dissolve into signification, leaving behind actual vines, actual loaves. Dodd suggestively calls these 'cryptograms'.[24]

John may have known Mark, but if he did he was as free with him as with any other source. His symbolic meaning underlines what action there is, and often replaces scenes of action in the Synoptics. There are no exorcisms in John, but light casts out darkness; there is no virgin birth, but Jesus' uniqueness and divine derivation are expressed throughout. Jesus' glory and possession of the Spirit are constant, so there is no need for a baptism scene or a transfiguration. What is implied in the Gospels is manifested in John. What is not manifest, however, is the Jesus who agonized in the garden, or who was tempted in the wilderness, because the incarnate Word does not have to wrestle with that kind of personal, human decision.

> Now is my soul troubled. And what shall I say? 'Father, save me from this hour? No, for this purpose I have come to this hour. Father glorify thy name' (John 12.27f.).

Moreover, in pursuit of meaning John uses a different chronology from the Synoptists. Jesus, for instance, does not begin his ministry in Galilee, as he does in Mark, but works from the first round the centres of Judaea and Jerusalem. There, early on, he cleanses the Temple of all lesser sacrifices, to leave himself, the one true sacrifice, there alone. For John the incident is the enacting of the *true* state of affairs. Similarly, he sets the crucifixion later so that Jesus may die just as the passover lambs are being slain: 'Behold the lamb of God'. And the resurrection is certainly not the watershed for John that it was for Paul, since Jesus' glory is most fully revealed in the cross (as John's church's reflected glory is in suffering?), and it is the crucified Christ who will draw all people to himself.

Characterization, as usual, fits the scheme. That is not to say that the scheme comes chronologically first in composition, and then Jesus is fitted in; it is rather that experience of Jesus' spirit reflected upon in a certain context produces the whole of character and action displaying the theme. The character of Jesus in John is both human and not human – most human indeed in his dying. In his life glory and knowledge shine out, condemning the Jews of the synagogue in their opposition, their preference for darkness over light. Jesus may indeed thirst on the cross (though that fulfils Ps. 69.21), but his request for water from the

Samaritan woman is not so much an expression of thirst as the springboard for the revelation of living water. In the same chapter (4.32–34) Jesus declares that he has no need of food, since his nourishment is to do God's will. Instead of bringing the good news Jesus is himself the good news; from being the man in the Synoptics who pointed to God, Jesus has become the one who points to himself as the expression of God's will and work. Yet Jesus remains the Logos which, although divine, abiding in God and God in him, is not all that God is, so Jesus is subordinate to God (5.19; 7.16).

Although so often in the gospel the flesh of the Logos appears only as the vehicle for the manifestation of his glory, the flesh suffers in a human way the scourging, the thorns, the crucifixion and the death. But at the same time the Johannine Christ knows in advance the glory of the cross and the return to the Father. He remains adequately omniscient and fully in control, so that when the last prophecy is fulfilled he can cry, 'It is accomplished'. With John as with Paul the incarnation of the pre-existent divine Wisdom-Word-Son is by God's plan consummated on the cross. Thus incarnation and death become an unsurpassable expression of the divine love. Again, in the Letter to the Hebrews occurs the same pattern of 'the heir of all things', transcendent from the start, who in obedience to God suffered the shame of the cross and was then exalted as the high priest of the new covenant.

This is all a far cry from Mark. The freedom of New Testament writers in their choice and use of materials, their developments, omissions, *aggiornamento* and resymbolization is staggering to those brought up with confessional standards, creeds and articles of belief. At their best such standards (known as symbols, but not symbolically) may hope to instruct, to affirm, to give a sense of cohesion and connection with the past. But the Grand Inquisitor remains a ghost in the machine, for often these benefits are gained at the price of wrestling with the presentation of Jesus as saviour today with the freedom and the faith of the New Testament, using faith in the Pauline sense of trust or the Markan sense of response rather than the Johannine sense of knowledge.

Before coming to my own effort in christology, using the Gospels, drama, history and my sense of the present, I wish to record one last moment when the dramatic nature of the gospel was at least partly realized in theology before the tradition became concerned exclusively with ontological questions of nature and hypostasis.

Tertullian

Tertullian, a third-century African Christian writing in Latin, was concerned with the 'economy' of salvation, that is, with God's action in the drama. This 'christology from above' occupied all the church fathers who developed clues from John's Gospel and the descriptions of wisdom, all understood in terms of the philosophies of the day, as Tertullian used Stoic concepts in his theology (and thus the process of *aggiornamento* went on).

There was no doubt for Tertullian that Christ was divine, but in opposition to a group known as modalist monarchians he had to distinguish between God and Christ while maintaining their unity. The modalists wished to justify the Christian practice of offering to Christ praise and prayer of the kind proper to God alone, and for that purpose blurred or denied all distinction between Christ and God. In his treatise *Against Praxeas* (one of their number) Tertullian marshalled a number of arguments to prevent this loss of individuality for Christ, including an appeal to those verses in John's Gospel which describe the Son as sent by the Father or praying to the Father, thus other than and subordinate to the Father. These verses were to prove awkward to assimilate when Christ was later said to be co-equal with the Father.[25] But Tertullian's most extensive rebuttal takes the form of his picture of the relationship between Father and Son, with its philosophical underpinnings.

Before all things God was alone. But even then he was not truly alone, for he had with him eternally his reason, his *ratio*, by which he silently made his plans. Tertullian understands this process of reasoning (whether divine or human) in a dramatic manner as an interior conversation with a partner who is in a sense 'other'.[26] God's reason is thus something which may become a personification like Wisdom, whose creation indeed Tertullian goes on to describe from Proverbs. Reason and Wisdom have the same *vis*, power, function, though different names. But in Tertullian's scheme God has not yet spoken, so this is a silent processing and a kind of gestation period within God as he thinks through and ordains what he is about to do. Then he speaks, bringing forth his Word full of divine reason and wisdom, and Word for Tertullian is *sermo*, discourse, articulated reason, not *verbum*. God who had already thought of all the substances of the world then creates them through his Word. The Word has the divine substance, but is other than the speaker. And in the other great biblical metaphor, the Word brought forth is also the only-begotten Son of God, distinct from, yet substantially related to, the Father.

Philosophically Tertullian argues that God is one substance. What he may have meant by substance is not my main concern here. Kelly describes it as connoting 'the divine essence, that of which God is, with the emphasis on its concrete reality'.[27] With the image of a spring which feeds a river which in turn flows into an irrigation canal, Tertullian describes the Son/Word and Spirit as the outflowing of that substance and therefore of one substance with the Father. If substance connotes what they have in common, what is to mark the distinctions among the three? At this point he introduces the word *persona*. The Father, the Son and the Spirit is each a *persona* in the work of salvation while they share the same substance.

Persona was a term which already had quite a history of diverse use before Tertullian took it up. It began by designating the mask worn in the theatre where the distance between performers and audience was so great that characters were identified by the masks they wore, which may also have served as megaphones.[28] Masks were used not to hide but to identify like badges, so later connotations of hiding behind a mask should not be imported. From that specific meaning the word extended its domain to include the part played by the actor, taking on the sense of 'character' or 'role'. The Greek word *prosopon*, used contemporaneously by Hippolytus to distinguish Christ from God, had a similar history in the theatre, but was also the word for 'face' or 'expression' as well as 'role'. In that other sense the Latin equivalent would be *facies* or *vultus*, but Tertullian does not use such passive reflecting terms of Christ.[29] He does use *facies* when discussing the biblical verses concerning seeing the face of God, and can say that the Father is the face of the Son.[30] But that happens in and through the Son's *persona* with dramatic symbolic resonances in view. Evans, an editor of *Against Praxeas*, comments that Tertullian 'retains in his mind the original sense of words which in ordinary Latin have had their primary meaning almost lost in metaphor'.[31]

The other sense in which *persona* was used in Latin, namely the character or capacity by which one acts in society, reflects the alternative social use of role and character in our own times, though without modern psychological self-consciousness or sociological awareness. One is known by who one is publicly, by how one speaks and acts, though this does not appeal to those who think that 'being' is entirely something private and innate. Yet modern notions of 'person' owe more to the Latin sense than the Greek.

The two meanings of *persona* virtually interlock in Tertullian who is recounting both the drama and the social activity of salvation. A phrase like *alii dabat filii personam* can hardly be given any other sense than 'he assigned the role of son to another'; but cases are rarely as clear as this. Because of the word's dramatic background it is not surprising that it occurs in situations of dialogue. Thus a quotation from Isaiah (45.14) which for Tertullian is an address to the pre-existent Christ is introduced with *Esias ad personam Christi*.[32] This use of '*persona Christi*' and not '*Christus*' *tout court*, which recurs in Tertullian, seems to indicate that it was the character or role of Christ he had in mind which is eternal and may therefore be invoked before Christ appeared on earth. *Ex persona* and *apo prosopou* were already in general use. Philo of Alexandria, for instance, in his *Life of Moses* distinguishes in this way between what God says by means of Pharaoh and what Moses himself says on behalf of God. In that case Pharaoh has been turned into a character in God's drama/action.

Tertullian created a vivid account of the divine economy of salvation which depended at every point on dialogue and interaction: God with his reason and wisdom, then God with his Word/Son and Spirit putting that reason and wisdom to work in creation, salvation and the guidance of the church. Tertullian had earlier argued vigorously for Jesus' humanness, but for him, as for other theologians of his time, that humanness, a separate substance from the divine, was something the divine (and therefore immutable) Christ *clothed* himself with. So the two-tier drama on earth as Tertullian sees it is:

> The Spirit on the one hand did all things in Jesus suitable to itself, such as miracles and mighty deeds and wonders; and the flesh, on the other hand, exhibited the affections which belong to it. It was hungry after the devil's temptation, thirsty with the Samaritan woman, wept over Lazarus, was troubled unto death, and at last actually died.[33]

Such convenient division of Jesus Christ's experience, which probably continues even yet in popular piety, together with the notion of Spirit clothed with humanity, will not do for today's conception of humanness, for humanity is there devalued. Moreover at that time the conception of God as immutable was paramount, and when that together with the notion of substance changes, other changes follow.

But there is an attractiveness about the active individuality of Tertullian's *persona* who enacted something, which was lost when *persona* came to refer to a 'person' *within* the Trinity rather than to particularity of action *ad extra*. By the time Boethius in the sixth century defined 'person' as 'an individual substance of a rational nature' all interaction and performance had disappeared. It is notorious that 'person' today does not mean what is enshrined in classical Greek christological dogma. I suggest that if a connection is sought between 'person' today, as someone who is conscious of him/herself in a network of relationships (business, family, neighbourhood, church, etc.), and 'person' in the past there is more possibility in '*ce goût du concret*' of the Latins, as Braun expresses it, than in '*l'esprit grec, porté aux abstractions*'.[34]

PART FOUR

Christology

7 · *Christological Form*

The form of classical christologies was dictated by answering the question 'Who is Jesus Christ?' in terms of nature and person. According to the parameters of the Chalcedonian definition, in Jesus Christ divine and human natures (*physeis*) concur in one person (*prosopon* and *hypostasis*) 'without confusion, without change, without division, without separation'. Mackey argues that at the time these Greek terms were introduced they were understood in a functional sense, so that the definition when it was first made averred that 'Jesus functions as man and as God.'[1] If that is the case, then what I wish to argue for in this chapter is in direct descent from Chalcedon.

Nevertheless in Western theology the two natures came to be regarded less as concerned with action or function and more as expressing constitutive substance. Such reification allowed the human and divine substantive natures to be treated as counters (one plus one) or as pendulum weights which had to be carefully adjusted somewhere between Nestorius (thought to have too much stress on the humanity) and Apollinarius (too much emphasis on divinity). The difficulty of maintaining the *unity* of the person of Jesus Christ under these conditions was extreme.

> Hence all the results of the endeavour to achieve a *living* presentation of the unity of the divine and human in Christ, ever since it was tied down to this expression, have always vacillated between the opposing errors of mixing the two natures to form a third which would be neither of them, neither divine nor human, or of keeping the two natures separate, but either neglecting the unity of the person in order to separate the two natures more distinctly, or, in order to keep firm hold of

> the unity of the person, disturbing the necessary balance, and making one nature less important than the other and limited by it.[2]

All the inbuilt difficulties Schleiermacher outlines here can be found in the history of christology, including alternating (rather than concurrent) divinity and humanity, a stress on divinity which overwhelmed and limited the humanity of Jesus and (since Schleiermacher's time) an emphasis on the human Jesus which offers no way of imaging concurrent divinity.

Schleiermacher's criticisms of the tradition subsequent to Chalcedon all have point. He asks in effect how one may speak of a divine 'nature' as if it were another species of nature to be held alongside a formally comparable human nature. He points out how 'person' and 'nature' have changed their meaning since fifth-century Chalcedon, and he speaks with the voice of modernity. Since his time (*The Christian Faith* was published in 1821) psychological and sociological content has been added to the sense of 'person' as well. Another subsequent development is an interest in Jesus' whole career as a person in the modern sense. So incarnation and atonement cannot be symbolized in unspecific 'impersonal' humanity, and Jesus' independent human individuality assumes far greater importance.

Yet christologies with an emphasis on ontology and substance, although highly metaphysical in nature, are not wholly different from those in the New Testament because their sense of salvation continued to underlie their constructions.

> What made the union of full divinity and full humanity in the one person of Christ important to them was the conviction that only one who was 'of one substance with the Father as regards his Godhead' could possess the divine properties of incorruptibility (*aphtharsia*) and immortality (*athanasia*), and only one who was 'at the same time of one substance with us as regards his manhood' could impart them to us.[3]

Thus once more it was the very understanding of salvation, in this case salvation from corruption and mortality, which led to the presentation of the saviour in a drama of substances which could account for that salvation.

As I shall continue to use the terms 'humanity' (or 'human nature') and 'divinity', I should perhaps explain how I understand myself to be using them, since, like most people today, I do not subscribe to any Platonizing notion of invisible 'real' substance in which things participate in order to be what they are. In the first place 'humanity' and 'divinity' are concepts. For any concept, including the concept 'humanity', at any time and place (and there have been many times and places) there will be a set of commonly accepted central defining conditions without which people would not be able to communicate at all effectively. We therefore have some notion what a contemporary in our own society intends by 'humanity'. But like all concepts it is socially engendered and used, so that its content is liable to change with changes in society, and to vary between societies (or their sub-groups). What it is to be human is conceived very differently post-Darwin, post-Freud, post-Durkheim and post-Marx (to name only four influences) from what it had been before. Events like the World Wars and the emancipation of women have had their effects on the concept too. Indeed the reappraisal of women shows that a concept can undergo radical change which contradicts its previous content, so that concepts do not simply develop organically. From being a timeless universal 'humanity' has become a time-full social concept of a general idea. Ontology is thus relativized in its expression, which must be social.

Concepts in use may have more or less agreed central conditions, but they will also have a penumbra where things are much less clear. 'Humanity' shares this characteristic. One could ask, for instance, the historical question – at what point did human nature emerge? Any answer is likely to be arbitrary. If it is with *homo sapiens sapiens*, is humanity adequately described by what distinguishes that evolution from all that had gone before? That may seem insufficient considering what humanity has gone on to. Again one may ask whether there is any degree of intellectual or physical handicap which removes its sufferer from what may be called humanity. The kindly answer to that question is 'no', since humanity is a word with overtones of value and few would wish to say that any member of the human species is without value. But if people with all levels of physical and intellectual handicap are included, the *logical* result is that it becomes harder to find central defining conditions for 'humanity' and the word comes to refer exclusively to the biological with nothing to say on activities or qualities. The value which tends to the extension of the word's scope ends by emptying it of content. Ambiguity of this kind is built into the social use of concepts, and what usually happens in practice is that limiting cases are bracketed out except in special circumstances. Yet it is important to emphasize the existence of such cases in order to keep concepts from appearing as clear and distinct ideas.

'Humanity' for me, therefore, is a tolerably workable late twentieth-century Western concept, differing in some respects from any similar concept in, say, Indonesia or Nigeria, and in other respects from the concept 'human nature' in mediaeval France. I call the concept 'tolerably' workable because although it communicates something there is not total agreement on what is central even among contemporary groups in the West, because what is valued or tolerated in humanity differs. If 'humanity' describes what people at a time and place value among biological humans at large (so that 'inhumanity' remains a deviation), 'person' as it has come to be used recently focusses that value in an individual. The cry is 'I am a person, not a thing/statistic/doormat', and depersonalization is seen to be the outcome of inadequate relationships. So a 'person' demonstrates or enacts what it is to be a valuable human.

For myself I would put first in this valuable humanness a sense of the self, of who one is, understood by introspection together with comparison and contrast with what is around. Yet that very requirement can be fulfilled only through an openness and sensitivity to what is going on in one's world. Where there is no sense of the self (for whatever reason), the world will invade the boundaryless individual, who then becomes a cipher. Such a person is not free. On the other hand, if the boundaries of the individual are too rigid and barrier-like, there is a loss of openness to the world around and a diminution of the constant taking in and giving out reflectively and sensitively in relationship which makes the person part of humanity in the world. Such a person is crippled in the capacity to love. Luther's description of the sinner as turned in on him/herself away from God is the religious aspect of the refusal or the diminished capacity to be human. From a self who is also open to the world may come, on the one hand, creative abilities of all kinds from cookery to science to poetry, and on the other relationships with other humans and with the environment which may reach the heights of reciprocity, care and love. These are the ideal possibilities in a world whose whole possibility was given by God. With the multiplicity and finitude of creation, however, these possibilities occur as we and the world are in process of both change and stability and as we wrestle with personal, linguistic, moral and social ambiguity. It is this sense of human being that I shall use for describing sin and salvation, and the same sense of freedom and love in the presentation of Jesus.

'Divinity' is very different from 'humanity'. In one sense it is also a human concept, social like all concepts, and thus changing as society changes. To the fathers, immutability was a central definition of divinity, because to them change implied loss and deterioration rather than new possibilities. For the same reason, incorruptibility and immortality loomed large as the characteristics of divinity imparted to the saved. This made for a very different picture of God from, say, the one in the prophet Hosea. But whatever the changes, the point of having a concept of divinity or divine nature is, as Stead argues, to assert God's independence of the human experience God is invoked to explain. To say that God is a substance functions as a 'claim that God is not limited or prescribed by our experience of him, but exists in his own right; in this respect he is analogous to an unknown physical object, say an undiscovered star. A star does not come into being by being discovered; and God is not brought into being by our human consciousness or metaphysical demands.'[4] In that sense substance has to be affirmed to let God be God above and beyond even the use of words like 'God' and 'substance', beyond historical and philosophical questioning or whittling at the edges of the concept. Human variety and change in the understanding of God take place all the time, but the affirmation is that nevertheless God is. Human nature, therefore, is humanity as it is currently intuited, valued and conceptualized; divine substance is that which transcends human intuition and conceptualization. So the two cannot be laid side by side in an ontology of Jesus Christ as if they were formally comparable.

Stead likened God in independent existence to an undiscovered star, an object, and that is correct, for the notion of God independent of anything else has to be of something with no external relations. Once, however, the affirmation of God's independence of humanity is made, human experience need no longer be bracketed out. That makes a decisive change, for the basis and point of the religious tradition is the avowal of relationship with God. So if God's existence is affirmed at all, it is affirmed not only as independent of humanity, but also as able to relate to what is not-God.[5] The capacity to relate is therefore to be seen as part of the being of God, and that is decisive for christology. The independence of God shows divine freedom, and the capacity to relate is divine freedom shaped by love. The immutability of God consists in the everlasting nature of God's independence of everything else, but also appears as the constancy of God's relationship with humanity and all creation.

For the church fathers there could be no *relationship* as we understand it between divine and human substances, so salvation took place through the divine taking on itself what we are (subject to change and death) so that we might become what God is (immortal). It was a case, therefore, of a movement between the natures which happened at one point rather than finding a *constant* connected relationship between humanity and divinity. Thinking in terms of substances, the fathers had to insist on no 'confusion' in the Chalcedonian formula, for one cannot mix human and divine to make a *tertium quid* (some third thing which is neither). Relationship, however, is not about mixing substances but about the capacity of God to love, understand and indwell creation, creating the possibility of responsive love from creation in its own way.

Again, to recapitulate a point made earlier, when relationship rather than substance is in view, knowledge and power in God cannot be totally described as abstract perfections independent of creation. It is part of God's nature to relate, and as far as creation is concerned, divine knowledge and power are used only to encourage and further relationship without overwhelming the other by negating freedom or over-riding response. For the sake of true relationship the force of God's power is therefore withheld, and God enters into the vulnerability of relationship with finitude, rejoicing when love and freedom combine, but also suffering rejection, inattention and the misuse of belief.

I have therefore taken freedom and love working together as the chief characteristics of God in relationship, as described at more length in Chapter 1. God freely and lovingly created, making possible the evolution of multiple, finite creatures free from divine control. But since that very freedom brings problems, God also accompanies creation in love. Humans are too limited to know what that might mean for non-human creatures, but for ourselves in the Judaeo-Christian tradition the effect of the divine presence has been described as salvation, as 'life more abundant' in the Johannine phrase.

From our human point of view creation and salvation are the primary actions of God, or rather they are two aspects of how God is in relation, for there has never been creation without the possibility of salvation, a creation cut off from the loving presence of God which is the divine initiative or presupposition of salvation. Thus God is known as creator and saviour. Other images for God like father or king take their reference from the creating-saving character of God, and express it in terms of lived experience. But precisely because it is a lived experience, the enactment in life of king/subject, father/child or whatever, these relationships are properly said to take place in roles. Creator and saviour are the primary divine roles which keep our beliefs about God from being amorphous and make response possible. In one sense they are dramaturgical, since they may be seen and enjoyed as framed in the tradition. But they spill out from the tradition into life. When congregations are urged to re-enact Abraham's faith or Nehemiah's determination the continuing reciprocity of the divine and human roles is understood. And as a matter of mutual relating here and now creator/creature, saviour/saved are roles which are enacted in personal and social life.

Roles are sometimes thought to be necessarily external and artificial, but that is not the case. I have argued this at greater length elsewhere, but some recapitulation is needed here.[6] Zizioulas, for instance, taking issue with Tertullian's use of *persona* writes: '*Persona* is the role which one plays in one's social or legal relationships, the moral or "legal" person which either individually or collectively has nothing to do with the *ontology* of the person.'[7] Certainly some legal uses of the word are restricted, but if social roles really have nothing to do with ontology then our development as persons has nothing to do with ontology, for without social relationships we cannot become what we might be. Illegitimate children hidden from society in shame had not in six years developed beyond infants of six months.[8] Their human being was arrested and undeveloped because they had not become themselves in the process of being daughter, granddaughter, neighbour, schoolchild, and so forth, the first roles children play in society. Certainly persons are more than roles, for they may reject or transform a role, and they will enact roles individually, as the many different ways of being a teacher illustrate. Yet humanity exists as selves in relation to others, not merely in isolation, so a role is an ontological vehicle, a term for the continuity of being-who-one-is-in-relation to others.

Thus every encounter with another does not have to start from an absolutely unspecified beginning. A father habitually *acts* (the very language is dramatic as well as social) towards his children in some respects differently from the way he acts in relation to a friend, while roles such as father and friend elicit and develop different things within a person. At the same time we interpret others, including their words, body-language and gestures, as we interpret what goes on in a play, for the being-in-relation of the other is thus revealed to us. Some roles on some occasions may be experienced as external, artificial and constricting, but that arises from the mismatch of the person and the constraints of a particular role rather than from an inherent defect in the notion of roles. Indeed in roles where people feel they can 'be themselves' they may not even realize that they are in a role. A role therefore spans who one is and what one does; it concerns who one is in action and relationship. In so far as it is concerned with what is actually done, a role is functional, but in that it reveals the person in action it is ontological.

It is thus no undesirable or merely external category which is being applied to God here, although all relationship with creation will constrain the infinite divine being, somewhat as a mother is constrained in relation to a child. Yet although there is more to the mother than any five-year-old can know, the woman is still herself in being mother (a role with continuity of behaviour) to her child. Likewise there is more to God than creation can comprehend or even experience, yet God as creator and saviour expresses a continuous being-in-relation to others and is so interpreted by humanity. Thus God's freedom and love are not abstract theological concepts but the character of God's action as creator and saviour.

Following John's Gospel, much has been made in theology of God's Word, and this emphasis on roles can be seen as an enlargement of that conception to include God's visible effects in action and relationship which evoke response. Again aesthetic drama and social praxis cannot be totally separated. To respond to God as creator and saviour is both to see all the world as a certain kind of living stage and also to be caught up in the action within it. For as Boff writes: 'This world is not simply a stage on which the drama of salvation is played out; it too is part of the drama.'[9] The response is both to enter imaginatively into the tradition, and also to enact it in present circumstances in our lives. Seeing and doing are both involved, for without praxis seeing can dwindle into onlooking, while dutiful doing without the dramatic vision is a form of legalism. The vividness of it all is rendered by God's Wisdom personified, who came to earth to seek people out and who herself had to be sought for her benefits. That made the notion of God's wisdom less abstract, for it was to a woman, a human figure, that response was made. The figure of Wisdom is a personification of the divine character in action, or, in my terms, a manifestation of God in the role of saviour.

To arrive at Jesus after speaking of Wisdom is to move from personification to person/*persona*, from *prosopopeia*, a figure of speech rendered vividly human, to *prosopon*, the part played by a human being. For the formal crux of this christology is that God in the role of saviour was incarnate in Jesus Christ. In his speech, actions, life, death and resurrection was seen, in this particularity of person, place and time, the saving character and action of God. There was already in Jesus' day a long tradition concerning God who saves, and also figures like Wisdom and Logos taking on God's creating and saving roles. So in spite of Jesus' own reluctance to be lauded or categorized, his saving effect was expressed by harnessing ideas of Wisdom and Word together with other roles of God's emissaries like Messiah and Son to this specific career, thus presenting Jesus himself in a role. Since the role is divine, part of the divine being, Jesus, unlike Wisdom, is its incarnation. It seems improbable that memories and stories of Jesus would have been retained if what I have called his 'saving effect' had not been experienced. In other words his person gave rise to his *persona*. At the same time it seems that it was *only* what pertained to this effect which held attention – thus there is little enough of his life in Paul – just because it was the person-in-the-role who was important. Strictly speaking we have no stories of Jesus, but only stories of Jesus as the Christ. Yet a role is the expression of a person-in-relation, not something divorced from personhood. So although we have no access to Jesus' 'private life' and cannot satisfy our modern curiosity concerning Jesus the individual, we are not necessarily out of touch with Jesus of Nazareth in encountering his depiction as Messiah.

Precisely because Jesus *is* presented in the role and not in the round, the identification with the divine role can be made. The epiphenomena, whatever they may have been, have been removed by the infant church and the evangelists, leaving nothing but the saving action. Jesus not only *brought* salvation, he *was* salvation, for he enacted it in the double sense of 'demonstrating what salvation is' (the dramatic) as well as 'bringing it about' (the social, practical or even legal sense of enactment). The comparison with Sir Thomas More in Bolt's *A Man for All Seasons* is illuminating. In history More, like Jesus, is a contingent person, contingently free. Yet from that life the play presents More as the incarnation of humanist ideals and Christian spirituality, or, as Bolt saw it, a man with a self which could not finally be surrendered to expediency. To enjoy and be moved by a play which presents this is to have a dramatic experience. But if, as Bolt hoped, the play evoked response and a rethinking of the self in present exigencies, More would be the occasion of a kind of conversion concerning the self. In a formally similar manner Jesus in the Gospels presents, focusses, enacts, incarnates and therefore makes vivid and critical the freedom God gives creation and the love wherewith God accompanies it. Unconditional forgiveness and healing are offered. So is the freedom to see or not to see, to be involved or an onlooker, to give oneself to the transformation of values which the cure of relationships involves or to remain part of the *status quo*. To see this in Jesus is to see God expressed humanly for humans; to respond to it is conversion.

Any christological model stands in some relationship of continuity and discontinuity with past tradition. In particular, if it fails to give expression to real humanity and true divinity in action together for salvation, it will have moved beyond the 'family resemblance' which gives the study its identity. In what follows, therefore, I shall work through much of the traditional christological agenda, relating it to this conception of the person and work of Christ.

Truly Man

Jesus was human in every way there is to be human by modern standards, not just by those of antiquity. For the church fathers it was necessary that Christ be essentially human, for unless divinity had assumed human nature, humanity could not be taken up into divinity and thus be cured of corruptibility and mortality. There is a different but equally compelling reason for insisting on the full humanity of Jesus – the contingent individual human Jesus who gave rise to the gospels – when relationship rather than substance is the principal category. Jesus was human, an individual with his own history, a self open to relationship. Being human, he was given by God the same freedom with the same love as the rest of creation. God did not overturn that freedom nor adopt Jesus as his instrument. Instead, it was out of Jesus' own freedom that he turned to God in love, that he was so filled and defined by the relationship that he could convey it vividly to others. Thus freedom and love characterize Jesus in their human contingency. Even from the pro-Jesus Gospel accounts it still appears that it could have been otherwise, for at any time he could have chosen differently: he could have taken a short-cut through his mission dispensing with freedom and love, as he was tempted to do; he could have made himself unavailable to all and sundry, protected by a ring of disciples; he could have avoided the cross whose later significance he did not know. But at every point this man chose in his freedom and in the love of a son for his father a life which showed his contemporaries what both divine and human freedom and love are like, what they can do and can suffer.

He is thus truly human in that there was no extraordinary component in his make-up which made his openness to God any more 'natural' than it is to any other man or woman. As Sobrino has emphasized, Jesus' life was a life of faith.[10] Moreover the contingencies in his life were not unlike the contingencies in any life. He is thus truly man in another sense. For if God created the world in freedom and love, granting freedom and seeking for response in the use of this freedom in love, then the Jesus of the Gospels represents the fulfilment of creation's purpose. This is what humanity is truly for in relation to God and the neighbour, while only a human can be this kind of fulfilment.

Yet just because Jesus *was* human, that fulfilment was contingent, in the sense that it did not involve omniscience or any other superhuman charactertistic. Jesus could sometimes be wrong, as when he expected the imminent arrival of God's fulfilment.[11] Moreover, he had to *learn* that his mission extended beyond 'the lost sheep of the house of Israel' through his encounters with, for instance, the Syro-Phoenician woman and the Roman centurion. It was Paul in Galatians who extracted the full force of this by declaring that in Christ there is neither Jew nor Greek (3.28), while the Letter to the Ephesians describes Christ as our peace, having broken down the wall of hostility between Jew and Gentile (2.14). Thus the effects of freedom and love in Christ go on being worked out. But Jesus himself was caught in the ambiguous processes of the world in that those who opposed, betrayed, tried or condemned him acquired a guilt they would not have carried without him. There is a sense in which he made them guilty through his innocence. Further, this ambiguous world is one in which things may always be differently interpreted, including Jesus' words and deeds. Therefore, as Pannenberg notes in a rare moment of Christian understanding for those who rejected Jesus, when Jesus claimed divine authority for what he did, this 'in the light of the egocentricity of the condition of human existence . . . necessarily made the impression of unlimited pride, of blasphemy'.[12] To be in the world at all is to be caught up in such ambiguity. Nothing in Jesus' life or Christianity's subsequent christology escapes this. Salvation then and now is not in the first place salvation *from* the ambiguous world, but the realization of relationships of love *within* it. None of this contingency makes Jesus any the less the fulfilment of God's desire for freedom used in love, but it does show that he was a *human* fulfilment.

Thus Jesus was a real member of the real world, and whatever is said of the traditional attribution to him of sinlessness has to be said in the light of that. Much depends on what is meant by 'sinlessness'. If it is taken to mean that he never, ever, said or did anything wrong to anyone, 'the one quite unspotted life that has been lived within our sinful race',[13] it not only makes his humanity less believable, it cannot be sustained. For one thing, we have no access to the largest part of Jesus' life, and the evangelists who were describing the Messiah were not likely to put in anything unanswerably discreditable about him, were such material available. For another, as Bonhoeffer once wrote:

> He was not the perfectly good man. He was continually engaged in struggle. He did things which outwardly looked like sin. He was angry, he was harsh to his mother, he evaded his enemies, he broke the law of his people, he stirred up revolt against the rulers and the religious men of his country.[14]

Even if all these occasions came out of his service to God, they still show that Jesus shared fully in a world where choices have to be made, so that priority given to one thing diminishes the importance of others. This is a world where 'being a good son to his Father' and 'practising the kingdom of God' could conflict with and diminish 'being a good son to his mother' or 'a loyal member of the religious tradition'.

But if sin is thought of less in terms of individual items of moral failure and more in Luther's sense of being a soul curved in on itself, totally preoccupied with itself in satisfaction or unease, then the picture of Jesus' sinlessness is rather different. There remains the fact that there is a good deal of Jesus' life unknown to us, but the traditions and the parables are full of a man turned imaginatively and practically to God and to others. In that sense Sebastian Moore is right to say: ' "This man eats and drinks with sinners" was the common taunt of decent, religious people. This is sin-free behaviour. Sin, our fundamental uneasiness with ourselves, *needs* outcasts, rejected classes of persons to "make ugly".'[15] Sinlessness may not always be a helpful attribution to make of Jesus, since it does tend to convey today a moral perfection which made the world safe for him and thus distances him from our own starting point. But with the reinterpretation of sinlessness in terms of openness to enabling relationship, it is possible to echo Paul that this man who knew no sin was made sin for us (II Cor. 5.21). He knew no sin – that is, he spent his life freely and fruitfully in relationship with God and his people; he was made sin because there was imposed on him the absolute denial and negation of relationship contained in a death sentence. And this, life and death alike, was 'for us'.

Truly God

To say in any sense whatever that Jesus Christ is truly God is to make an affirmation of faith which is not susceptible to demonstration for the sceptical. Nor am I here concerned with the experiences by which people come to make the affirmation. The role of a christology is to give a model for understanding the attribution which is rationally coherent within itself and imaginatively suggestive so that it enables belief and life.

Divine substance exists independently of humanity and cannot be grasped in human terms. Yet God's freedom and love can be revealed out of the possibility and actuality of relationship given in creation and salvation. It is a characteristic of God's being to relate creatively and savingly, and it is the relationship which is known. To say that Jesus Christ is truly God, therefore, is to say that God in relationship with creation was present and effective in his action. The point can be made more explicitly by underlining the difference between 'Jesus Christ illustrated the divine role' and 'Jesus Christ enacted the divine role'. Only the second version is incarnation. Illustrations may be of something absent or theoretical, and they may be partial. But to enact, with its dramatic and social force, is to make present and effective all one needs to know. Thus Jesus Christ is Immanuel, God with us, at the same time as he is a first-century Jew with a particular set of historical contingencies. We cannot in this world know God except in historical contingencies. When God relates to creation, that relation, whether perceived in terms of word, spirit or incarnation, can take place only in a particular historical situation with all its polyvalence, limitation and openness to change.

What Jesus did, according to the Gospels, was to live out consistently the effects of his own relationship with God. In so doing, without intending that explicitly ('Why do you call me good? No one is good but God alone', Mark 10.18), Jesus made visible and tangible in historical particularity a God who did not demand the keeping of the law, or even a baptism of repentance like John. 'God is a power who is ready to give unconditionally, to forgive, to heal, to create new chances, for anyone without distinction and without limit, now.'[16] Something of this belief could have been found earlier from the prophet Hosea in the illustration of Israel free to be the erring wife, whom Yahweh nevertheless loved and would not abandon. Likewise, the accessibility of God was personified in Wisdom. Jesus, however, enacted what Wisdom personified and Hosea had illustrated, with God a participant in the action for those with eyes to see. 'Jesus had expressed, explained and embodied Yahweh's appeal to Israel . . . his search for a close relationship with his people.'[17] Yet this enactment took place out of the coming together (the concurrence) of God's love and Jesus' free human response: a response nurtured within the Jewish tradition, and thus orientated towards God, yet a response free to judge that tradition where it stifled relations of love.

In the Chalcedonian formula the divine and human natures of Jesus Christ were said to be concurrent but not, among other things, confused. This remains an important point, for God is God and humanity is something quite other. 'Concurrence', however, means running side by side in dynamic co-existence. It describes what can happen in a relationship where two people are 'of one mind' in our latter-day idiom (which has nothing to do with having only one mind between the two of them). Each is him/herself, for this is not a matter of one active and one passive will, but both concur in the sense of agreeing in what they are doing together and acting as one. In a relationship concurrence is more than a theoretical agreement, so the importance of this formal analogy is that concurrence is known in action. Similarly, christological concurrence concerns Jesus and God in their relationship *as it is displayed in living and acting* to the end, so that human action which made no divine claims for itself had divine effects and therefore came to be perceived as itself the enactment of God, who alone can save.

God in relationship is truly God, Jesus truly human with all that entails including temptation, finitude and error. Jesus does and says what he sees to be necessary in his circumstances. That represents his own speech and action variously presented by the evangelists. But what 'Jesus sees to be necessary in his circumstances, is evoked, directed and given character by God's relationship with him and his with God. By making the *relationship* visible and effective in what he said and did, Jesus made *God-in-relationship* visible (drama) and effective (praxis). To those with a little faith these were the words and actions of salvation: 'God was in Christ'.

Pre-existence

There was never a time when God did not accompany creation in love, judgment and forgiveness, time having begun at creation.[18] Through the aeons of evolution in all its changes and variety, with disasters for many species and survival for some, God was present. Since our language is human, reflecting human experience and values, we have no proper words for what concerns God and non-human creation. Our sense of relation is built on human relations with things or on personal relationships with human values like love. To project such ideas on to the rest of creation is to practise the pathetic fallacy, as if nature had human feelings, while it is equally inappropriate to speak of God and non-human creation in terms of a human relating to what is not human. Nevertheless, given belief in the constancy of God, something divine and non-human in all its variety, which we cannot express, which is analogous to a relationship of love such as humans experience, related and still relates God to non-human creation. God's presence continued through the arrival of the hominoids and all the versions of *homo* until the point was reached where men and women could express and respond humanly to a relationship with God. Even from that point, whenever it was, to Jesus' day, millennia passed as God accompanied creation. In other words, although salvation is again a human term appropriate to the transformation of relationships as humans understand them, there has never been a time when God has not 'saved' in freedom and love. Nor, since God is constant, will there be any time in the future (time and creation being coterminous) when the divine presence is not permeating the world with its offer, humanly expressed as possibility (creation) and love, judgment and forgiveness leading to newness of life (salvation). Thus the cosmic divine role with its own character (its Logos, to give a slightly different slant to a traditional term) is everlasting, pre-existing and post-existing Jesus.[19]

In one sense, therefore, to maintain the dramaturgical model made earlier, the life of Jesus is a play within a play, a brief human play within an everlasting divine one, but a play which has been found to render divine cosmic meaning humanly. There is some analogy here with *Hamlet*. Hamlet engages the travelling players to perform a particular play which enacts the kind of dealing he believes to have occurred among his father, uncle and mother. 'The play's the thing Wherein I'll catch the conscience of the King.' The performance made vivid, involving and critical what was true outside the play. In the same way Jesus' human enactment of the seeking, saving, forgiving God 'catches the conscience' more compellingly than any exposition of cosmic truths, but nevertheless conveys these truths. Thus, in formal similarity to *Hamlet*, Jesus enacts what is true outside his life. The healing, exorcism, availability and love to the uttermost which Jesus in his own openness to God enacted in first-century Palestine express in these particular circumstances the divine desire for wholeness and love everywhere and always, and thus simultaneously express in human enactment the transcendent divine role, the logos. The difference from *Hamlet*, therefore, is that God is as much a part of the inner as of the outer play, attracting but never coercive and effective when responded to.

This account of the pre-existence of the divine role has some affinities with first-century conceptions of God's Word and Wisdom, in so far as these were primarily considered to be characteristics of God, whose personification and activity were a vivid *façon de parler* rather than the attribution of separate eternal subsistent beings. Yet narrative acquires its own momentum, and the pre-existent figures solidified and multiplied. Torah, the Jewish law, acquired pre-existence and descent from heaven, which gave it rigorous authority. The heavenly man, the unfallen Adam of Genesis I and the Son of God were other eternal subsistences differentiated from yet always closely connected with God, working on earth on God's behalf and often having particular significance for the eschaton, the end of the age. At an earlier time 'the word of the Lord', active but unpersonified, had come to the prophets who were themselves 'sent by God' to speak God's message to the people. By first-century Judaism, when God seemed distant and silent and there were no more prophets, the Word itself became a distinct subsistence and celestial emissary. One might almost say that the standard imaginative way in which the commerce of heaven and earth was understood at the time was through pre-existent figures descending to offer knowledge and salvation.

It is therefore not surprising that Jesus, believed to be Messiah and validated by the spiritual force of the resurrection, itself an anticipation of the end, was almost instantly assimilated to this role-pattern.[20] Christ as Son of God absorbed the characteristics of Wisdom (Col. 1.15–20) or incarnated the Word (John I), but transcended all such beings. Thus in John Jesus, the Word, himself imparted the Spirit (another emissary), while Paul wrote that 'at the name of Jesus every knee should bow *in heaven*' (Phil. 2.10) and argued that Jesus superseded the law. From the heights of being in the form of God to the depths of the form of servanthood and crucifixion, from being the instrument of initial creation to being the victor who will finally lay all things before God's feet, Jesus Christ represented the total dimensions of God's dealings with creation. Paul can refer to such pre-existence in passing, in the process of making another point, such as the encouragement to humility in Philippians 2, so the attribution was clearly not controversial. It was also widespread enough to appear in such different strands of the New Testament as the prologue to John's Gospel and the Letter to the Hebrews.[21]

It is one thing to see how an attribution came to be made in the first century and another to ask whether it can in any sense be made today. Certainly it cannot be made in the same sense, for it depends on the conception of God as distant, vertically transcendent and connecting with the earth through emissaries. If Jesus were to be firmly connected with God, it was a virtual necessity that he be interpreted in this way when his significance was dwelt upon. But in this christology I have understood God to be present *with* creation so that transcendence radiates out from every particular presence, and to be in relationship with all creation without any intermediate bridge. That means that no one is required to act on God's behalf from heaven. Emissaries, as such, are not needed and Jesus is rather the intensification to visibility of what is always the case with God.

There are also good theological reasons for distancing oneself from notions of pre-existence. When Paul and others predicated that of the man Jesus (as they seem to do, as well as of the Son, the heavenly man and so forth) they opened the way to a diminution of his humanity, so that Jesus became the divine in human form. John Knox traces the first indications of that in Paul himself.[22] Such thinking cancels out, among other things, the freedom and faith of the human Jesus of Nazareth. Yet that freely given human response is more important to a christology of the concurrence of the human and divine than any doctrine of the pre-existence of the Christ. 'Manhood, to be sure, has been affirmed of him' John Knox allows, 'but generally speaking it has been so amplified, supplemented or otherwise altered as no longer to be recognizable as the manhood we know.'[23] Neither manhood nor the humanity of Jesus' response in word and action can be preserved by a form of kenoticism which leans on Paul's phrase 'he emptied himself' to suggest that Jesus Christ divested himself of pre-existent divinity to 'take the form' of servant humanity. (It is interesting in this case to compare English translations of Philippians 2 to observe the dogmatic pressure on translators to be specific on what was given up, although the Greek is simply 'he emptied himself'.) The case against kenoticism may be stated briefly. Either the pre-existent Christ gave up all his divine attributes to become human or he did not. If he did not, he was a docetic Christ, only seeming to be human, but with more than human capacities. Yet if he did yield them all, the divine was metamorphosed into the human, then back to divinity, and that the church has never affirmed.[24] God can never be other than

God. Comprehensively, then, one may say that to be truly human includes being a member of a race and an evolved species on earth, conditions which preclude a divine prehistory, but not the possibility of salvation becoming visible in divine concurrence with a human being. Pre-existence on the first-century pattern, however, as contingent as Paul's belief in the elemental powers of the cosmos, is not the only way to connect Christ eternally with God.

The transcendent Christ

What God is like and what God does are construed by Christians primarily through what they find in Jesus Christ, seeing in his life eternal realities enacted under contingent human conditions of time and space. Precisely because the ultimate reference in a presentation of Jesus *is* divine and eternal, the New Testament makes use of the then current motifs to express that aspect in pre-existence and post-existence. In contradistinction to that contingent though traditional account with its picture of a certain vertical action at a distance which, because it involved God, then required elongation before and after, I have affirmed the one God's intimate, involved saving role before, during and after Jesus' enactment of it. There is an everlasting relationship between God and creation through time which has all the dimensions and splendour Paul focussed on Christ. Yet Christ remains the Christian focus. To focus is to give particular clarity to the general and indistinct. For Jesus Christ to be able to do this, an alternative account of his transcendence of the particularities of Jesus of Nazareth has to be given. Two matters are at issue here: First, the eternity of Jesus Christ, for if nothing at all is said of post-existence the worst kind of adoptionism could be implied, whereby God used and discarded Jesus, merely taking from the man what was needed like Hegel's omnivorous World Spirit. The second concerns the Christ-shaped understanding of God which has fashioned the Christian church in times and places far removed from first-century Palestine.

The eternity of Jesus Christ is the eternity of salvation. Admittedly it is impossible to think or write at all coherently about eternity, since we are creatures whose perceptions are necessarily temporal and spatial, whose knowledge extends metaphorically within a paradigm or by paradigm shift, whose descriptive categories come in symbiotic binary opposites (good/bad, long/short, i.e., we do not know what goodness is without evil, or length without brevity) and whose concepts are never precise or free from change. Eternity functions as a regulative, limiting concept for the temporal nature of all discourse. Only on the basis of what is believed about the constancy of the eternal God in relationship with the world may any kind of affirmation about what is eternal be made in the halting language of belief and hope. Therefore if it is believed that creation came into being out of the freedom and love of God who seeks as response relationships of freedom and love with and within creation, then the realization of such moments, in which God is always present and concurrent with the human, has eternal and divine as well as human and temporal significance. Thus in Jesus' parables the seed grows secretly with its evident harvest later, thus the alms given in private have their value awarded by God. In the same way the Beatitudes promise an eternal consequence for a present state, while in the well-known parable the sheep are eternally distinguished from the goats. The pattern of a present state or action, often hardly noticed by humanity, which is validated by God, is a recurrent theme in the Gospels, and leads C. F. Evans to suggest that 'if the good action is good because, being done in faith and out of non-possession, it leaves the door wide open to God's use and consummation of it, it can be said to be an action which is *capax resurrectionis* and in the long run cries out for something like resurrection'.[25] In Chapter 2 I called such actions moments of the kingdom of God. They are the fruit of human creation, harvested for eternity, when humanity in entirely contingent and ambiguous conditions aligns itself with God's spirit to produce such effects as 'love, joy, peace, patience, kindness, goodness, faithfulness, gentleness, self-control' (Gal. 5.22).

If such resurrection to eternity with God is an inherent possibility within all human positive response, how much more is that true for the one whose response was so powerful that others were saved and an entire movement was founded on belief in God's saving love? Christian actions take their character by analogy with Christ's: if they in their actions as selves in relation are fruit, he is the first fruits, the sign offered to God of a harvest to come (Lev. 23.10). Paul called Christ the first fruits in his resurrection from the dead (I Cor. 15.20, 23) in keeping with his view that death and resurrection were the moments necessary for salvation. But without denying the force of these I am concerned to move salvation, resurrection and first fruits back into the life of Christ as well.

Such emphasis on the life is a corollary of believing in God's presence *with* creation rather than in a divine distance in transcendence. When God is thought of primarily as distant, as happened in the first century and in those later centuries when Christian theology was being classically formed, the *significant* moments of divine connection with Jesus Christ have to be those of the descent from the divine area and the return to it, hence the moments of incarnation and death/resurrection/exaltation alone. (Of course transcendence need not be spatially 'up', but we are creatures of spatial and temporal consciousness and tend to image and think of God as located somewhere. For almost its whole history christology has been predicated upon the notion of a distant God whose outreach was the Logos, the Christ.) On the other hand, when God is thought of as present with creation, though also exceeding creation infinitely, God is able to concur, to share dynamically in the actions of the life of Jesus Christ, and then the significant moments become the ministry and death, with resurrection, so to speak, the divine amen on the total concurrence. Through the paradigmatic instance of Jesus it becomes possible to say that any divine concurrence with the human bestows eternity on human action, with all the incorruptibility and deathlessness the church fathers craved.

Moreover human action is the action of a self-in-relationship, so if the action becomes eternal, what then of the self who enacted the relationships? There are immense philosophical difficulties in conceiving the continuity of a discrete post-mortem 'self' – Jesus' or anyone else's. What would constitute continuing identity? Is any identity possible without the continuance of a material body? There seems to me to be no way of avoiding some version of these difficulties, given that I wish not to separate actions (which could be remembered by God without any eternity of the self) from the person acting. It is not possible to enter that debate fully here, yet

I propose a change in the terms in which it is usually discussed, namely post-mortem experience as some form of linear continuity of the ego (that is, a self without relations). Apart from its other difficulties, such linear continuity pushes the arrow of time into eternity and is that very time-bound thing, a 'development'. Instead of that what is eternal may be the synthesis of the conscious self expressed in such responses of freedom and love as were possible within life's circumstances. That would give variety without vicious ambiguity, since what is unfree or unloving would be consigned to the non-being to which it properly belongs. In that case not only the action but the person open to and enabling good relationships enjoyed in life is in concurrence with God and thus is part of creation in God eternally, eternally conscious of freedom and love. Efforts to describe what that might mean, and to account for limiting cases like stillbirths who have had no chance to exercise freedom and love, would be an unprofitable exercise of the imagination, for the constancy of God's freedom and love is to be trusted. The principle, however, remains that whatever or whoever is concurrent with the divine shares in divine eternity. From creation's point of view eternity is, so to speak, contagious on account of the divine concurring with the creaturely. On the other hand the rich man who ignored the beggar at his gate avoided both the contagion and the kingdom.

It may be objected here that most human selves' response to God is far too 'rudimentary and inadequate' in Lampe's terms for this to be what is eternally celebrated.[26] People require more 'creative and saving work' after the dissolution of the physical body to fit them for life with God. That would be a valid way of looking at things if creation really had as its purpose individual 'soul-making', the purification and perfection of individuals. But that remains an egocentric account of what creation is about. For in that case what is to happen is that we are to be perfected so that *our* life-project comes at length to a satisfactory end. That would be another version of personal glory ('Glory for me'), even if it is glory reflected from God. (That leaves aside the philosophical questions of identity and whether a perfected Ruth Page would still be Ruth Page.) But *God's* purpose, as envisaged in this book, is relationships of freedom and love with and among creation. Why not, therefore, find what is eternally constituted as participating in God by means of concurrence in those moments and those selves in which this purpose bears fruit? That could be what God wants from creation rather than our own desire for individual personal eternity.

These 'moments' (short or long) would not be a matter of 'works' in the pejorative sense, or 'merit', both of which are quantifying, self-regarding notions incompatible with action in freedom and love. The *surprise* of those who enter the kingdom in the parable of the sheep and the goats on account of their concern for others is the yardstick for comprehending the attitude of freedom and love. In the moment of action, attention is given to the other without calculation so that eternity, as far as the doing is concerned, is a by-product rather than an aim. In this way eternity in God's presence would be the experience of selves in relationship concerning what in each self was 'saved' not as a matter of Christian confession or intellectual belief, but as salvation worked out in action with or without orthodox belief. Belief may make all the difference in sensitivity and enlarged response, but actions of freedom and love may take place without it.

When this understanding of eternity is applied to Jesus it is clear that his self was expressed in his love of the Father and of the neighbour. So that self, having concurred with God, is, in language which has to be pictorial, 'taken up' into God, making a difference to God and to God's continuing relationship with humanity because of the saving effects which began and continued through him. So the continuing identification of Jesus Christ with God's salvation is not misplaced. Christ, Lampe writes, 'is the archetype of new life, which is eternal life because it is life in communion with the eternal God'.[27] That communion began in Jesus' life, and just as salvation is found in that life as well as in Jesus' death, so eternal life is an aspect of his living and his dying, not something which began at the resurrection.

This account puts serially what in John's Gospel is collapsed together. For John Jesus in life *is* the Logos, is glorious, with the result that all contingency is excluded. Instead, I understand Jesus to have enacted the word of salvation in faith and freedom, and only therefore to be the Christ, having enacted the Logos expressing the divine *raison d'être* of creation eternally. The word of God which pre-existed and post-existed Jesus is salvation within the possibilities of creation. Jesus enacted this role and is thus the *enacted* Logos, the logos made visible in and through contingent action by a particular individual. The glory John insisted on is the glory of the enacted Logos in the eternity of God's presence. To be premature with the glory is to deny the need for Jesus' human faith, freedom and love in concurrence with the divine. To deny the glory is to consider Jesus Christ at best an episode in the life of God. Out of his own response of love Jesus made the difference of an enacted Logos to God. To put it this way, of course, requires the kind of *aggiornamento* of thought John himself practised, in this case to a belief that creation adds to the experience of God in relation. If God is thought of as perfect and unchanging from everlasting and thus without real relationship with creation, Jesus Christ could not have made the difference of an enacted Logos, giving human shape to the role of God in salvation.

God's saving presence continues in the world, and that remains fundamental, as it was for the concurrence with Jesus in action. Nevertheless, the possibility and nature of such concurrence is made visible to Christians in Jesus Christ, who is now both the man to whom the evangelists and others responded and the eternal character of the enacted Logos beyond any particular time and place. So salvation anywhere may be said to be through Jesus Christ. For Paul, Christ signified everything to do with salvation – its environment, shelter and clothing as well as its enactment. Christ is thus the name for the condition of human and divine concurrence (to concur with God was to be in Christ) although the initial derivation is from one 'born of woman, born under the law' whom God raised from the dead. But for Paul it was also important that Christ transcended Torah as God's Wisdom and that he would defeat the hostile elemental spirits of the universe. So although the earthly features of Jesus, so to speak, have become blurred in the vision of the eternal Christ, that Christ is the saviour in a specific earthly setting which plays a part in the presentation. There is no salvation in general but only the discovery of God's love and forgiveness in particular circumstances with the consequent blossoming of freedom and love within a given society. Therefore the eternal Logos which is Jesus

Christ is recalled, re-enacted and re-earthed time and again in contingent, ambiguous and imperfect cultural conditions to continue to give human shape to the role of God. Indeed there are probably more varieties of Christ than there are of Jesus, and necessarily so.

The dramaturgical model gives a useful way of envisaging what happens. The play of plays, the serious, painful and joyful play which all creation is about, concerns God in freedom and love seeking and provoking freedom and love within the multiplicity and contingency of the world. A moment when that became luminously clear for those with eyes to see was the life and death of Jesus. Here was the human play which in its human and limited fashion enacted the divine drama. This is a different concept from the older notion of a two-tier drama whereby what happens on earth is a human counterpart to a simultaneous enactment in heaven. As I keep insisting, God is here with us, involved in action with us, rather than a celestial onlooker or the deviser of a Platonic blueprint for human participation. There is no above and below. For creation there is one overall play, the play in which its life is involved in God's purposeful presence. That play, however, has to be understood by women and men and to be found vivid and involving. For that its enactment in the play within the play, that is, the life and death of Jesus with their saving effects, becomes paradigmatic – an enacted Logos *then* which being eternal may be applied to all situations *now*.

There are two ways of presenting this enactment. One begins from a re-presentation of Jesus' first century life using current results from historical research as warrants for some of the presentation, but using these in a coherent narrative whole with literary characteristics. Moreover, theological representations differ from historical accounts which raise no christological questions in that they are shaped to express the tension and fruitfulness of divine concurrence with the human, however that is understood. Such concurrence may be intended as a conclusion arrived at from the play, as the possibility of personal integrity is arrived at from seeing *A Man for All Seasons*. Just as the effectiveness of that play requires of its audience some openness to the perception and valuing of integrity, so the presentation of Jesus requires for its effectiveness some openness to the possibility of God and an imaginative response to the imaginative construal. To the extent that society currently values realism and history, and because historical study is frequently illuminating and corrective although always revisable, but not because some simple timeless truth *wie es eigentlich gewesen ist* is possible, this mode of presentation, pioneered in its narrative realism by the evangelists, continues to be effective.

On the other hand, some presentations follow the pattern of Paul or the freedom of John to reshape the play. To use Pauline practice but Johannine language, such plays presuppose the life of Jesus and take from it what assists in presenting the eternal logos in Christ applicable to their situation. From my earlier argument that should not be considered an illegitimate move, since the eternal logos transcends the particularities of Jesus of Nazareth. Like the first group, such presentations will in the end be literary and imaginative in character. Historical warrants may have less importance, though these accounts do share with the first group the basis from which it all grew, namely, that there was such a person to whom such a response was made. Again, presentations of Christ the Logos of God are effective only when there is openness to belief in God and an imaginative response of vision and commitment to the persuasiveness of the presentation. The theme of all presentations has always been salvation, although classical christology was so metaphysical that that could be obscured. Today presentations of the Christ are immediately concerned, like Paul, with salvation here, now in this context. Plays of the first kind, which show salvation in process then, in the first century, require that the present application be realized by the audience, or provide commentary to show what is involved today. Both types of play render the environment ('in Christ', Jesus as the way), the values and the direction of our own enactments.

I have written of two types of play, but these are not hermetically sealed off from each other; rather they represent two ends of the spectrum of possibilities. A presentation centring on Jesus has what its author believes to be pointers towards his specialness (otherwise, why bother?), while a Christ-figure will not even be recognized as such unless there remains the pattern of action or values in Jesus' life and death as displayed in the New Testament.

Yet a drunk who goes by night
Towards the Scroggs Hill farm
May see a blaze of light
In a sod hut, and there
A girl with a child on her arm,
The rounded Maori face,
A blue dress loosely worn,
And mercy to swamp despair
At the gorgehead of grace
Where the Christ of fire is born.

From which he would come down
To the bride no worm can touch
To the gravel roads of the town,
School, store and bowling green,
To the old in their bleak hutch
And the chaingangs of the young
Struck wild by summer's horn,
And praise the living scene
With an unwounded tongue
In the land where I was born.[28]

Here the New Zealand poet James K. Baxter re-earths Christ among the Maori people and ordinary townships of his own country – caught absolutely in 'school, store and bowling green'. The Christ of fire brings warm, purifying and inspiring grace which transforms the ordinary in the midst of its ordinariness. In Chapter 1 I quoted another poet, Francis Hope, whose training and perception was for 'the flat and documentary truth' but who was tantalized by unspecific 'visions of otherness revealed/In the exactitudes of place'.[29] These visions are given content, value and direction for Baxter in his eccentric Christianity by the figure of Christ, and that is how the eternal enacted Logos works, expressing humanly the involvement with God 'in the land where I was born'.

J. K. Baxter was a *pakeha* (a white New Zealander). Maoris themselves are concerned to express *Karaiti te Maori*, Christ the Maori. They began effectively with a religious musical of that name, using their traditional communal styles of action song and lament. Thus the very means were different from the

Western method of conceptualization. The effects were electric. This was no longer the 'pale figure' the Europeans had brought with them:

> For me he became not just a man – but a Maori. He enters into my culture and readily accepts the 'dynamics' of my culture that I have to build upon in order that I may know him more fully. It is vital to me as a believer within a particular culture.[30]

There may of course be dangers in any cultural invoking of the enacted Logos, for the culture itself provides ingredients, attitudes and values which will shape the final presentation. Thus another *pakeha* questions the use of *Ariki* (Lord) for Christ, since the person of the pre-European *ariki* was *tapu* (sacred, untouchable).[31] Would a Maori Christ thus become too lofty and sacred to approach instantly? But such dangers (which only appear as dangers if one's values are different) lurk in *any* cultural presentation, including those with a long European history. Europeans with their use and misuse of Christ the King are not in a position to be critical of *ariki*. *Karaiti te Maori* is one instance of the current explosion among non-Western countries of the depiction of Christ as one from their culture – not Jesus of Nazareth, but the divine Logos of the human possibility of freedom and love where they are. Similarly blacks in America, to whom the white Christ is part of white domination, may not be able to see and respond to freedom and love from such a figure. For them the concurrence with God remains and salvation occurs when Christ is black.

If there are ever-increasing numbers of presentations of Jesus and of Christ, are there any criteria by which to judge among them? Clearly those who appeal to historical warrants in their presentation are vulnerable to the normal criteria of historians. This, as I argued in Chapter 4, is not a simple matter in accounts of Jesus because New Testament scholars are various and their findings revisable. I myself found a further complication, in that two occasions of importance for my presentation, the temptations and the agony in the garden, when Jesus seems most human and vulnerable, were private incidents, so who could have known of them? Luke turns temptation into a triumph for Jesus, just as John plays down the fear of Jesus before death. But Mark leaves both more naked. It is possible that Mark is depicting a Messiah who is an example to his church in resisting temptation and suffering for God's sake, but these incidents seem to run counter to Mark's strong Son of God character, so perhaps they may indicate an early tradition among the disciples. Through my own response to their poignancy and the possibility that they might be historical I included them in an account which was intended to be at least historically aware.

On the other hand, after much debate on both sides of the question, I omitted from my account Jesus' encounter with the woman taken in adultery (John 7.13–8.11). This shows exactly the kind of Jesus I wished to describe – accessible, not bound to rules, more concerned to make both accusers and accused think about themselves than to condemn. But the story is a wandering piece of tradition, of uncertain provenance, inserted incongruously into John's Gospel.[32] Grollenberg calls it a story 'which went the rounds among the first Christians' and his comment on its conclusion is apt:

> The impersonal law had vanished from sight along with those who required conformity to it. Now the woman had become a person instead of a 'case': Jesus was talking to her. He asked whether she too saw the situation for what it was. Then he gave his judgment. What she had done was bad. But he did not blame her or threaten her. He simply showed her that she was free.[33]

By discussing this incident here I have, of course, circumvented the historical hesitation which prevented me from using it earlier. But in this kind of way decisions on what may go into a historically conscientious account of Jesus and what has to be left out are finely balanced, rarely certain, while other motives are simultaneously in play. Although historical criteria are so tentative, they remain the most easily applied.

Another identifiable criterion is the notion of 'family resemblance' among the various different but overlapping accounts in the tradition and at present. But that works only for individual comparisons, not for the search for a common denominator among them all apart from the name Jesus Christ and a reference to God. It would be hard to say even what would be ruled out by the family of presentations. The depiction of an angry or cynical Jesus, for instance, could appeal to the cursing of a fig tree for not bearing fruit out of season (Mark 11.12–14) or the apparently callous remark that the poor are always going to be there (Mark 14.7). Even an account of Jesus as a man intensely aware of his relationship with God has to cope with the wealth of parables which do not mention God. It is no wonder that John Austin Baker could write: 'The total picture does not hang together; and unless we are prepared to believe in a Jesus who was both confused and confusing cannot be correct.'[34] Therefore people select what is of value to them, therefore presentations differ and 'family resemblance' has to be very loosely invoked. The traditions conveniently accumulated by Jaroslav Pelikan in *Jesus through the Centuries* are so various that nothing firm emerges.[35] What, for instance, is there in common among 'The Rabbi', 'The King of Kings', 'The Monk who rules the World', 'The Teacher of Commonsense' and 'The Poet of the Spirit', to give only a few of Pelikan's chapter titles? Much of that variety persisted in spite of orthodox doctrinal metaphysics and shows the continuing dramatizing proclivities of believers within their own situations. Yet 'each of the almost infinite – and infinitely different – ways of construing that name (Jesus Christ) has been able to claim some warrant or other within the original portrait (or portraits) of Jesus in the gospels'.[36]

To those who wish 'objective' controls and agreed criteria certifiable by the churches this may not seem very satisfactory. But the variety has arisen precisely because Jesus has been so valued by diverse people in so many different times and places, and that is more a stimulus to re-presentation than a cause for despair. Difficulties of course remain. One could say truly that an angry or cynical Jesus is not what the Gospels at large depict, but the curse on the fig tree is still there. I could make no use of it myself in my selection, but I have to acknowledge its presence in the Gospels. Yet I am not impressed by English criticisms of the excessive emotionalism of Jesus in the Gospels' portrayal.[37] These may have much to do with a regrettable national preference for repressing emotion in public, and I would be more impressed if they came from, say, an Italian. What that illustrates is that criticism is most likely to be concerned with the *values*, including social values, expressed in a presentation of Jesus or of Christ the Logos, and although these will again be as various as the presentations embodying them, their effects are available for scrutiny. Thus 'gentle Jesus meek and mild' has very little appeal today, but there was a time in the nineteenth century when such gentleness was valued. Yet the gentleness of Jesus – and of women who were acknowledged at the time to be more Christlike than men – was valued in the sense of being split off from everyday business and political practices to be put on an irrelevant pedestal far from power or the possibility of interference.[38] This was a way of privatizing and neutralizing any effectiveness of both women and Christ.

From that sociological comment emerge the two criteria which may be continually brought to bear on any presentation, though even then the findings may not be clear-cut. First, does this Jesus or this Christ actually save? In the terms of this book does he bring about (enact) the release from unfreedom and lovelessness of a soul curved in on itself? Does he incarnate God's *universal* love and open one's eyes to the possibilities of creation as moments of the kingdom? Clearly these questions are asked in line with what I believe about God and particularly how God relates to the world, for such conceptions are logically and theologically prior to evaluating a presentation of Christ. Such questions as I have asked have to be put today to all versions of the tradition, and to all christological orthodoxies, for, as Husserl once remarked, survival may be the hypocritical form of forgetfulness. It is less demanding to rehearse once more the two-nature orthodoxy than to encounter an unsettling present saving figure. It may also be that Christs of earlier times are now powerless to save because they no longer convey concurrence with the divine, so, like the religious law Jesus bypassed for this reason, they may put distance and difficulty between people and the kingdom.

The second criterion is whether this Jesus or this Christ is free to judge in any sense. It is, after all, the infinite God with whom we have to do through Jesus Christ as enacted Logos. Facing that question prevents the domestication of God in Christ to something merely relevant, merely reinforcing, like the Aryan Christ of the German Christians, or to something irrelevant like gentle Jesus. This matter was raised starkly for theologians in Latin America, for they inherited a tradition with two main and complementary renderings of Christ.

One was Christ the King, richly dressed like a celestial Ferdinand of Aragon. In the name of this powerful Christ a powerful church could rule and secular power might be legitimated. George Casalis asks:

> Why do we think of the glorified Christ as a heavenly monarch and transfer to eternity the traits of earthly kings? Is this how we justify the anguish of our peoples? Is this not the very image of all the crushing oppression carried out by paternalistic powers, so sacred and so implacable?[39]

Perhaps, he suggests, in the light of all the abuse of power which has been evident in the Christian church, it is regrettable that the primitive church used the expression *Kyrios Iesous*, Lord Jesus: 'What does this mean – the demythologization of the emperor or the ideologization of Jesus?'[40] Could such an imposing title have remained inoffensive?

If Christ the King, the image of the Conquistadores, appeased the ruling power, the other image, the woeful Christ hanging on the cross dead from suffering and grief, appeased the poor, for it reflected their suffering and their destiny. As Hugo Assmann describes them:

> The dolorous Christs of Latin America, whose central image is ever the cross, are Christs of impotence – an impotence interiorized by the oppressed. Defeat, sacrifice, pain, cross. Impotence, powerlessness, is accepted 'undigested', recognized in advance and submitted to. Defeat is not perceived as a temporary reversal to be overcome in struggle. It appears as an inevitable necessity, as a condition of the privilege of living.[41]

In combatting these Christs in the name of Christ the Liberator, liberation theologians may put too much hope in recovering 'the historical Jesus' as a criterion, but they show clearly the need for the basic questions whether this Christ saves by empowering others in freedom and love, and whether this Christ is free to judge the *status quo*. I shall return to what I understand by judgment in the section on salvation. But here it has to be said that this is not only judgment on individuals and their relationships, or judgment on institutions, but also judgment on the christology itself with its presentation of Christ. When that is understood, christological models and their imaginative construals may be held with commitment but do not become an ideology in the bad sense. Any christology, including this one, is deconstructible, or, to use the ancient theological equivalent, requires the *via negationis*, for not only will it be inadequate to its subject, it cannot be effective for everyone, always. New presentations will continue to be written, for as Boff comments:

> Each generation must come face to face with the mystery of Jesus and in the attempt to define Jesus it will define itself. Each generation will give him its names of honour and glory and will thereby insert itself into the christological process that began at the time of the apostles.[42]

'Each generation', Boff wrote. Now these generations are seen to include black Americans, Africans and Asians, men and women from the islands of the Pacific, indigenous people from countries once colonized with a white Western Christ. They portray within their own culture the logos of God which is God's saving character in human shape, perceived in the freedom and love of Jesus. But now also 'each generation' *actively* includes women in whose experience the enacted Logos may be re-earthed and re-enacted. Yet that proposal appears to arouse far more opposition than the notion of African or Asian male Christs. But the principle is exactly the same. Just as the Jewishness of Jesus may be irrelevant to, for instance, Maoris, so the maleness of Jesus may be irrelevant to women in the perception of the enacted logos. I say 'may be irrelevant' because that is not always and everywhere the case, but it is a case which has to be affirmed.

Women are quite right to complain that there has been an assumption of necessary maleness throughout the history of christology, as present in this century as in antiquity or the Middle Ages. The occasional modern statement of such maleness is the tip of the iceberg of the continuing pervasive assumption. Thus in an otherwise widely sympathetic book on *The Atone-*

ment J. W. C. Wand could write: 'What prevents Wisdom from becoming an entirely satisfactory representative of God is that it is generally pictured as a female figure.'[43] From this one may only deduce that male figures are entirely satisfactory representatives! This is a completely unwarranted assumption concerning the mystery whom we call God, an assumption whose arrogance is breathtaking, especially in relation to the gracious tone of the rest of the book. That was published in 1963, and so overt an expression might not be acceptable in responsible print today. But as it represents the continuation of centuries of masterful tradition women may wonder whether it remains a silent premise.

Another feature of maleness which has been popular in christologies is men's warm appreciation of 'sonship' into which believers are incorporated as an extension of the relationship between Son and Father. I have in fact used 'Son' infrequently in this book. It is a Johannine account of the relationship and is hardly mentioned in the other Gospels. 'Sonship' is certainly a term used in the New Testament, but from that very point it has excluded women. It is a metaphor employed by men thinking about men, for a relationship which includes women is something other than sonship. Once more Wand has a revealing sentence: 'We are dealing with the relations between a loving father and his wayward sons.'[44] Again, in spite of the fruitfulness of his rethinking of *God as Spirit* as recently as 1977, Geoffrey Lampe provides some clear examples of this exclusion: 'Through Jesus God acted decisively to cause men to share in his relationship to God, and that same God . . . brings believers into that relationship of "sonship" towards himself.'[45] What this shows is the unconscious, not intentionally dismissive, but in practice annihilating assumption of the continuity of maleness, probably from God, certainly through Christ, to believers. This hegemony does not offer freedom and love to women.

Jesus was, of course, a man. For some women that is enough to make it impossible that he be their saviour, but that is to raise maleness to the same level of importance that it has assumed for men (or, to be fair, many, perhaps most, men). Instead of that I believe maleness to be one of those true features of Jesus' life, like his Jewishness, which played an essential part in making Jesus who he was but is contingent to Jesus of Nazareth and need not be part of the enacted saving relationship with God which is the eternal Logos. This christology has been centred on action (both drama and praxis), not on ontology. Male ontological assumptions are therefore irrelevant. Maleness is not divine just as Jewishness is not divine – neither are femaleness nor Maoriness. These are features vivid and involving to ourselves in which the freedom and love of God is enacted so that it becomes a lived experience.

With that attention which is also renunciation of our self-absorption we may also understand features which do not involve us. But to make any of them *necessary* is a form of imperialism and a denial of the freedom and love in relationship which the whole thing is about. From the Gospels, moreover, no one would derive the image of an imperialist male Jesus – that by its very exclusiveness could not be part of the paradigmatic enactment. As Rosemary Ruether points out: 'The role played by women of marginalized groups is an intrinsic part of the iconoclastic, messianic vision.'[46] She also concludes that the maleness of Jesus has no *ultimate* significance and that its use for domination is misuse. 'His ability to speak as liberator does not reside in his maleness but in the fact that he has renounced this system of domination and seeks to embody in his person the new humanity of service and mutual empowerment.'[47] It is this character of freedom and love actually implemented in human conditions which makes Jesus the saviour and the enacted logos. *Anything* actually experienced as running counter to that character (whether intended by the writer or not) cannot meet the first decisive question for presentations of Christ – does this Christ save? The second decisive question was whether this Christ judged, and male Christs are as much in need of judgment as any other, especially when they appear to give uncritical comfort to the maleness of men.

Women at the moment are establishing that out of their experience theological patterns and values may be different from those expressed in the traditions. But women and men cannot for ever do theology only in terms of their femaleness or maleness, since wholeness of relationship requires both, and since the problems each causes the other have to be acknowledged rather than dealt with neurotically, as in the past. Indeed it is an argument towards the need for the possibility of a female Christ that male sexuality can sometimes be disastrous for women. The first thing which made me sympathetic to the idea of a female Christ, to what Ruether calls 'Christ in the form of our sister', was a poem written by a woman who had been brutally raped, and who therefore was insecure in relation to all men. (May I recall here that Wand and the tradition he represents thought that *men* were the ideal representatives of God?) In her case male sexuality was precisely the origin of unfreedom and unlove, so there was no hope in looking to a male Christ for salvation. It was on seeing the representation of a *female* figure on the cross that the woman began to be healed. So I conclude this section with her poem as an account of salvation which meets the criteria of a presentation of Christ.

O God
through the image of a woman
crucified on the cross
I understand at last.

For over half of my life
I have been ashamed
of the scars I bear.
These scars tell an ugly story,
a common story,
about a girl who is the victim
when a man acts out his fantasies.

In the warmth, peace and sunlight of your presence
I was able to uncurl the tightly clenched fists
for the first time.
I felt your suffering presence with me
in that event.
I have known you as a vulnerable baby,
as a brother, and as a father.
Now I know you as a woman.

You were there with me
as the violated girl
caught in helpless suffering.

The chains of shame and fear
no longer bind my heart and body.
A slow fire of compassion and forgiveness
is kindled.
My tears fall now
for man as well as women.

You, God,
can make our violated bodies
vessels of love and comfort
to such a desperate man.
I am honoured
to carry this womanly power
within my body and soul.

You were not ashamed of your wounds,
you showed them to Thomas
as marks of your ordeal and death.
I will no longer hide these wounds of mine
I will bear them gracefully,
they tell a resurrection story.[48]

Uniqueness, universality and finality

God is unique: there is no other – no competitor for finality or ultimacy. God is not a tribal deity with responsibility, so to speak, only for the geographically and historically bounded tribe, but the infinite who is also creator and saviour of what is not-God in all its creaturely finitude, weakness and error. All the major religions of the world have this universal transcendent reference, although Theravada Buddhists, among others, would not express ultimacy in such personal terms. In his 'field theory of religion' John Hick allows for both approaches by calling the ultimate 'the Real' known either in *personae* or *impersonae*, the first of which has some affinities with what I have called the 'roles' of creator and saviour.[49] The abstract term 'Real' is a necessary reminder of the mystery of God for, as Hick says, 'infinity is an experience-transcending concept'.[50] The sense in all religions of what Christians call 'salvation' Hick characterizes as the humanity-transforming move from a consciousness centred on the self to one centred on the Real.

Hick's term 'the Real' expresses both abstraction and value (most people would probably prefer the real to the unreal). Abstracts are useful for indicating transcendence, but they are hard to live by, so what makes each religion distinctive in itself and potentially transforming is how the value of the Real is expressed more particularly and vividly within it. Christian imagery, liturgy and theology give such expression to the Christian faith. My own account begins with the Real, infinite and mysterious, experienced and responded to within the Judaeo-Christian tradition as the free and loving God who companions creation seeking and encouraging freedom and love in response. That is a sense of God by which one may live and worship. Even that sense, however, is made decisively lively and available to me as a human being by the account of Jesus as a man in whom salvation became visible, for his response was so thorough that he not only received freedom and love from God but gave it to others, thus concurring with the divine saving purpose and becoming the enacted Logos by which Christian churches orientate themselves to the Real.

There is a sense in which for Christians who have given the matter thought, Christ must be unique and the definitive revelation of what God is like – otherwise, presumably they would not be Christians. Christologies may vary, but in all their accounts there has been no one like this man. This, for me, is neither an ontological uniqueness nor a uniqueness of actual action – as John 14.12 says, 'greater works than these will he (who believes in me) do because I go to my Father'. Concurrence with the divine is a human possibility not limited to Jesus. But the 'great work' of incarnating freedom and love to the point of becoming paradigmatic for an entire movement based on worshipping God in these terms is unique and final within that movement. The understanding of the paradigm has often changed, but there is such a surplus of signifiers in the New Testament that changes can take place without lessening the focus on Jesus Christ pointing, as Jesus himself pointed, to God. There is also a sense in which the universality of Christ has to be affirmed if he is believed in any way to encapsulate the character of the infinite God in relation to humanity. There is no time, place or person outwith the divine presence. Similarly, there is no country, class, colour or gender in which Christ may not be rooted as the vivid human enactment of relationship with God. No one is *a priori* excluded. Anyone may come to God through Christ. But to say 'anyone may come' is very different from saying 'everyone must come', and to affirm the uniqueness and finality of Jesus Christ within the Christian tradition even with its universal horizon, is not to affirm that Jesus Christ must be unique and final for those in other religions of the world.

In that case the uniqueness, universality and finality of Christ is a confession of faith within the Christian church. To believe that 'everyone must come' to God through Christ is once more the form of imperialism which denies freedom and love even as it preaches that message of salvation. Moreover it diminishes God back in the direction of a tribal deity, for it credits the divine with a very limited operation and no joy from all of creation for most of its history, but only some joy from some of creation in the last two thousand years. The strong words of the New Testament – there is 'no other name' by which people may be saved (Acts 4.12); no one comes to the Father except through the Son (John 14.6); what took place in Jesus Christ was 'once for all' (Heb. 9.12) – appear from exegetes to have less than the exclusive sense in which they have often been used. James Dunn, for instance, calls John 14.6 homiletic rather than doctrinal and after considerable discussion concludes:

> The exclusiveness claimed for Christ may simply be a way of bringing home (to John's church) the strength and urgency of that claim in a world full of alternative and enticing mediators and deities. That seems to be the main thrust of the Johannine claim, not the outright denial that God's spirit and word may well be experienced elsewhere in the world. It would certainly constitute an unchristian narrowing of the gospel if it were to be denied that the Word of God was never heard or Spirit of God never experienced outside an explicitly Christian context.[51]

As God – word, spirit or presence – is constant and never out of saving character, so experience of God wherever it occurs may be salvific.

It is also suggested that 'one and only' language in the New Testament is comparable to declarations of love: 'This is the one and only man/woman for me'.[52] However that may have been in New Testament times, it certainly appears to me that in an inescapably pluralistic religious world in which many religions have by any standards produced saintly men and women (centred on the Real, not on themselves), while all religions have a mixed history of better and worse, the confessional *pro me* and *pro nobis* (on my behalf, on our behalf) aspect of affirmations of faith have to be realized. That does not prevent the recommendation of Christianity in life and word, nor the objection to what is 'intolerable' in Langdon Gilkey's term[53] in other religions or our own, but it does preclude the automatic condemnation of men and women of other faiths as excluded from the transformation of divine salvation expressed in their terms.

Nor would such a stance make affirmation concerning Christ's finality *pro nobis* any less whole-hearted. Avery Dulles objected: 'If this (Christ's absolute uniqueness) is obscured, the Christ-event will not elicit the kind of worship and thanksgiving needed to sustain the Christian community in its vibrant relationship to God.'[54] Would that the relationship were always vibrant! For myself, however, I would have more trust in both God and Christian communities. The most relevant comparison here is the liveliness of commitment possible within one branch of the Christian church while being aware that there are others. I can see that there are other ways of being the church than the Presbyterian one into which I was born and to which I belong. I acknowledge, indeed rejoice in the existence of saintly people in other churches and in mine. Some things seem to me better in other churches and some in my own, while there is better and worse in the history of the Church of Scotland as in any other church. It is contingent that I am a Presbyterian Christian, that my formative experience of the church was within the Church of Scotland, but the decisive point is that I am enabled to worship and encouraged to live a Christian life within it while ecumenical experience gives me a perspective both critical and appreciative of my own church. This argument is not diminished by the fact that occasionally people change churches, as others occasionally change religion.

In the same way the critical point about Christ is that people are enabled to worship God and are encouraged to live a life orientated on 'the Real' through him/her. Where that happens the revelation is final in the sense of decisive *pro nobis*, even though most Christians are Christian because they were born in a Christian country or community. Again, dialogue with other faiths gives one a much needed perspective on one's own. One may be glad rather than dismayed to find what Christians call salvation occurring in other faiths, for what can be better than that salvation should occur? It increases rather than lessens my thankfulness to God for the salvation I know. But just as ecumenicity within the Christian church does not lead to the creation of one super church, so the acknowledgment of God's effects in other religions does not lead to an artificial syncretism. Rosemary Ruether expresses well the relation between universal and particular in this case:

> True universality lies in not trying to make one cultural synthesis that can embrace all possibilities. Such a synthesis will always be limited, and thus become a new cultural imperialism that ignores or denies truth outside its limited construct. True universality lies in accepting one's own finiteness, one's own particularity and, in so doing, not making that particularity the only true faith, but allowing other particularities to stand side by side with yours as having equal integrity. Each is limited and particular, and yet each is, in its own way, an adequate way of experiencing the whole for a particular people at a particular time.[55]

Salvation

Whatever the difficulties with cosmic dramas of pre-existence and descent, there is no comparable obstacle in recognizing the kind of experience which gave rise to that manner of identification of Jesus' work with God's work, an experience interpreted as relationship with God in newness or abundance of life. Without such experience, still taking its rise from a presentation of Jesus, there would be no point in attempting a christology, nor in teasing out the sense in which Jesus Christ is truly human and truly God. Salvation is the stone flung into the pool with consequential ripples of christological belief. 'Salvation', however, has been given many different meanings, some more passionate than others, some more cerebral, metaphysical, moral or social. That is not surprising, for salvation is always an experience of divine rescue and transformation in a context concerning particular people. It particularizes the universal constant love of God in specific imperfect circumstances and is realized individually, however social its implications may be. It will therefore be differently experienced and expressed as circumstances change, together with the categories by which circumstances are understood. It cannot be otherwise while salvation continues to be a lived experience.

I have called this section 'salvation' rather than 'atonement', a term which has been used for the reconciliation, the bringing together 'at one' of God and wayward, suffering, dying humanity. It is certainly possible for humanity not to be at one with God, but the way in which this lack of concurrence has traditionally been described seems to me to be an inadquate account of relationship. It is agreed that it is not God who has to be reconciled with humanity, but humanity with God. But that has been taken to imply that there is effective estrangement in the relationship such that God's love and forgiveness cannot be applied in the human situation. In that case the death of Christ, imaged as sacrifice, ransom or redemption price, is said to create a bridge across which divine and human may come together once more so that God's benefits may flow to humanity. The use of these images in theories of atonement has been based on the notion that if one person is irresponsive or selfish in a relationship, that relationship no longer exists until or unless some decisive act cures the estrangement and restores communion. Such a pattern may indeed happen, but it does not begin to describe a relationship spoiled on one side but characterized on the other by love in freedom – a love which does not have to be earned. Love does not consider a relationship broken, is not for ever entertaining the wrong done to it, but keeps all avenues open hoping for the free response of the other.

> Love is patient and kind . . . Love does not insist on its own way; it is not irritable or resentful . . . Love bears all things,

> believes all things, hopes all things, endures all things. Love never ends (I Cor. 13.4–8).

That was the action of the father of the prodigal and it is equally the action of God. If God is constantly companioning the world in love, there has never been estrangement on God's side, and since forgiveness is part of love's maintaining openness to relationship, God's forgiveness precedes any act intended to propitiate or expiate. 'We cannot say that God was unforgiving until Christ came and died on Calvary; nor can we forget that God's work of reconciliation goes on in every age.'[56] There is an almost logical point here, for if God rather than humanity 'provides the atonement, then forgiveness must precede atonement; and the atonement must be the form of the manifestation of the forgiving love of God, not its cause'.[57] To forgive, however, is also to forget, so God's judgment takes seriously all the better and worse that occurs in this world, sets aside from memory into virtual non-being what is not worth remembering and remembers the rest eternally, thereby giving it eternal life. Past failure, therefore, is over, in the sense that it does not interfere with the continuing possibility of relationship with God. That relationship is in place even if people never discover it, but to discover oneself loved, forgiven and stirred to action is to be transformed in person and relationships.

The death of Christ is thus not on its own his 'work'. His person and work cannot be separated, for his work was not the achievement of a salvation otherwise unprocurable but the visible enactment of God's saving relationship, the making vivid and immediate of what is always true. 'His work is but his person in movement.'[58] 'Your sins are forgiven', Jesus said to the sick, and 'Your faith has made you whole'. The sick had not willed themselves better, nor had they faith in the sense of correct beliefs concerning Jesus. Rather they had come with some trust and some hope to put themselves in Jesus' hands. In that way the trust which God places in humanity and the risk God thereby takes, described in Jesus' parables of the father or master delegating authority to son or steward, was answered in the case of the sick by their trust or hope of healing which brought them to Jesus. In the christological terms of this chapter they aligned themselves with the concurrence of divine and human in the action of Jesus Christ and were healed, forgiven. In the same way, 'seeing' brings about salvation, not in the Gnostic sense of having secret knowledge, but in the sense of having caught a vision of a love which shows up one's lovelessness, fragmentation and self-absorption together with hope and trust of forgiveness and new life. Thus Zacchaeus was made whole from his social isolation and economic exploitation of others through his response to Jesus and thus to God in Christ. The endless accessibility of Jesus to all who would come to him, his compassion and his criticism, his behaviour directed freely towards people and not towards possessions or rules for living are not just example or illustration of something else, but the enactment in one set of imperfect human conditions of the salvation made possible by God's love. In its first happening Jesus' life was drama and praxis together. In the written Gospels it is drama ready to spill over into praxis through response.

Although there is always God-given freedom in human experience there is not always human freedom. People are acted upon by other people and by circumstances beyond their control. In like manner Jesus, who in his ministry used his freedom actively and thereby embodied the seeking, saving activity of God, was acted upon rather than acting in his suffering and death. Every prop, every shared understanding or movement of sympathy was knocked away from him. He was tried on grounds of political expediency and social control. He was betrayed by one of his disciples and deserted by the rest. His judges could not comprehend him and he was caricatured by soldiers who later did their duty in crucifying him before mocking onlookers. Jesus' love for God and God's mission brought him to this pass, but where was God in all this horror? It took resurrection, not to undo the pain, but to show that God had been in it all, enduring the contradiction of love but not removing his saving, forgiving presence. In the terms of John's gospel 'the light shines in the darkness and the darkness has not overcome it' (John 1.5). Or, as Paul claimed triumphantly, nothing, no 'tribulation, or distress, or persecution, or famine, or nakedness, or peril, or sword . . . will be able to separate us from the love of God in Christ Jesus' (Rom. 8.35, 38).

Injustice, suffering, mockery and desertion are things which happen in this world, and they happen not outside the caring companionship of God but within it. The persecutor who denies relationship and the persecuted who suffer are both part of the pain which companioning the world brings God. Since humans and indeed all creation have freedom, salvation is not an easy matter of divine *fiat*, and even less of predestination, so it includes the patient enduring of grief and pain in God's constant openness to and love for a creation absorbed in itself. God's presence in all the circumstances of the death of Christ enacts in a specific situation of human failure and pain the divine presence in all such situations.

There too God's presence is a saving presence when attended to, for a relationship of love saves. Salvation is powered by the love of God active towards human response, forgiving past and continuing failures, comforting, stimulating and enabling wholeness of people and relationships. Whatever the cost in divine suffering, God's presence with the sick who are not healed and with those who are oppressed in circumstances they cannot change is as real and as saving as in any other condition. Salvation is discovered to be a reality by people in the circumstances they find themselves in, while no one has control over or enjoys all their circumstances. The incurable and the oppressed are at the far end of a spectrum of actual unfreedom on which every human being has some place. In the multiple finite world for ever being shaped by those with the power to make a difference, the use of whatever freedom is available to one creature may inhibit or destroy some freedom in another.

That can happen on any scale within creation. The freedom of oppressors to oppress, the freedom of cancerous cells to multiply, like the freedom of a man to drink, drive and kill, or of meteorological conditions to produce avalanches or tornadoes are instances where human or non-human freedom brings grief and misery. God, having given freedom to all of creation will not intervene by removing that, but suffers the result of the divine gift when it goes awry. Even in such cases to believe that God is not absent in any of that pain and to see this paradigmatically expressed in the suffering and death of Christ ('He saved others, himself he cannot save') is to respond to God and be changed in the midst of circumstances which do not change. Wholeness and personal renewal always take place in the midst of things as they are, but one's vision of how things are and what can be done within that is transformed. Thus Jesus is the visible embodiment of God's love suffering contradiction as the negative effects of creation, but continuing nevertheless to companion the world. Jesus did not suffer everything, just as he did not experience everything:

> Was he married, did he try
> To support, as he grew less fond of them
> Wife and family?
>
> No,
> He never suffered such a blow.[59]

Yet Jesus saves and is the enacted Logos because he incarnates the *whole* pattern and values of God's relationship in action and suffering.

The traditional account of the atonement which this most resembles is that of Abelard in the twelfth century, although, clearly, there are also differences. Abelard was equally convinced that love was not only the motive for God's seeking and valuing sinners, but also the means of salvation. Love is effective; love saves.

> The love exhibited in the incarnation and death of Jesus Christ is creative, transforming love. It first acts to restore the inner life of man, whom sin has alienated from God and neighbour.[60]

This happens as grace and in Abelard's dramatic descriptions is realized through 'seeing'. As he wrote to Heloise:

> He bought you not with his wealth but with himself. He bought and redeemed you with his own blood. See what right he has over you and how precious you are . . . What has he seen in you, I ask you, when he lacks nothing, to make him seek even the agonies of a fearful and inglorious death in order to purchase you? What, I repeat, does he seek in you except yourself? He is the true friend who desires yourself and nothing that is yours, the true friend who said as he was about to die for

> you: 'There is no greater love than this, that a man should lay down his life for his friends.'[61]

Christ thus illuminates the understanding and transforms the heart towards God and neighbour. The obstacle to reconciliation lies in humanity, not in God, so 'the drama of Christ's advent, ministry, death and resurrection . . . is the mighty act of God in removing the obstacle, lodged in the heart of the sinner, to man's fellowship with the divine Father'.[62] Such an action cannot be received casually, as cheap grace, for as Abelard reiterates, the 'seeing' includes a realization of the cost and suffering for God, and it requires, in Weil's terms, the renunciation of our egocentricity. 'Even though God is eternally forgiving, his mercy would be too easily counted as indulgence if he had not revealed its cost to him in the incarnation and death of his own Son.'[63] It is an implication of redemption, moreover, that Christ's self-giving becomes an example to follow.

It is a mistake to suppose that 'Abelard transposed (atonement) wholly to the subjective realm'.[64] As Weingart points out, Abelard's thinking is thoroughly theocentric.[65] He concentrated on God's action in transforming the sinner because if the problem lies with the sinner, it is the sinner who has to be changed, not God. As Rashdall wrote in support of Abelard: 'Christ's whole life was a sacrifice which takes away sin in the only way in which sin can really be taken away, and that is by making the sinner actually better.'[66] Better, not perfect, that is cured of being boxed up in sin. For Abelard that was entirely the work of God, all God's grace. I, on the other hand, have understood part of God's grace to be the gift of freedom to creation such that the response is human and free. Nevertheless God's encompassing presence in love and suffering is the gracious context in which the response is made. Both God's gift and human response are needed, thereby obviating categories like 'objective' and 'subjective', for as Keith Ward notes: 'Bluntly put, redemption cannot be intelligibly said to be accomplished unless people are actually redeemed.'[67]

A second criticism of Abelard which, if true, would stand against my presentation as well is that his account does not deal adequately with guilt. There are probably two things involved here: the gravity of sin itself and its psychological weight on the sinner. 'The resolution of guilt needs more than a loving demonstration that the hurt does not matter.'[68] It is certainly possible to be facile or sentimental over God's love and forgiveness, and there is Heine's remark which would permit anything and excuse everything: 'God will forgive; that's his job.'[69] (Yet the depths of divine grace are such that it forgives and sets aside the casual trivializing of forgiveness.) Abelard himself is neither casual nor facile. He uses traditional metaphors for God's saving action such as the redeeming of sinners at great price, but the wonder is that sinners should be so valuable to God that God endures the 'hurt' their opposition and redemption cause. Forgiveness does not mean that the hurt does not matter either to God or to the redeemed, for it is in 'seeing' the uttermost effects of sin on God in Christ that a perspective is gained on guilt's proportions. Human hearts are changed by seeing guilt of that dimension forgiven out of love. This is Abelard's theocentricity once more, for instead of concentrating on people penned up egocentrically by their own guilt he directs attention to the effects on God of that guilt while forgiveness is found in comprehending that divine love is not deflected by the weightiest of sins, nor by a sinner *incurvatus/incurvata in se* through brooding on personal guilt.

'Guilt' is originally a legal term, and it may be that Abelard's account (which is nowhere expressed in full) is felt to be inadequate because it does not declare a sinner guilty and worthy of condemnation. In that case sin is thought to be taken seriously only when it is both condemned and suffered for, as Christ is said to suffer in our place in other accounts of atonement. Abelard in fact uses but does not emphasize the language of Christ submitting to God's wrath against sin. His own emphasis, however, can be seen as much more concerned with rehabilitative than with punitive justice, God being more interested in the cure than the punishment of the sinner.

The requirement of punitive justice in relation to guilt is often expressed as a deep psychological need which Tillich describes as acceptance of the 'demand that (the Christian) himself suffer infinite punishment and the message that he is released from guilt and punishment by the substitutional offering of Christ'.[70] That may not be justice in the ordinarily understood meaning of the term, since an innocent man suffers for the guilty who do not suffer, but it is held that Jesus Christ's suffering does deal seriously with God's righteousness and the gravity of human sin. If that is a psychological point I have to say it is one which escapes me. Guilt certainly needs to be taken seriously and casual forgiveness would not do that. But divine forgiveness which is not separable from God's suffering as well as joy is not casual just because it is always offered unconditionally.

Rahner is surely right when he declares: 'Theology has been too long and too often bedevilled by the unavowed supposition that grace would no longer be grace if it were too generously distributed by the love of God.'[71] Grace does not overlook sin, for real forgiveness is not possible without taking it seriously and deliberately 'forgetting' it, blotting it out for eternity.[72] This is not the 'forgiveness' Stevie Smith mocks:

> I forgive you, Maria,
> Things can never be the same,
> But I forgive you, Maria,
> Though I think you were to blame.
> I forgive you, Maria,
> I can never forget,
> But I forgive you, Maria,
> Kindly remember that.[73]

What possibility of future relationship is there with that 'forgiveness'? God cannot be understood in these terms, nor can the grace of forgiveness dispensed by Jesus during his life. In the vivid picture of Col. 12.4 God nails the bond against us to the cross and thereby cancels it. In that legal metaphor we are made innocent and that happens once for all. (Hence all the difficulties of the church in the first centuries over post-baptismal sin.) In the metaphor of personal relationships, however, forgiveness is part of the continuous process of relating, and the blotting out it involves means that some of each one's life is lost while some is always sifted out for eternity. Schubert Ogden expresses it thus:

> Just as the reality of God as the Creator is not something belonging to the past of nature and history, but is their ever present primordial ground, so the reality of God as Judge and

Redeemer is not a particular event of the future, but the ever-present final consequence of each passing moment in the stream of time.[74]

Moreover talk of guilt in the legal sense assumes as the only effective relationship that between judge and accused, while sin becomes the only human thing which matters to God, leaving all the positive aspects of creation irrelevant. But between God and each individual human there is something much more like personal relationship in which God knows pleasure as well as pain. To remain with guilt, however, legal models should give way to models of interpersonal guilt. Sin takes place in and between individual people and groups, even if the results poison society. If one within a marriage, a family or a friendship spoils a relationship through some form of selfishness, punishment is of no avail (except, perhaps, in the limited form of training for the young: but we are not young being trained, we are adults with responsibility). For the relationship to continue in wholeness the seriousness of the matter, which includes the guilt of the one, the suffering and readiness to forgive of the other, has to be recognized by both and then put behind them. That deals very adequately with guilt *within* a relationship.

The real psychological hurdle for many people is to be forgiven without that forgiveness having been *earned* by anyone, and to say the simple words 'I'm sorry' with nothing in their hands, not even Christ's death as propitiation. There is much practical disbelief that forgiveness may be truly unconditional. That may be why atonement theories of justice where salvation is earned by Christ and we plead his merits continue to be popular. Such accounts were common during the Reformation when a disavowal of the merit of all human works was offset by an emphasis on the merits of the divine work. 'Work' was still seen to be necessary.[75]

Yet justice may be seen to be the approximation to love which is all that a *society* with its large numbers is capable of.[76] It is a necessary but clumsy surrogate for love and freedom *en masse*, where relationships are formal. Thus Christ is said to have altered the status of *all humanity* in relation to God by the justice of his atoning death while individuals are incorporated into this new status. Without denying the need for justice and fair relationships in society and God's concern over the suffering injustice brings, one may argue that the case with God is different. God's dealings are not with humanity at large but endlessly in relation to each person with his or her relationships, so for describing God and Christ there need be no surrogate for the kind of love and forgiveness which happens between two people in an acknowledged relationship. It is also possible to stress guilt in an almost masochistic manner so that the sinner acquires importance on account of his or her sin, rather than being valuable as an object of God's love. The thought then would be that 'my sin is too important (rather than too great) just to be forgiven'. But this is another manifestation of human egocentricity.

Abelard, like other theologians in the Western tradition who followed Paul, concentrated his conception of atonement on Christ's death. Therefore the forgiveness Jesus gave in his life and his actually making people whole do not enter his picture. But once Jesus' living and dying are seen as equally important the notion of an atoning death dissolves, for all that atonement was believed to bring is present already in Jesus' life together with the relegation to outer darkness of self-regarding irresponsibility or self-preoccupied lack of concern for the sick and the imprisoned and so forth. Thus, when George Hendry considers how Jesus 'dispensed forgiveness to men from the beginning of his public ministry, with never a suggestion that it was contingent upon any work he did' he sees Christ as 'the human agent of God's grace' in a way which in effect enlarges Abelard's account:

> The grace of God is his will to have fellowship with sinful men, and its primary work is to be seen, not in the removal of the obstacle to that fellowship, but in the establishment of the fellowship which removes the obstacle.[77]

To say that love saves, therefore, is to say that love desires and initiates a relationship which is itself saving, a saving process within the stream of history characterized by freedom and love. Hendry still says, however, that Christ came to bring forgiveness, as though God had not forgiven in the Jewish tradition or did not forgive outside the Judaeo-Christian tradition. One of the most poignant expressions of forgiveness in fact comes from the

Psalms: 'If thou, O Lord, shouldst keep account of sins, who, O Lord, could hold up his head? But in thee is forgiveness and therefore thou art revered' (Ps. 130.3, NEB). Ogden again captures the wider view:

> The claim 'only in Jesus Christ' must be interpreted to mean, not that God acts to redeem only in the history of Jesus and in no other history, but that the only God who redeems any history – *although in fact he redeems every history* – is the God whose redemptive action is decisively re-presented in the word that Jesus speaks and is.[78]

'The word that Jesus speaks and is': that is to say that Jesus is not a sign of something else, but the enactment of the thing itself in time and space. That point rebuts the other critisicm of Abelard, potentially applicable to me, that Jesus Christ is merely a demonstration:

> As Harnack pointed out, if Christ came only to demonstrate the love of God, there is no real necessity for the cross, and none even for the incarnation.[79]

The cross, however, like the incarnation, is *necessary* only if redemption is *earned* by it. That might represent part of Paul's view, but then Paul was not concerned with Jesus' life and could use legal and sacrificial metaphors which in time led to horrific, unloving accounts of atonement. The cross, representing both human opposition and human and divine suffering, is not necessary but highly probable for a life in which freedom is exercised in love. The crucifixion of Jesus was contingent upon the freedom of men to oppose or desert him. Given the history of the world it seems highly probable that such opposition and self-preservation might occur, but in no way necessary. Nor may the incarnation be called 'necessary', since it was contingent upon Jesus' free response to God. 'Jesus, Christians would say, acted in response to God's call to him, *though he need not have done so*.'[80] From that Keith Ward argues that God cannot be said to have intended the incarnation in Jesus, since 'such incarnation depended always upon Jesus' free choice and so could not be complete until Jesus' death. But God could take that completed life and use it for a special contingent purpose, within the context of his universal purpose for the world.'[81] God's universal purpose Ward identifies as redemption, while God's contingent purpose is a particular way of redemption. In a similar way I have written of God's universal purpose of salvation into freedom and love being contingently but really enacted in the life of Christ.

Neither incarnation nor the cross were therefore necessary; rather, they were the fruitful and fearful result of faith concurring with God. But that still leaves the matter of 'demonstration'. The first question to ask of those who write of 'mere demonstration' is whether they have never been moved, shaken or changed by anything they have *seen*, as opposed to being convinced by intellectual constructs or moral arguments. A demonstration of love (like a demonstration of hate, naked power or generosity) is capable of bringing about real change when seen by people not too curved in on themselves to notice. If the opposing argument then becomes that this change affects only the spectator, it colludes with the silent and undesirable premise of some atonement versions that it is God who has to be changed for salvation to occur. Abelard frequently emphasized the moral effects on the believer of seeing Christ's death and it has sometimes been believed that this moral pedagogy was all his account contained. In that case the demonstration would be only a pattern to follow, like steps in a dance. But Abelard intended far more, as I do with the dramaturgical model. The demonstration is one of visible, effective salvation, which, when seen with personal involvement, continues to effect salvation. For that reason 'enactment' with its overtones of 'bringing about now' is a much more adequate word than 'demonstration'. This was a 'manifestation', in McLeod Campbell's language, of God's goodness and love awakening response 'which a simple intimation of divine clemency and goodness could not quicken'.[82] Moreover, 'no manifestation of power meeting me can so assure me that I am meeting God as the manifestation of love. Therefore they greatly err who seek an external evidence of power, instead of an internal evidence of love, in considering the claim of anything to be received as from God.'

Into what situations, then, does this manifestation of love arrive? The short answer is that it is present in every situation, but it is worth enlarging that a little. To begin at the end there is dying and death. Pannenberg points out that this is a rare motif in contemporary writing on salvation.[83] He revives the notion of Jesus' death as an 'inclusive substitution' the Godforsakenness of which, as he sees it, was cancelled by the resurrection so that all Godforsaken death is overcome. I find the resurrection not so much a cancellation of the past as an affirmation of it – here too was God. But Pannenberg is right to say:

> No longer will anyone die alone and without hope, for in community with Jesus the hope for one's own future participation in the new life that has already appeared in Jesus whose content is community with God has been established.[84]

Jesus has made visible what is always true of God, and one of these truths is that death, like suffering, is not Godforsaken. Even though in our finite language we can only make pictures of 'community with God' in eternity, the divine constancy of relationship endures beyond this life.

In life, however, salvation concerns persons who are selves-in-relation. It takes marooned individuals out of their isolation, thus enabling love, and creates freedom by giving submerged individuals their personhood. Its primary locus is neither the individual nor the collective, but the process of living as selves with networks of relationships. Each self has some freedom, not only as a gift from God but also within society, even though the latter may be, in Gandhi's words, 'less than that of a passenger on a crowded deck'.[85] Anyone who has seen a packed Indian ferry will know what he means. Yet he continues that each has 'freedom of choice as to the manner in which he uses that freedom'. It is through that area of freedom that salvation may become effective, evoking response, making known a relationship (a 'fellowship' Hendry called it) which transforms the self and its relations.

There are many different ways of being *incurvatus/incurvata in se*, so preoccupied with the self that the salvation inherent in God's presence cannot be attended to. Beauty may be an obsession, or plainness, or disability. Anxiety, apathy and self-congratulation, all of which bind people to themselves, may be the result of intelligence or stupidity, poverty or riches. A sense of worthlessness which makes relationships impossible may be as consuming as a sense of worth which despises others. It is possible to demand from all relationships the constant propping up of one's ego with consequently more than psychological effects on those relationships. It is equally possible to seek comfort, advancement and power for the self, or the extended self in family, class, business or nation in such a way that relationships are manipulated towards that end while relationships which do not serve that end are actually or virtually denied. Thus selves are expressed in relationship, so that, for instance, a theologian who writes a panegyric on love but has no consideration for a secretary is more securely known in the relationship than in the rhetoric. Even sin in the sense of moral failure does not simply involve the individual, but that individual in action and relationship. Criminal offences are made possible by relationships which are warped, as in some murders, or denied, which makes it possible for one to steal from another, or, for that matter, to pollute the environment.

In the midst of all this selfishness and failure in relationships God is, so to speak, stirring us up, saying, 'Look, look', giving us countless possibilities to see how things may truly be. While anything may open one's eyes and be a moment of the kingdom, the ground, the criterion and the goal of all understanding of salvation is for Christians the action of God in Jesus Christ. There both those who thought themselves worthless and those who marginalized others see the value Jesus gives to the poor, the upsetting of expected relationships in his parables, his fidelity through suffering and mockery to death, indeed a whole life and death lived in concurrence with God. Out of each person's area of freedom some response is possible, though it may not be well-informed, or total. The response is a giving of oneself, an entering into the play with the forgiveness of what is past and the possibility of transformation. The play is everlasting, but Jesus Christ, the enacted Logos of God, continues to encapsulate and enact the saving relationship of God with humanity which can be salvation for our time and our relationships.

Salvation as relationship with God is in part a comforting experience as the warmth of forgiving love and the sense of being valued make secure. But it is also disturbing and transforming. There is joy and risk in entering any relationship of love, and the risk in this case is what transformation involves. Not only is the self lifted out of its egocentricity and fragmentation (what Paul called dying and rising with Christ), but relationships are transformed in the process. Respect for the other as God respects our otherness replaces manipulation; a realization of the other's intrinsic worth to God, true even of one's enemies, replaces instrumentalism or withdrawal. God has forgiven us and we have to learn to forgive others. Thus God becomes a comforting, strengthening, unsettling presence when attended to in every relationship, personal, social or national.

The difficulty and the hope of such transformation are profoundly illumined in the writing of Protestant and Catholic theologians in Ireland endeavouring to understand and transcend the bitter division of their communities in the north.[86] What is remembered on both sides in Nothern Ireland is in one sense times when freedom and love have been disastrously absent, but these are not the same times for each community. The problem the theologians are faced with is the reconciling of two contrary sets of memories kept alive in the present to provide identity by difference and opposition. It is not surprising that they dwell considerably on forgiveness, which is explored sensitively by, among others, the Protestant Alan Falconer and the Catholic Gabriel Daly. Forgiveness, Falconer insists, is not a weakness but the renunciation of destructive power for integrative power. He quotes from Arendt: 'Forgiving, in other words, is the only reaction which does not merely re-act but acts anew and unexpectedly, unconditioned by the act which provoked it and therefore freeing from its consequences both the one who forgives and the one who is forgiven.'[87] For Daly forgiveness is one of the principal signals of transcendence: 'When true forgiveness occurs, there is God.'[88] In a manner which recalls the emphasis I put on the concurrence of divine and human as a human possibility made visible in Christ, Daly wishes 'to argue for the immanent, if imperfect, presence and manifestation of divine forgiveness in human forgiveness. The recognition that Jesus' acts of forgiveness were divine acts in a human mode and were inspired by human compassion can be made the christological basis of communitarian forgiveness.'[89] It is desirable and laudable, he says, to bring in legislation to reduce the occasions of hostility between the communities, but such external means are limited. The relationships which are at the core of the problem will not be healed until there is understanding and forgiveness.

What I have called 'the difficulty and hope' of forgiveness in all the sorry history of Irish troubles is not, of course, simply an Irish problem. Britain has a history of responsibility there and recently Europe, the Middle East and the United States have also become involved. Of British response (and recognizing Irish responsibility as well) Enda McDonagh writes:

> Without a real sense of Irish suffering British Christians or politicians are never going to understand the depth and difficulty of our common problems. It is not, to begin with anyway, a matter of apportioning blame but of recognizing British power and so British responsibility and so the need to understand. Without sharing the sufferings, being inhabited by them, understanding will not come. Neither will the commitment nor the capacity to help resolve it, to help overcome the chaos which is at least partly of British origin and British sustenance. Such openness to Irish suffering is a particular responsibility of British Christians.[90]

God, who understands, suffers 'with his people. And they are all his people, Protestant and Catholic, Unionist and Nationalist, British Army, UDR, UDA, and IRA . . . The mutual infliction of suffering is a self-inflicted wound on oneself and one's compassionate God.'[91] What McDonagh asks for here, then, is that British Christians in following God should be like God vulnerable rather than untouched, suffering rather than outraged at what happens and has happened in Ireland. He does not suggest, though well he might, that British Christians seek the forgiveness of the Irish for their share of responsibility.

His experience leads McDonagh to ask tough questions of forgiveness.

> The forgiving voices of particular family members faced with the killing of one of their own is properly impressive. It rekindles faith in the loving possibilities of human beings . . . For the offence which the bereaved suffered, and it can be enormous, they can be forgiving and seek to take the whole

> family with them. Such forgiving may and should lead the killers to repentance. The bereaved cannot give the killers direct forgiveness, nor can the latter, after the victim's death, receive it.[92]

This is not the situation I described earlier of forgiveness *within* a relationship which is the model of God's forgiveness, for killing is the most terminal expression of a disavowal of relationship, and it is the impossibility of forgiveness from the dead thereafter that McDonagh describes. But what of God's relationship to both the victim and the killer?

> Can God from on high as it were forgive the murderer on behalf of the victim? What kind of involvement with the victims by God does this suggest? What kind of God does it suggest?[93]

McDonagh does not immediately answer his own questions, but in the picture with which I have been working, God, who is not 'on high' but part of the very situation of the murder, *does* forgive the murder – not because murder is a peccadillo and grace is cheap, but because God continues in hope that there will be 'repentance', that breaking into consciousness of the want of freedom exercised in love resulting in a turning round in one's tracks. To that end the murder is judged and consigned to oblivion, to the loss of both God and the murderer, but the relationship in which God freely accompanies the other in love continues.

The victims are victims for historical reasons and ultimately because God lets creation be in freedom – to bear fruit or fail most horrendously. The relationship of God to the one who became a victim was as real, as redolent of possibility, as that with the murderer. The suffering of God at the blindness of killing and the pain of death is suffering on the divine scale. God shares, too, in all the reverberations of bereavement. When the victim's family forgives, there is a resounding moment of the kingdom, fruit produced from an unlikely fig tree. When they do not forgive I am in no position to judge them, never having been called on to forgive on that scale. But where there is no forgiveness, the war goes on. Only forgiveness, that serious consideration of the injury and the decision not to make it definitive for future relationships, can in the end break the series of reprisals, whatever other constitutional actions have to take place. Jesus forgave. He called on Peter to forgive seventy times seven. The kind of God all this suggests, in answer to McDonagh's final question, is, in the personal language humans use, one whose sensibilities are never blunted by the long recital of human failure, who understands reasons on all sides far better than the most acute analyst, who is engaged, involved with the people in the midst of it all far beyond any church's walls, who desires that the divine gift of freedom be exercised in love and stirs up people and possibilities for that perception (this is written on Holy Saturday, the climax of perceptibility), who rejoices when love is enacted but suffers with those who suffer and from those who are violent (any kind of violence), yet will not leave creation to its own desolation.

To whom in the end are we not all related? The very things which give any person an identity in the world – in my case I am a theologian who is British (Scottish!), white, middle-class, female and Protestant – all carry with them a history of relationships in one's favour or against one, which are crying out for transformation from wilful ignorance, set expectations, apathetic non-involvement or instrumental manipulation. Moreover the fact that it is in the area of human freedom that salvation finds its entrance is more than sufficient reason for working to enlarge that area of freedom in the midst of actual unfreedom to make it possible for humanity to respond without being ground down by history, biology, poverty or failure – and that despite the perception that all action in a multiple finite world will have an ambiguous character.

The demand is tremendous and would be impossible if it were not for three things. First there are perceptible moments of salvation (of the kingdom) happening now for those with eyes to see. They may be as small and fleeting as the encounter between black and white I described in Chapter 3, or they may be larger acts of forgiveness or generosity. Such happenings, especially on a large scale, are rarely pure and never simple, but they do occur. Even when the world is at its grimmest and most divided, salvation keeps breaking in. (In the quotation echoed here it was 'cheerfulness' which kept on breaking in.[94] The equivalence may stand!) Secondly, there is the understanding of God, who knows all possibilities and limitations better than we know ourselves. God knows that we cannot give heart and soul to every cause – and there is relationship with the environment to be added now to the human list as well. Openness is only possible where there is a sense of the self, and too many demands overpower that sense. God knows, too, that no solution to any problem can be perfect. The imperfect parameters within which all human work is done by imperfect humans is a condition but not an alibi well-known to God who let such conditions be. Thirdly, there is God's continuing love, forgiveness and support, made vividly effective in Christ Jesus, so that while there may be one particular moment of its discovery, salvation is also a relationship continuing in oneself in relation to God as well as being an everlasting possibility looked for and worked for within the world.

8 · *Jesus Christ, Saviour*

Salvation in parable

There is a whole cosmology of creation and redemption contained within Jesus' story of a loving father who had two sons, one a prodigal. The parable effectively begins with the father letting go, allowing his younger son an unheard-of degree of self-determination. Moreover the father gives him his 'share of the inheritance', thereby expressing trust in the lad and treating him as an adult. There is nothing on the father's side to stand in his way. Just so God the creator, having given the universe the possibility of coming into being (having 'fathered' it), lets go all domination and prescription, allowing creation its freedom to become what it may with what in the course of time it inherits. Time and again in Jesus' parables God is pictured as letting go, or departing himself, for in the spatial relationships imposed by narrative that distance from authority is the only way to represent the freedom and possibility of independent action by others. Attention then focusses on this action, but because the father is also God, the action matters in a cosmic perspective, for ultimately it is all response to the creator who let it be.

In its finite freedom from external direction, creation has produced various kinds of flourishing and a similar variety of failure. Each son in the parable flourishes and fails in different ways, and as befits a story, they begin by making response to their father at opposite ends of the spectrum: one stays at home and works, a 'successful' son in that respect, the other departs entirely to have a good time. Within these two boundaries of possibility every other kind of partial or intermittent response is comprehended. The story then centres on the prodigal, the youth with no restraints who appears to flourish as long as he has money, but who becomes a hyperbolic instance of failure, suffering and degradation from the folly with which he dissipates what had come to him. All the lesser failures of creation are included in his case. He is left without a single relationship, and there is no solution for failure in the world he now inhabits. At that nadir the son succeeds in reaching a decision ('repentance') and with a new humility sets out to return to his father's house, to be a servant there.

In a story a man can be in only one place at a time, but given that condition Jesus portrays the father being as beforehand as possible. Watching from the roof-top, he sees his son coming, and before the prodigal can complete his return and his humble request, his father meets him on the road with a total acceptance and welcome which sweep away his sense of having lost his place. Clearly the father had suffered from the absence of his son, and yearned for his return. Metaphysics, unlike stories, is not bound to serial events in space and time, so what Jesus represents as the father looking out for the son may be portrayed as the omnipresent God who accompanies creation at all times in love like the father's, suffering its waywardness, a healing, persuasive presence when attended to, but not an intrusion overriding the decisions of others. Therefore, when prodigals of any kind turn round, they find they are already accepted, loved, forgiven.

In the midst of the reunion a sour note is struck by the elder brother, who has not failed as conspicuously as the other, but who is not free to enter into the love and generosity of the moment. He is the type of the observer of rules. The father is no less loving with him, acknowledging his worth, but encouraging him to enlarge his own vision and to share his father's joy. The story does not tell how he responded, but the elder brother has as much to discover as the younger one about the way love liberates from selfishness. So each son may be saved from his own kind of egocentricity through the effectiveness of the father's unselfish, generous, accessible love.

Jesus' parable is in the end a story and cannot be allegorized, but the presuppositions from which it is told, and its implications for understanding the relationship between God and humanity, are cosmic. There is nothing here concerning God's righteousness, his justice, victory or election, and there is no place for sacrifice or ransom. The story is concerned entirely with salvation brought about by the power of love to those blighted in and by their circumstances. It ends in joy, yet it is not a tale of cheap grace. Everyone in it suffers in some way. It is more a story of the pain of offering grace and the difficulty of accepting it than a story of easy forgiveness. To this someone might say, 'That is all very well. But Jesus told this story during his life. After his death and resurrection other accounts which give meaning to these events have to be included.' That is certainly true, but these other accounts cannot violate the spirit of this story or they are describing someone other than the loving father of variously deficient sons and daughters.

A story indeed cannot tell the whole story. For one thing, there is no one else in its world except its own characters, so no confusing contingencies occur to spoil the story-line. In life all manner of contingencies, the needs and demands of others, the multiplicity of competing interpretations of all events, render circumstances far more complex than those in Jesus' tale. Moreover, since this is a story, we do not know what happened next among the three characters, and whether the prodigal settled down. In the world we experience, on the other hand, response to God is made in the midst of complexities and ambiguities which continue after that response has been made. Nevertheless, whatever qualifications have to be borne in mind, what remains fundamental is that it is the quality of the love of God which changes everything, a love more vividly portrayed by the story than by the statement. That is not cancelled out by Jesus' other stories of servants judged for their selfishness, for these men show no sign of self-perception, no chink in their self-sufficiency and greed for possession through which love and forgiveness could enter in. God's judgment which consigns to oblivion is thus a last sad resort wherever there has been nothing for love to latch on to and concur with. Even then God, like a battered wife who loves and therefore will not leave her husband, continues to accompany the most closed and selfish life in love and hope.

Salvation is made possible by this character of God who enters into the fears and failures of every situation, not to 'conquer' them in the bellicose language often favoured by theology but to present (make present) the alternative way in which life may flourish through response to others and to the God who let it all be. Because each set of circumstances has its own specific imperfections, the effects of salvation as a lived experience have been differently portrayed. In the first century they included release from the fear of demons and other hostile cosmic powers. They have been seen as freedom from the change, decay and disintegration of the flesh and as the setting aside of the verdict on personal, private sins. Salvation has given meaning in a world found meaningless and liberation in a world of oppression and exploitation. Even within these general interpretations it has been experienced differently in individual circumstances. In each case there is a sense in which nothing changes: death and decay continue; the effects of sin and selfishness go on reverberating; the world continues to be ambiguous and the powerful continue to oppress the powerless. But when life in this world is experienced in the larger context of the eternity of God's powerful love, evil in its many forms loses its finality and thus its apparent inevitability and hold on creation. This frees (saves) people from acquiescence in things as they are individually or socially, and replaces the inertia of fatalism with the hopefulness of love. It gives point to thought, commitment and action, which relies on the continuing gracious companionship of God. For when that relationship is known and lived, all other relationships are evaluated in its light, and that changes everything.

Thus salvation, in its initiative and foundation, is not demanding of humanity, and indeed could not be, for it concerns God's character as love, whatever the failures and finiteness of creation. What is hard, perhaps, is the simple human acceptance of this enduring love as the only force God opposes to all evil, and as the *unconditional* forgiveness of our own sins. Love like this cannot be earned, it can only be received with open hands. Given that acceptance, however, salvation begins to work like leaven, like light in our own world as people, cherished, forgiven and transformed put their new allegiance and values into practice. Thus the working out of the salvation which is given freely is the life-long endeavour to renew the relationships of the world from their obstruction, diminishment or selfishness. That is demanding, and its results will never be purely and totally good in an ambiguous world of multiple finite freedom, but God continues to accept, to forgive, to rebuke and to encourage those involved in the process.

This is a Christian account of salvation. Other religions have various other ways of facing the imperfections of the world. But what gives the Christian version its specific content, its belief in the goodness of a God concerned about the world, who 'saves' those who could not save themselves? The Christian answer is to point to Jesus Christ in the belief that in his life, death and resurrection salvation became visible.

Salvation visible

In the entire career of Jesus, in it and not through it or beyond it, the saving relationship God has with humanity has paradigmatic expression. To see this is not like seeing the point of a proposition or an argument, it is more like discerning the point of a play, a play whose theme is life and salvation, and whose protagonist, while it is always Jesus of Nazareth, is also and simultaneously God. The Gospels are more drama than they are explanation, more a showing of the Messiah/Christ than a telling how this might be. In them Jesus not only teaches the life of the kingdom of God, but is shown enacting it, conveying it in his forgiveness, healing and exorcism, in his openness to everyone and his compassion for the poor. Paul was scarcely concerned with what happened in Jesus' life, but he still constructed a whole cosmic drama out of the death and resurrection, which represented the defeat of principalities and powers, so that Jesus became the second Adam, undoing all the harm which the first Adam brought about. Thus the original enactment demands continuing dramatic representation.

In the terms I have been using, the life, death and resurrection of Jesus show what it is for divine and human freedom and love to flow together, thus fulfilling the possibilities of creation in ordinary human circumstances. The man Jesus in his freedom responded to God with an openness which put up no obstacles and held nothing back. He could not be deflected even by his misunderstanding mother (Matt. 12.46–50). In one sense the relationship was secure and private, with the warmth and trust of son to father. But it was also compelling, for it was in the joy and urgency of his knowledge of God that Jesus launched into his mission. But that does not make the response any the less his, and human. He had to make decisions on the manner of his ministry, tempted to the demagoguery of miracle, so much more potent then than now, but finding that spectacle could not convey the God he knew. Instead he put into action the way he did know God, the way of love freely offered.

This was something for everyone to share, whatever their state of ritual purity or moral uprightness. There were no prior conditions.

> Just imagine: it did not matter if you had never observed the law, had collaborated with the Romans, had extorted money from fellow Jews, had resorted to prostitutes, or whatever. You had only to turn to Jesus' God and it would be all right.'[1]

Shocking as this acceptance of prodigals is to the elder brother type, the accessibility of Jesus was God's accessibility, his invitation God's invitation. Thus with never-ending generosity Jesus connected with people where they were. His recognition of sickness, demon possession and social ostracism was his own reaction, but also a visible enactment of the concern of God over all that cripples life and relationship – including riches, privilege or religious righteousness where these close one person off from another. There are no barriers to God, so Jesus ignored or denounced humanity's social barriers and healed the physical barriers.

But God's accessibility is not something to be discovered only in pain and suffering, as if God had no part and pleasure in the good things of creation. Jesus was no ascetic, and the principal demonstration of this in the gospels is that he 'came eating and drinking' (Matt. 11.19) with Pharisees, with tax collectors and sinners, with anyone who would share a table with this man who had no table of his own. All that is to say that his way was the way of fellowship and companionship in preference to the way of judgment on all enjoyment. What that reflects is that God is present with pleasure in moments of enjoyment like a shared meal, just as God is present in compassion in life's tragedies. But good things themselves may make people so comfortable and satisfied that they trust in these goods and fail to respond to God and their fellow creatures. So Jesus, at table with property owners, could tell unsettling stories of the generosity of a hirer of labour, of the father of the prodigal, or of unprofitable servants. Table fellowship was maintained, but the religious imagination of his hosts was teased by intimations of the radical love and freedom of God.

No one was bludgeoned into believing what Jesus said or represented. His audiences, the poor and sick, the wealthy and established, were free to respond or to pass by. His disciples were free to leave (John 6.66f.). Love cannot work by compulsion. It can only draw the other to itself to explore the riches and grace of the relationship. Jesus is like Wisdom, who set up her table and *invited* people to dine with her and gain insight (Proverbs 9.1–6), for, in the metaphor from Revelation (3.20) Jesus knocks at the door, but only when it is opened by the other does he come in to dine in fellowship. So the response, the 'seeing' or 'hearing' and 'doing' rests with the individual, but when people do respond to Jesus, however feeble their contrition or hope or understanding, Jesus responds to them in turn, making present and real God's salvation – 'your faith has saved you'.

Jesus also forgives. He does not have to die to win forgiveness for humanity in its imperfection and egocentricity. God, like the father of the prodigal, is more ready to welcome those who are sickened by what they have done than people are to acknowledge their need of forgiveness. Moreover, like the father of the elder son God lures people persuasively out of the narrowness of their vision – and that is equally salvation, knowledge of the freedom in love of God. Thus there is never a loss of relationship between God and humanity, although humans may put up their own barriers against the divine and lose all awareness of its existence. Forgiveness is a *divine* gift, as Jesus' contemporaries pointed out to him. But it was a spontaneous part of his putting into action the way of God with the world. God's relationship of love with creation has always included forgiveness so that the relationship might continue. Therefore what Jesus enacted in forgiving was that pre-existent relationship made visible and particular in time and space. Jesus presented (made present, immediate) the concern of God over the distress and presumption of humanity, and he offered salvation in terms of a wholeness and transforming relationship with this God.

Jesus' trial, crucifixion and death are part of what it is for God to be present with the world. Jesus disturbed religious and political powers enough for it to be expedient that he die. For if mutual love between God and humanity happens in this world, with the result of divinely inspired freedom from fear and selfishness, it cannot for ever avoid the clash with those in power whose vested interest in things as they are opposes the unsettling effects of salvation. Private spiritual enlightenment offers no problems to authority, but when the transformation of relationship with God becomes the criterion for transforming *all* relationships, so that salvation is something worked out as well as received, any present equilibrium is threatened. On the one hand this shows the character of salvation like leaven, bubbling away in society. On the other it is the tragic aspect of life that the appearance and action of love may become the occasion of hatred. Love does not generate hatred, but its occurrence may turn the propensity to hate into action. 'Love to the loveless shown', as the hymn has it, gives the possibility 'that they may lovely be', but also the continuous possibility that love will be opposed, denied or rejected. The cross of Christ is the very symbol of all that is cross-grained, frightened, uninvolved and unloving in humanity. It enacts humanity's short way with God.

There is a very perceptive moment in John Fowles' novel *The French Lieutenant's Woman* when a young Victorian, secure in his beliefs in science and progress, looks at the 'tortured athlete' on the cross and finds the calling of his time 'to uncrucify'; 'to bring about a world in which the hanging man could be descended, could be seen, not with the rictus of agony on his face, but the smiling peace of a victory brought about by, and in, living men and women'.[2] That expresses so well the confidence of the nineteenth century in Europe and America that by scientific advance and the practical means of education, sanitation and the extension of the franchise moral and social enlightenment would supersede all that the cross represents in the way of brutality and suffering. 'Progress', where it occurred, was no pointless exercise with its enlargement of comfort and opportunity, but it did not uncrucify Christ. It did not remove lovelessness and the denial of relationship. These create the poverty we seem to have always with us, as we suffer them from others and inflict them ourselves.

When that state is seen in the light of love its own darkness is shown up, like the darkness round the cross, or the darkness people preferred because their deeds were evil (John 3.19). Love's judgment is that it can work in the light, it can accompany and attract what is in darkness, but where darkness is preferred it has to be left to its own futility. John's Gospel is full of such imaginatively compelling pictures of light and darkness. But what these in their stark opposition cannot convey is the actual mixture of the two in a largely grey world where divisions into good and bad cannot be made too easily or too dismissively. Thus, perhaps, the hopefulness of God, for nothing is entirely and simply dark. Nor can the opposition of light and dark convey the vulnerability of God who in the everlasting openness of love continues to suffer its rejection and diminishment.

Thus the cross is not only the outcome of the ferment of salvation meeting the obduracy of power, and the symbol of evil wishing to erase the inconvenience of transforming love. It also demonstrates how far love will go in faithful companionship of humankind. In entirely human terms Jesus, who could have stayed in Galilee, or gone home to settle down like many disillusioned young revolutionaries, chose to come to Jerusalem, and in spite of the agony of prospection in the garden of Gethsemane, accepted the beatings, the mocking and the slow death. Love and fidelity brought Jesus to his end. In that Jesus discloses God, he discloses a God who chooses always to accompany his people in love, offering them transformation, no matter what the opposition and the cost in suffering. God is wounded for our transgressions and bruised for our iniquities. Freedom in creation creates the possibility of the misuse of freedom. God suffers from this on a divine scale just as humanity does in its own life. But without that freedom to fail in relationship, a freedom to assert power and dominion over others without love, there would not be the freedom to respond to God, to acknowledge love and its transforming power, and to order the world according to its values. The divine gift of possibility which brought about Pilate also brought about Jesus.

Jesus endured some of the suffering a human life can hold. But the pain of God's love is like the everlasting pangs of childbirth, very real pain, but pain with hope in it, and joy over new birth, although children may fail to be born to love (John 16.21f.: Hos. 13.13).[3] God 'mothers' as well as 'fathers' the world. What translated Jesus' sufferings into the cosmic dimension, making them also the birth pangs of what followed, was the divine affirmation which the disciples experienced as resurrection. The resurrection is not the happy ending to the story of Jesus, but the setting of that story into the entire context of God's relations with humanity. The resurrection, therefore, gives the perspective from which the story of Jesus is turned to human drama enacting divine truths. His life is a presentation, an enactment of what God is like and how God acts. All the New Testament writers move within the cosmic setting given to Jesus' life by the resurrection. Even Mark, the most apparently down-to-earth, tells the story as of a secret Messiah. Paul saw God in Christ reconciling the world to himself, and John proclaimed: 'The light shines in darkness and the darkness has not overcome it' (John 1.5). The ultimate power which was there at the beginning and will be there at the end is inextinguishable love.

Salvation here, now and for ever

'Love never ends'; there is neither geographical nor historical limit to the offer of divine salvation. At all times and places where self-centredness, individually or socially, brings about unfreedom, lovelessness or pain God is in the midst urging salvation, enjoying its occurrence but suffering its contradiction along with those who suffer; all the while continuing in hope and faithfulness – what the Hebrew scriptures call 'steadfast love'. It has always been like that and it will always be like that.

Humans, however, tend to be absorbed in the passing show or, more often, their own concerns, and thus take a shallow or blinkered view of the possibilities of that creation in which they have a place. In relation to all such egocentricity God is like a child tugging at his oblivious mother's skirts, seeking to gain her attention so that she can see in her way what he sees in his. 'I was ready to be sought by those who did not ask for me; I was ready to be found by those who did not seek me. I said, "Here am I, here am I" to a nation that did not call on my name' (Isa. 65.1). Other metaphors for this activity of God might be the warning bars on a road which make motorists slow down and attend to hazards, or an interpreter who enables people to attend to and thus deepen appreciation of a work of art. The common element in these metaphors is the gaining of attention: an attention which makes one notice what one would otherwise miss; an attention which enlarges response; an attention which makes one aware of fragility and vulnerability. Attention to God includes all of these, and part of God's activity is persuasiveness to attend and respond.

There are many events and experiences which may arrest attention and focus it on God, but for Christians the standard and paradigm of them all are the words, actions and suffering of Jesus which made love and forgiveness perceptible humanly to humans. Such salvation can come through a human man only when God, the author of salvation, is in dynamic concurrent relationship with him. Here was God in the role of saviour and Jesus in the role of Messiah. A role is an ontological vehicle, so although this concurrence was known in Jesus' action, it implies the freely chosen alignment of all Jesus was with the being of God in relationship with creation. Action and the self who acts in such concurrence with the eternal God becomes itself eternal as the fruit of creation from the seeds of possibility and the husbandry of steadfast love. For all eternity Jesus, who opened the eyes of his followers, whose spirit was experienced as God's spirit and in whose name a movement grew rejoicing in and practising the way of salvation, is the Christ of God. He is also the enacted Logos, the one who out of his own freedom and love put into action the chracter of God humanly, and is thus the one through whom God may fix the attention and catch the conscience of humanity. As enacted Logos Christ was not a pre-existent being, nor a Platonic form, but the first fruits of freedom and love in creation in relation to the Christian church, providing its values and direction, relating it all to the God who continues to companion creation freely.

As enacted Logos Jesus Christ transcends the necessity of the particularities of his life in first-century Palestine – such as his Jewishness, his maleness, his expectation of the imminent Day of the Lord – while the character of God in action to save remains forceful for belief and action. That character is constant and constantly engaged, but the divine-human relationship always happens here, now, in whatever circumstances and with whatever language and concepts here and now is experienced. Thus in all accounts of Jesus in the first century, or of Christ active in contemporary society, the issues and failings of the present remain the inescapable perspective from which presentations of the saviour are made, interweaving the *status quo* with the given from the past as it impinges on the present. Indeed in this 'post-modern' world where attention is dissipated through the continuous inundation of diverse information the very need to attend has to be emphasized and built into the dramatic model of christology. More, perhaps, than any other age we should see God in Christ acting to engage the attention away from contentment with endless serialism and fragmentation. *Then* the issues of relationship and what constitutes (or denies) love and freedom here and now may be addressed. And they may be addressed in the world where they happen, not in Christian retreat from the undoubtedly formidable difficulties. Such accounts of Christ here, now, have been made by women and men all over the world, and they are true accounts when they make salvation present to their hearers with all the transformation, indeed the eternal transformation that brings, together with the divine judgment of non-being on all that works against freedom and love in relationship with God and one's neighbour. This saving action of God in Christ is the Christian confession of faith, a possibility open to all, yet not the only connection with creation made by what is ultimately Real and to us a mystery.

This book has been concerned with a christological model, and with the divine and human values of freedom and love incarnate in Christ and offered to all. The end of such a book is not the place to begin an analysis of contemporary society for the concrete application of the model. Yet sprinkled throughout what I have written have been pointers to that application. Instead, this short chapter has fallen, without my intending that, into a trinitarian kind of pattern with God the Father who gives freedom to creation and labours like a woman in childbirth for its response in love; the Son in whom that character is enacted rendering it immediate and effective, communicable from one human to another; the Spirit, not as the descent of the dove from somewhere else, but as the wind which blows where it will, the urgent presence of God which, like the weather, humanity cannot control, but which is always there, stirring up response. All of that is one God, eternal, yet here, now, known to us as creator and saviour, the originator and companion of creation in all its response to possibility. Thus the conclusion of this christology is the memorable prayer from Ephesians (3.14–19) which begins and ends with God:

> For this reason I bow my knees before the Father, from whom every family in heaven and on earth is named, that according to the riches of his glory he may grant you to be strengthened with might through his Spirit in the inner being, and that Christ may dwell in your hearts through faith; that you, being rooted and grounded in love, may have power to comprehend with all the saints what is the breadth and length and height and depth, and to know the love of Christ which surpasses knowledge, that you may be filled with all the fullness of God.

Notes

Prologue

1. W. Plomer, 'A Church in Bavaria', *Celebrations*, Jonathan Cape 1973, pp. 14f. Used by permission of the estate of William Plomer.

2. Edwin Muir complained, 'The Word made flesh here is made word again', 'The Incarnate One', *Collected Poems*, Faber and Faber 1960, p. 228. The iron wordiness he objected to certainly is objectionable, but had the flesh never been made word again dramatically we would not know of it.

3. Wallace Stevens, 'So-and-so Reclining on her Couch', *The Collected Poems*, Vintage Books, Random House 1982, p. 295.

4. F. Young, *Can These Dry Bones Live?*, SCM Press 1982, p. 93.

1. God

1. The picture of God in this brief chapter was presented more fully and argued for in my *Ambiguity and the Presence of God*, SCM Press 1985.

2. Julian of Norwich, *A Shewing of God's Love*, Sheed and Ward 1974, p. 9.

3. D. Hume, *Dialogue on Natural Religion*, Hafner Publishing Co. 1969, p. 41.

4. The canonical book of Hosea is in a 'disturbed textual condition' (W. Zimmerli, *The Law and the Prophets*, Blackwell and Harper and Row 1973, p. 69), but that does not, I believe, affect what I am drawing from the book.

5. C. V. Camp, *Wisdom and the Feminine in the Book of Proverbs*, Almond Press 1985, p. 219. The description of Wisdom is derived largely from this book and thus concentrates on the Palestinian Jewish rather than the Hellenistic rendering. The Greek Wisdom of Solomon portrays Wisdom like the Immanent Logos permeating the world (cf. Heb. 1.3)

2. Jesus

1. Cf. E. Trocmé, *Jesus and his Contemporaries*, SCM Press 1973, pp. 123f.

2. Graham Greene, *Monsignor Quixote*, Penguin Books 1983, pp. 59ff.

3. G. Vermes, in *God Incarnate: Story and Belief* ed. A. E. Harvey, SPCK 1981, p. 63.

4. F. Hope, 'Jesus', *Instead of a Poet*, The Bodley Head 1965, p. 47.

5. C. H. Dodd, *The Parables of the Kingdom*, Fontana Books 1961, p. 29.

6. Fyodor Dostoevsky, *The Brothers Karamazov*, Penguin Classics 1987.

7. L. Boff, *Ecclesiogenesis*, Orbis Books, Maryknoll 1986, p. 5.

8. L. Grollenberg, *Jesus*, SCM Press and Westminster Press 1977, p. 51.

9. A. Nolan, *Jesus before Christianity*, Darton, Longman and Todd 1977, p. 32.

10. Cf. E. P. Sanders, *Jesus and Judaism*, SCM Press and Fortress Press 1985, pp. 61–76.

11. J. P. Mackey, *Jesus: the Man and the Myth*, SCM Press and Paulist Press 1979, p. 150.

12. P. Lapide, *The Resurrection of Jesus*, SPCK 1984, p. 83.

13. Sanders, *Jesus and Judaism* (n. 10), p. 302.

14. Ibid., p. 305. The emphases are mine, but refer to the points Sanders considers of particular importance.

15. G. O'Collins, *The Calvary Christ*, SCM Press 1977, p. 52.

3. *The Imaginative Construal of God*

1. These problems have been usefully collected together in John Bowden, *Jesus: The Unanswered Questions*, SCM Press 1988 and Abingdon Press 1989.

2. J. McIntyre, *The Shape of Christology*, SCM Press 1966, p. 11.

3. Cf. my *Ambiguity and the Presence of God*, SCM Press 1985, pp. 35–82.

4. Ibid., p. 57.

5. John Fowles, *The French Lieutenant's Woman*, Signet Library 1979, p. 282.

6. 'Christianity, growing up within Judaism, took for granted the major tenets of the Christian faith – its monotheism, its belief in God as creator, and Lord of history; its conviction that God had revealed himself to Moses and the prophets, and that the Scriptures were the witness to this revelation,' M. D. Hooker, *Continuity and Discontinuity: Early Christianity in its Jewish Setting*, Epworth Press 1986, p. 16. There were, of course, also differences, which Professor Hooker explores.

7. D. Kelsey, *The Uses of Scripture in Recent Theology*, Fortress Press and SCM Press 1975.

8. Ibid., p. 163.

9. J. McIntyre, *Faith, Theology and Imagination*, The Handsel Press 1987, pp. 160f.

10. W. Shakespeare, Sonnet 116.

11. K. Barth, *Church Dogmatics*, II/1, T. & T. Clark 1957, pp. 257–321.

12. K. Barth, *God in Action*, T. & T. Clark 1937, p. 11.

13. K. Barth, *The Humanity of God*, Collins 1961, p. 50.

14. K. Barth, *Evangelical Theology*, Fontana Library 1965, p. 16.
15. Barth, *The Humanity of God* (n. 13), p. 48.
16. Ibid., pp. 76f.
17. Ibid., p. 77.
18. Rudolf Otto, *The Idea of the Holy*, Oxford University Press 1925.
19. Barth, *The Humanity of God* (n. 13), p. 82.
20. Cf. ibid, pp. 61f., for some defence of universalism, including: 'This much is certain, that we have no theological right to set any sort of limits to the loving kindness of God which has appeared in Jesus Christ.'
21. P. F. Knitter, *No Other Name?*, Orbis Books, Maryknoll and SCM Press 1985, p. 241.
22. S. Weil, *Waiting on God*, Fontana Books 1959, p. 103.
23. Barth, *The Humanity of God* (n. 13), pp. 88–96.

4. *The Imaginative Construal of Jesus*

1. John Bowden, *Jesus: The Unanswered Questions*, SCM Press 1988 and Abingdon Press, 1989, p. 45.
2. Ibid., p. 32.
3. E.g. J. Jeremias, *New Testament Theology*, SCM Press and Scribners 1971, pp. 36, 61–8.
4. Ibid., p. 68.
5. J. I. H. McDonald, *Kerygma and Didache*, Cambridge University Press 1980, pp. 26f.; James Barr, '"Abba" isn't "Daddy"', *Journal of Theological Studies 39*, 1988, pp. 28–47; id., '"Abba, Father"', *Theology*, Vol. XCI, May 1988, pp. 173–9.
6. Barr, '"Abba, Father"' (n. 5), p. 179.
7. R. G. Collingwood, *The Idea of History*, Oxford University Press, 1946 p. 244, my emphasis.
8. C. F. D. Moule, *The Gospel According to Mark*, Cambridge University Press 1965, p. 86. This is a commentary for general readership and therefore will not express all that Moule would wish to say in scholarly detail. Yet it is intended to incorporate modern scholarship, and the general tendency of Moule's interpretation is clear.
9. Ibid., p. 87.
10. D. F. Nineham, *Saint Mark*, Penguin Books 1963, p. 291.
11. D. R. Catchpole, 'The "Triumphal" Entry', *Jesus and the Politics of his Day*, E. Bammel and C. F. D. Moule (eds.), Cambridge University Press 1984, pp. 332f.
12. Ibid., p. 330.
13. Ibid., p. 319.
14. J. Neusner, *What is Midrash?*, Fortress Press 1987, p. 8.
15. For the virgin birth cf. J. D. G. Dunn, *New Testament Theology in Dialogue*, James D. G. Dunn and James P. Mackey (eds.), SPCK 1987, pp. 65–71.
16. Frank Kermode, *The Genesis of Secrecy*, Harvard University Press 1979, p. 82.

17. Dunn, *New Testament Theology* (n. 15), p. 69.

18. R. Alter, *The Art of Biblical Narrative*, George Allen and Unwin 1981, p. 12, cf.: 'Almost the whole range of biblical narrative, however, embodies the basic perception that man must live before God, in the transformation of time, incessantly and perplexingly in relation with others. (p. 22).

19. F. Stern, Introduction to *The Varieties of History*, ed. F. Stern, Macmillan 1970, p. 25.

20. A. Schweitzer, *The Quest of the Historical Jesus*, A. & C. Black, 1950, p. 111.

21. G. Tyrrell, *Christianity at the Crossroads*, reissued George Allen and Unwin, 1963, p. 47.

22. P. Tillich, *Systematic Theology*, Vol. 2, Chicago University Press and Nisbet 1957, reissued SCM Press 1975, pp. 150–2.

23. J. Barr, *Fundamentalism*, SCM Press and Westminster Press 1977, pp. 76, 82.

24. E. Zola, *Le Roman Experimental*, cited in L. R. Furst and P. N. Skrine (eds.), *Naturalism*, Methuen 1971, p. 30.

25. Ibid., p. 54.

26. R. N. Stromberg, *Realism, Naturalism and Symbolism*, Macmillan 1968, pp. xviif.

27. E. Renan, *The Life of Jesus*, Watt & Co. 1947, p. 98.

28. F. W. Farrer, *Life of Christ*, Cassell, Potter and Gilpin n.d., p. 679.

29. R. Gutteridge, *Open thy Mouth for the Dumb: the German Evangelical Church and the Jews 1879–1950*, Blackwell 1976, p. 22.

30. H. S. Chamberlain, *The Foundations of the Nineteenth Century*, Vol. 2, John Lane 1911, p. 134.

31. G. Bornkamm, *Jesus of Nazareth*, Hodder and Stoughton and Harper and Row 1963, p. 13.

32. J. Moltmann, *The Crucified God*, SCM Press and Harper and Row 1974, p. 83.

33. D. Cupitt, 'One Jesus, Many Christs?' in *Christ, Faith and History*, S. W. Sykes and J. P. Clayton (eds.), Cambridge University Press 1972, p. 137.

34. The phrase is used by F. Kermode of the literary classic which, like the biblical stories, continues to endure through time: *The Classic*, Faber 1975, p. 140.

35. L. Wittgenstein, *Philosophical Investigations*, Basil Blackwell 1953.

36. E.g. P. K. Feyerabend, 'Problems of Empiricism, Part 2', in *The Nature and Function of Scientific Theory*, ed. R. Colodny, University of Pittsburgh Press 1971; Jacques Derrida, *Writing and Difference*, Routledge and Kegan Paul 1978.

37. T. Eagleton, *Literary Theory*, Blackwell 1983, pp. 146f.

38. L. Boff, *Jesus Christ Liberator*, Orbis Books and SPCK 1980, p. 292.

39. N. Perrin, *The Resurrection Narratives*, SCM Press 1977, p. 69.

40. Ibid., p. 71. cf. C. F. Evans, *Resurrection and the New Testament*, SCM Press 1970, p. 150: 'The resurrection of Jesus is his effective presence now with the believers and the continuance in some form in this world of what he had been. He is risen in the world and not out of it.'

41. Ibid., p. 128.

42. Ibid., p. 15.

43. U. Wilckens, *Resurrection*, St Andrew Press 1977, p. 23.

44. J. P. Mackey, *Jesus: the Man and the Myth*, SCM Press and Paulist Press 1979, p. 99.

45. G. W. H. Lampe, in G. W. H. Lampe and D. M. MacKinnon, *The Resurrection*, Mowbray 1966, pp. 30f.

46. D. Cupitt, *Christ and the Hiddenness of God*, Lutterworth Press 1971; reissued SCM Press 1985, p. 142.

47. Lampe, *Resurrection* (n. 45), p. 34.

48. I. Kant, *Religion within the Limits of Reason Alone*, Harper Torchbooks 1965, p. 55.

49. Gregory of Nazianzus, *Epistola* 101.7.

50. For some sense of the diversity see J. Pelikan, *Jesus through the Centuries*, Yale University Press 1984, p. 198.

51. Kermode, *The Classic* (n. 34), p. 121; cf. 'The coexistence in single text of a plurality of signifiers from which, in the nature of human attentiveness, every reader misses some – and, in the nature of human individuality, prefers one – is, empirically, a requirement and a distinguishing feature of the survivor (p. 133).

52. Ibid., p. 134.

5. *The Dramaturgical Prototype*

1. *Drama*, Liddell and Scott, *Greek-English Lexicon*, cf. Aristotle, *Poetics*, III–IV.

2. Martin Esslin, *An Anatomy of Drama*, Temple Smith 1976, p. 10.

3. Ibid., p. 22.

4. For the distinction, but not total dichotomy, between 'showing' and 'telling' cf. Wayne Booth, *The Rhetoric of Fiction*, Peregrine Books [2]1987, pp. 3–20.

5. Aristotle, *Poetics* VI.

6. Raymond Williams, *Drama in Performance*, Pelican Books 1972, p. 178; cf. Martin Esslin, *The Field of Drama*, Methuen 1987, p. 113; 'It will be evident that these "clef" or "key" signifiers must depend on the basic assumptions of the society and that their power and effectiveness will depend on the audience's familiarity with the *conventions* under which dramatic performance is practised in a particular culture, or sub-culture.'

7. Williams, *Drama* (n. 6), p. 180.

8. Cf. R. Gaskell, *Drama and Reality*, Routledge & Kegan Paul 1972, p. 5; 'Modern drama, like modern life, takes place for the most part in drawing rooms and kitchens. Insulated, except on rare occasions, from the onset of darkness, we can forget that man is an animal who lives by the fruits

of the earth and dies.'

9. René Wellek and Austin Warren, *Theory of Literature*, Penguin Books 1973, p. 42.

10. Cited without reference in Gaskell, *Drama* (n. 8).

11. Ibid., pp. 60f. Ruqiya Hasan makes the same point about unitive theme, which she also calls a 'regulative principle' and an abstraction 'closely related to all forms of hypothesis-building'. That would turn a play into a persuasive argument for adopting the hypothesis. (R. Hasan, 'Rime and Reason in Literature', *Literary Style*, ed. S. Chapman, 1971, pp. 309–10).

12. F. Dürrenmatt, 'Problems of the Theatre', in *Perspectives on Drama*, J. L. Calderwood & H. E. Toliver (eds.), Oxford University Press 1968, p. 35.

13. Esslin, *Field of Drama* (n. 6), p. 116.

14. H. Rosenberg, *The Tradition of the New*, Paladin Books 1970.

15. Ibid., p. 126.

16. Ibid., p. 128.

17. Ibid., p. 134.

18. Ibid., p. 136.

19. Ibid., p. 138.

20. T. S. Eliot, *The Use of Poetry and the Use of Criticism*, Faber and Faber 1964, p. 126.

21. Esslin, *Anatomy of Drama* (n. 2), p. 110.

22. Eliot, *The Use of Poetry*, p. 153.

23. R. Bolt, *A Man for All Seasons*, Heinemann 1971, Introduction, p. xi.

24. Ibid., p. xiii.

25. Ibid.

26. Ibid., p. xiv.

27. D. Knowles, *The Historian and Character*, Cambridge University Press 1963, p. 7.

28. A. G. Dickens, *The English Reformation*, Batsford 1964, p. 73.

29. Knowles, *The Historian and Character* (n. 27), p. 8.

30. Bolt, *A Man for All Seasons* (n. 23), p. 93.

31. G. R. Elton, *Reform and Renewal*, Cambridge University Press 1973. Elton does not give great praise to More. Like many historians he is impatient with the kind of hagiography which has surrounded More and he wishes to redress the balance.

32. Bolt, *A Man for All Seasons* (n. 23), p. xvii.

33. In this respect *all* well known story lines, from fairy tales to classical drama, exert the same pressure. When Giraudoux, with war in possible prospect in 1935, wrote *La guerre de Troie n'aura pas lieu*, the focus is on the striving of Hector to prevent the Trojan War, which the audience knows will take place.

6. *The Presentation of Jesus*

1. A. Wilder, *Early Christian Rhetoric*, SCM Press 1964, p. 77.

2. J. Knox, *The Death of Christ*, Abingdon Press and Collins 1958, p. 19.

3. Wilder, *Early Christian Rhetoric* (n. 1), p. 62.

4. Ibid., p. 13.

5. M. Esslin, *The Field of Drama*, Methuen 1937, p. 30.

6. Wilder, *Early Christian Rhetoric* (n. 1), p. 75.

7. Cf. C. H. Talbert, *What is a Gospel?*, SPCK 1978, p. 98: 'Our gospels belong to the debates over the legitimacy of the various forms of kerygma in early Christianity, that is, over arguments over which Jesus is the "true" Jesus and which way of life is the "true" Christian way.'

8. B. Chilton & J. I. H. McDonald, *Jesus and the Ethics of the Kingdom*, SPCK 1987, p. 113.

9. Ibid., p. 122.

10. Naturalistic plays with realistic sequence and motivation form one of the conventions to which contemporary society is accustomed, and in some there is no attempt at metaphoric depth. David Lodge finds such plays aberrant in drama at large: 'Naturalistic "fourth wall" plays which have dominated the commercial stage in our era must be seen as "metonymic" deviation from the metaphoric norm which drama displays when viewed in deep historical perspective . . . Such naturalism is, arguably, unnatural to the theatre' (*The Modes of Modern Writing*, Edward Arnold 1978, p. 82).

11. Esslin, *Field of Drama* (n. 5), p. 163.

12. Lodge, *Modes of Modern Writing* (n. 10), p. 3.

13. M. Hooker, *The Message of Mark*, Epworth Press 1983, p. 10.

14. Ibid., p. 13.

15. G. B. Caird, *St Luke*, Penguin Books 1973, p. 47.

16. F. Hahn, *The Titles of Jesus in Christology*, Lutterworth Press 1969, p. 11. Morna Hooker explicitly calls 'Son of God' a role, whether in God's address to the king in Ps. 2.7 or more generally concerning Israel's relationship with God. Similarly she turns the question whether New Testament writers identify Jesus with the Suffering Servant into 'whether Jesus is understood to be exercising the role which is described in Isaiah 53', *Pauline Pieces*, Epworth Press 1979, pp. 57f., 68.

17. Cf. W. E. Phipps, *Was Jesus Married?*, Harper and Row 1970.

18. J. L. Houlden, *Patterns of Faith*, SCM Press 1977, p. 33.

19. This description of Paul's christology, which probably developed over time and admittedly is nowhere systematically spelt out, comes largely from C. K. Barrett, *From First Adam to Last*, A. & C. Black 1962.

20. C. K. Barrett, *New Testament Essays*, SPCK 1972, p. 130.

21. C. H. Dodd, *The Interpretation of the Fourth Gospel*, Cambridge University Press 1953, pp. 285, 280.

22. C. K. Barrett, *The Gospel according to St John*, SPCK [2]1967, p. 48.

23. J. L. Martyn, *History and Theology in the Fourth Gospel*, Harper and Row 1968.

24. Dodd, *Interpretation* (n. 21), p. 137.

25. M. F. Wiles, *The Making of Christian Doctrine*, Cambridge University Press 1967, pp. 126ff.

26. *Against Praxeas* 5.

27. J. N. D. Kelly, *Early Christian Doctrines*, A. & C. Black 1968, p. 114. Cf. G. C. Stead, *Divine Substance*, Oxford University Press 1977, p. 161. The Stoic notion of substance which Tertullian used had some form of spiritual corporeality, unlike Plato's or Aristotle's account, and that may have aided the dramatic nature of Tertullian's conception. The account I give of Tertullian here is, of course, partial, concentrating only on his dramatic thinking and vocabulary.

28. F. L. Volpe and M. Magdalaner, *Drama*, Random House 1967, p. 12.

29. This point is made by R. Braun, *Deus Christianorum*, Presses Universitaires de France 1962, p. 222.

30. *Against Praxeas* 14.

31. E. Evans, Preface to *Tertullian's Treatise against Praxeas*, SPCK 1948, p. vii.

32. *Against Praxeas* 13.

33. *Against Praxeas* 27.

34. Braun, *Deus Christianorum* (n. 29), p. 241.

7. *Christological Form*

1. J. P. Mackey, *Jesus: the Man and the Myth*, SCM Press and Paulist Press 1979, pp. 243f.

2. F. D. E. Schleiermacher, *The Christian Faith* (1821), T. & T. Clark 1928, p. 394.

3. G. Hendry, *The Gospel of the Incarnation*, SCM Press 1959, pp. 25f.

4. G. C. Stead, *Divine Substance*, Oxford University Press 1977, p. 273.

5. Cf. Chapter 1 and my *Ambiguity and the Presence of God*, SCM Press 1985, pp. 119–34.

6. Cf. ibid., pp. 152–61, for a fuller discussion and defence of roles.

7. J. D. Zizioulas, *Being as Communion*, Darton, Longman and Todd 1985, p. 34.

8. W. J. H. Sprott, *Human Groups*, Penguin Books 1977, p. 23.

9. L. Boff, *Jesus Christ Liberator*, Orbis Books and SPCK 1980, p. 275.

10. J. Sobrino, *Christology at the Crossroads*, SCM Press 1978, pp. 79–117.

11. On Jesus' ignorance cf. ibid., pp. 100–2: 'The limitation on his knowledge is the historical condition that makes real his trusting surrender to the Father and his solidarity with humankind' (p. 102).

12. W. Pannenberg, *Jesus – God and Man*, Westminster Press and SCM Press 1968, p. 362.

13. H. R. Mackintosh, *The Person of Jesus Christ*, T. & T. Clark 1912, p. 400.

14. D. Bonhoeffer, *Christology*, Fontana Books 1966, p. 112.

15. S. Moore, *The Fire and the Rose are One*, Darton, Longman and Todd 1980, p. 79.

16. L. Grollenberg, *Jesus*, SCM Press and Westminster Press 1977, p. 41.

17. Ibid., p. 108.

18. Augustine, *Confessions* XI.10. For reasons of chaos theory entirely different from Augustine's, Ilya Prigogine writes: 'Time and the universe have been born at the same moment' ('The Rediscovery of Time', *Beshara*, Abingdon, Issue 9, p. 30).

19. Thus also G. W. H. Lampe: 'The concept of "pre-existence" serves to express the conviction that the creative and saving work of God embodies his constant and unchanging faithfulness' (*God as Spirit*, Clarendon Press 1977, reissued SCM Press 1983, p. 120).

20. Included in the large literature on the subject are M. Hengel, *Son of God*, SCM Press and Fortress Press 1976, which approves the development, and Lampe's *God as Spirit* (n. 19), which does not.

21. Cf. Hengel, *Son of God* (n. 20), p. 91, for the speed with which this christology grew.

22. J. Knox, *The Humanity and Divinity of Christ*, Cambridge University Press 1967, pp. 32f.

23. Ibid.

24. Cf. D. M. Baillie, *God was in Christ* (1948), Faber and Faber 1963, pp. 94–8.

25. C. F. Evans, *Resurrection and the New Testament*, SCM Press 1970, p. 36.

26. G. W. H. Lampe, *God as Spirit* (n.19), p. 160. John Hick has also described such continuing post-mortem development in *Death and Eternal Life*, Macmillan 1976.

27. Ibid., p. 161.

28. J. K. Baxter, 'Ode', *Collected Poems*, Oxford University Press 1988, p. 306.

29. Cf., p. 25 above.

30. Tete Tawhara, *Christ the Maori*, unpublished paper.

31. James Irwin, *Towards a Maori Theology*, unpublished paper.

32. For the history of the pericope see e.g. John Marsh, *Saint John*, Penguin Books 1968, pp. 681–4.

33. Grollenberg, *Jesus* (n. 16), pp. 56f.

34. John Austin Baker, *The Foolishness of God*, Darton, Longman & Todd 1970, p. 152.

35. J. Pelikan, *Jesus through the Centuries*, Yale University Press 1984.

36. Ibid., p. 4.

37. Thus Bertrand Russell preferred Socrates to Jesus, since the philosopher was 'bland and urbane towards the people who would not listen to him, and it is, to my mind far more worthy of a sage to take that line than to

take the line of indignation' (*Why I am not a Christian*, George Allen and Unwin 1957, p. 22).

38. Cf. R. R. Ruether, *New Woman, New Earth*, Seabury Press 1975, pp. 19–23.

39. George Casalis, 'Jesus – Neither Abject Lord nor Heavenly Monarch', in *Faces of Jesus* ed. J. Bonino, Orbis Books 1984, p. 75.

40. Ibid.

41. Hugo Assmann, 'The Actuation of the Power of Christ in History', in ibid., p. 135.

42. L. Boff, 'Images of Jesus in Brazilian Liberal Christianity', in ibid., p. 13.

43. J. W. C. Wand, *The Atonement*, SPCK 1963, p. 83.

44. Ibid., p. 60.

45. Lampe, *God as Spirit* (n. 19), p. 11.

46. R. R. Ruether, *Sexism and God Talk*, Crossroad Publishing Co. and SCM Press 1983, p. 136.

47. Ibid., p. 137.

48. I have come across this anonymous poem only in a newsletter and have not been able to locate it 'collected' anywhere.

49. J. Hick, *An Interpretation of Religion: Human Responses to the Transcendent*, Macmillan, 1989.

50. Ibid., p. 258.

51. J. D. G. Dunn, in *New Testament Theology in Dialogue* ed. J. D. G. Dunn and J. P. Mackey (eds.), SPCK 1987, p. 79.

52. Paul Knitter, *No Other Name?*, Orbis Books and SCM Press 1985, pp. 184–6.

53. L. Gilkey, 'Plurality and its Theological Implications', in *The Myth of Christian Uniqueness*, J. Hick and P. Knitter (eds.), Orbis Books and SCM Press 1987, pp. 44–6.

54. A. Dulles, *The Resilient Church: The Necessity and Limits of Adaptation*, Doubleday 1977, p. 78.

55. R. R. Ruether, 'Feminism and Jewish-Christian Dialogue' in *The Myth of Christian Uniqueness* (n. 53), p. 142.

56. Baillie, *God was in Christ* (n. 24), p. 191.

57. J. McLeod Campbell, *The Nature of the Atonement* (1855), Macmillan, 1895, p. 16. *Uniqueness* (n. 53), p. 142.

58. Mackintosh, *The Person of Jesus Christ* (n.13), p. 326.

59. Stevie Smith, 'Was He Married?', *The Collected Poems of Stevie Smith*, Penguin Twentieth Century Classics, London and New Directions, New York 1975, p. 389. Used by permission of the executor.

60. R. E. Weingart, *The Logic of Divine Love: A Critical Analysis of the Soteriology of Peter Abailard*, Oxford University Press 1970, p. 125.

61. Personal Letter 4, *The Letters of Abelard and Eloise*, Penguin Books 1974, pp. 151f.

62. Weingart, *Logic of Divine Love* (n. 60), p. 128.

63. Ibid.

64. Hendry, *Gospel of the Incarnation* (n.3), p. 117.
65. Weingart, *Logic of Divine Love* (n. 60), p. 131.
66. H. Rashdall, *The Idea of the Atonement in Christian Theology*, Macmillan 1919, p. 454.
67. K. Ward, *The Concept of God*, Blackwell 1974, p. 200.
68. F. Young, *Can These Dry Bones Live?*, SCM Press 1982, p. 27.
69. 'Dieu me pardonnera: c'est son metier', *Souvenirs de la vie intime de Henri Heine*, Princesse de la Rocca, Paris 1881, p. 125.
70. P. Tillich, *Systematic Theology*, Vol. 2, Chicago University Press and Nisbet 1957, reissued SCM Press 1975, p. 172.
71. K. Rahner, *Theological Investigations*, Vol. IV, Darton, Longman and Todd 1966, p. 180.
72. Cf. M. Paton, 'Can God Forget?', *Scottish Journal of Theology*, Vol. 35, no. 5, pp. 385–402.
73. Stevie Smith, in *Me Again*, Virago Press, London and Random House, New York 1983, p. 228.
74. S. M Ogden, *The Reality of God*, Harper and Row and SCM Press, 1977, p. 210.
75. Cf. G. Lampe, *Reconciliation in Christ*, Longman Green and Co., 1956, p. 21.
76. Cf. R. Niebuhr, *The Nature and Destiny of Man*, Vol. 1, Nisbet, 1946, pp. 313ff.
77. Hendry, *Gospel of the Incarnation* (n. 3), p. 134.
78. Ogden, *Reality of God* (n. 74), p. 173.
79. Hendry, *Gospel of the Incarnation* (n. 3), p. 117.
80. Ward, *Concept of God* (n.67), p. 192. My emphasis.
81. Ibid., p. 198.
82. McLeod Campbell, *Nature of the Atonement* (n. 57), p. 21.
83. Pannenberg, *Jesus: God and Man* (n. 12), p. 45.
84. Ibid., p. 269.
85. Cited by M. M. Thomas, *The Acknowledged Christ of the Indian Renaissance*, SCM Press 1969, p. 194.
86. A. Falconer (ed.), *Reconciling Memories*, The Columba Press 1988; cf. also *Northern Ireland: A Challenge to Theology*, Occasional Paper 12, Centre for Theology and Public Issues, New College, Edinburgh.
87. A. Falconer, 'The Reconciling Power of Forgiveness', in *Reconciling Memories* (n. 86), p. 92, citing H. Arendt, *The Human Condition*, Chicago University Press p. 241.
88. G. Daly, 'Forgiveness and Community', in *Reconciling Memories* (n. 86), p. 109.
89. Ibid., p. 113.
90. E. McDonagh, *Between Chaos and New Creation*, Gill and Macmillan 1986, p. 142.
91. Ibid., p. 140.
92. Ibid., p. 56.

93. Ibid., p. 57.

94. 'I have tried too in my time to be a philosopher; but, I don't know how cheerfulness was always breaking in (Oliver Edwards, cited in Boswell's *Life of Johnson*, 17 April 1778).

8. *Jesus Christ, Saviour*

1. L. Grollenberg, *Jesus*, SCM Press and Westminster Press 1977, p. 53.
2. John Fowles, *The French Lieutenant's Woman*, Signet Books 1970, p. 285.
3. Cf. the description of 'The Woman in Travail', Frances Young, *Can These Dry Bones Live?*, SCM Press 1982, pp. 43ff.

Index of Names